HOUSE OF HORRORS

House of
HORRORS

The Shocking True Story of

Anthony Sowell,

the Cleveland Strangler

Robert Sberna

Black Squirrel Books • Kent, Ohio

For my parents, Charles and Mary Sberna

And to the memory of the eleven victims of these horrible
crimes, and their families and friends who waited so long
for closure . . . and to those who are still waiting

© 2012 by Robert Sberna
All rights reserved
ISBN 978-1-60635-186-4
Manufactured in the United States of America

 TM
BLACK SQUIRREL BOOKS™
Frisky, industrious black squirrels are a familiar sight on the Kent State University
campus and the inspiration for Black Squirrel Books™, a trade imprint of The
Kent State University Press
www.KentStateUniversityPress.com

Cataloging information for this title is available at the Library of Congress.

16 15 14 13 12   5 4 3 2 1

Contents

Acknowledgments

Over the two years that it took to research and write this book, I was helped by many people. I'd like to thank, in no particular order, Latundra Billups, Shawn Morris, Tanja Doss, Vanessa Gay, Gladys Wade Thomas, Lori Frazier, Cuyahoga County Prosecutor Rick Bombik, John Parker, Cleveland City Councilman Zack Reed, Ray Cash, Renee Cash, Assad "Sam" Tayeh, Debbie Madison, Melvette Sockwell, Cavana Faithwalker, Leander Thomas, Leona Davis, Tressa Garrison, Ja'Ovvoni Garrison, Roosevelt Lloyd, Robert Harris, Karen Clemons, Florence Bray, Antonia Dozier, Barbara Carmichael, Adlean Atterberry, Art McKoy, Melanie GiaMaria, Rufus Sims, Steve Miller, Marie Kittredge, Christine Panchur, Treasa Mays, Laura Bozell, Kathy Cornell, Clark Broida, Inez Fortson, John Hunter, Jim Allen, Christine Shobey, Donald Smith, Yvonne Williams-McNeill, Bobby Dancy Sr., Joanne Moore, and Fawcett Bess.

Much gratitude to the Cleveland Police Department, particularly Lt. Richard Durst, Sgt. Dan Galmarini, Sgt. Ronald Ross, Deputy Chief Ed Tomba, and Chief Michael McGrath.

Thanks also to Michelle Pallo, Dr. James Knoll IV, Lori James-Townes, Dr. Phillip Resnick, Dr. Cathleen Cerny, Ed Gallek, Rebecca McFarland, Dr. Diana Goldstein, Walter Bansley III, Renee Hotz, Tom Sheeran of the Associated Press, former Cuyahoga County Coroners Dr. Frank Miller III and Dr. Elizabeth Balraj, and the *Plain Dealer*'s Stan Donaldson, Rachel Dissell, Marvin Fong, Dave Andersen, and Jo Corrigan.

And finally, a special thanks to Will Underwood, director of the Kent State University Press, and his talented team—Mary Young, Christine Brooks, Susan Cash, and their colleagues.

"I thought you were my friend . . ."

September 22, 2009

In the dull gold haze of sunset, faint shadows lay across the yards and houses of Imperial Avenue in Cleveland's Mount Pleasant neighborhood. The evening is warm. At most houses, windows have been opened to catch the occasional breeze. Residents are sitting on their porches, alone or in pairs. Their muted conversations and the infrequent passing cars are the only street sounds at this hour.

Like most of the homes in the neighborhood, the colonial at 12205 Imperial was constructed in the 1920s as a duplex. Cream with brown shutters, the house has living quarters on the first and second floors. A double-decker porch, spanning the width of the house, faces the street. The third floor, originally an attic, has been converted into a small apartment.

Since the summer of 2005, the large house has only been occupied by one person: Anthony Sowell. His neighbors, most of whom know him only as Tone or Tony, consider him friendly yet reserved—perhaps even a bit odd. On some evenings, he can be seen sitting in the darkness of his second-floor porch silently watching the neighborhood.

The porch is empty tonight. On the unlit second floor, the windows have been closed and the blinds drawn. A single plastic lawn chair sits in the middle of the bare living room. A hallway leads from the living room to a small bedroom, where thirty-six-year-old Latundra Billups is facedown on the wood floor, desperately clawing at the electrical cord that Tone has tightened around her neck.

Lanky, but deceptively strong, Tone is lying on top of her, pulling steadily and forcefully on the ends of the cord. Although Latundra has managed to slip her fingers between the cord and her neck, she is unable to ease the crushing pressure. Her fingers, trapped beneath the ligature, are now painfully squeezed against her throat.

For the past hour, Tone has subjected Latundra to a brutal sexual assault while strangling her—at first with his hands and then with the electrical extension cord. He is methodical and sadistic: several times during the attack, he tightened the noose until she neared unconsciousness—and then eased the pressure to revive her.

Believing that Tone will eventually release her, Latundra, a single mother of five, has somehow willed herself to remain composed.

But now he jerks the cord, constricting her airway, and Latundra understands that he has more than rape on his mind; he intends to kill her. Terrified, adrenaline fueling her, she bucks and rolls her body, attempting to dislodge him. As she thrashes on the floor, jagged splinters from the worn hardwood pierce her legs and torso.

Desperate now, she tries to pull the cord away from her neck, but her energy is depleted. Her body spasms, and then she stops resisting. Tone pulls the noose even tighter. He holds the pressure until at last she goes limp. Just before she passes out, Latundra prays that she will see her children again.

. . .

Several hours earlier, Latundra, a petite, medium-complected black woman called "Lala" by her friends, had been walking home from a relative's house when she saw Tone walking in the same direction. He invited Lala to come back to his place for a drink.

Lala first met Tone in March 2007 when she moved to Imperial Avenue with her three youngest children. She'd been introduced to him by his live-in girlfriend at the time, Lori Frazier.

Lala had known Frazier since the two were in their teens. They hadn't seen much of each other over the past decade, but when they discovered they were Imperial Avenue neighbors in 2007, they also found they had a common interest: crack cocaine.

Lala had smoked crack a half-dozen times with Frazier and Tone, either at her own house or on the third floor of his. In late 2007, after Frazier moved away from Imperial Avenue, Lala continued to party with Tone on occasion. When she had an urge to get high, she'd make what she called a "pit stop" at his house. She'd tell her children she was going to the corner store, then dash to Tone's for a quick fix.

But when Tone invited her to his house on that late afternoon in September 2009, she was initially hesitant. In recent months, she'd heard disturbing rumors that he'd been physically abusive to several women who had partied with him. One of the women, an acquaintance of Lala's, said that Tone had held her hostage in his house for nearly an entire day, raping her repeatedly. The woman hadn't reported the attack to the police, explaining to Lala that she was reluctant to testify against Tone because her family would learn that she was a drug user.

Lala was fairly certain that her friend had told the truth about being attacked. But the opportunity to smoke crack outweighed her fear of being alone with Tone. And, rationalizing, she reminded herself that he'd always been nice to her. On the walk to his house, she suggested that they purchase crack. Tone gave her fifty dollars and waited for her on a street corner while she went to a nearby house.

When they arrived at 12205 Imperial, he led Lala to the second floor. He usually entertained guests in the third-floor sitting room, but he explained to Lala that it was too dirty for visitors.

In the second-floor living room, Tone sat in the lawn chair with Lala beside him on the hardwood floor. They chatted, shared a crack pipe, and drank—King Cobra malt liquor for him and Wild Irish Rose wine for Lala.

Eventually, as daylight faded, they moved to a small bedroom, which contained only an extension cord and a tattered blanket on the floor. As they sat on the blanket, Lala began to feel nervous in the stark surroundings. She asked Tone if the rumors were true that he had assaulted two women. He shrugged off the accusations, denying he had ever mistreated any women.

He then leaned toward her and asked, "Have I ever done that to you?" Lifting his hand to her pink sweater and brushing her breasts, he stared at her, "You wouldn't give me sex anyhow, would you?"

Lala noticed a disconcerting change in his demeanor, an intensity that she hadn't seen before. "Oh, stop making jokes," she said, feigning a casual air.

He then removed his shirt, and she saw the raised outline of a cardiac pacemaker under the skin of his chest. A shiver ran up her spine as she recalled that one of the women who had been attacked by him had mentioned seeing the pacemaker outline.

Tone then told her to stand up. She was confused but slowly got to her feet. In a firm voice, he ordered her to turn around and face away from him. Putting his hands around her neck, he squeezed forcefully.

"What are you doing?" she shouted, turning her head to look at him. In reply, he punched her in the side of her face. She was dazed, tears welling in her eyes.

After instructing her to remove her pants and lay down on her back, he performed oral sex on her. She began crying. "Shut up. Doesn't it feel good?" he asked.

She was then told to roll over onto her stomach. He lay on top of her, spreading her legs apart with his knees. She felt pressure against her vagina and realized he was pushing his penis into her. Just as he penetrated her, he looped the extension cord over her neck. Before he could tighten the loop, she instinctively inserted her fingers under the slack cord. Lala pulled against the cord, but the tourniquet tightened against her fingers, trapping them against her neck.

Kicking and rolling, she fought for her life. During the struggle, a can of malt liquor spilled on the floor. Lala skidded on the slippery surface, but she was unable to dislodge him. He violently yanked the cord, lacerating her fingers and squeezing her throat. Unable to breathe, the pain in her chest unbearable, she saw flashes of white light, and then blackness.

· · ·

When Lala's eyes snapped open, she was surprised—and grateful—to be alive. She inhaled sharply, sucking oxygen. She wasn't sure how long she'd been unconscious, but she could see through the room's window blinds that it was night. (She'd later learn that she'd been unconscious for three hours.) Her sudden awakening startled Tone, who had been sitting in a chair next to her, smoking a cigarette. He sat up straight, also surprised that she survived. Silently, he stared at her in the darkness.

She felt dizzy and her neck ached, but she was determined to get out of Tone's house. She stood up unsteadily and began putting her pants on. Her sweater had been torn and it reeked of malt liquor. Amid the room's stale beery odor, she smelled feces. She realized that she had lost control of her bowels during the strangulation.

"Where are you going?" he asked.

When she told him she was going home, he said, "You aren't leaving. I'm going to have to kill you and myself because I know you're going to tell the police."

Although Lala's sense of relief dissipated, she wasn't frightened by his threat. "If he tries to jump me again, I'll be ready this time," she thought.

Lala also sensed that Tone's voice and his mannerisms had lost the forcefulness that she'd seen earlier. Maintaining her composure, she assured him that she wouldn't report the incident to the police. In an attempt to engage him in conversation, she pointed at her ripped sweater and said, "I thought you were my friend, but look what you did to my sweater."

Tone then apologized and offered to replace it. When told that it cost a hundred dollars, his mood darkened and he accused her of "playing him." But, after a pause, he said, "If you come back tomorrow, I'll give you fifty dollars for the sweater and we'll get high."

She was stunned by his offer. Could he seriously think that she'd ever come back here?

Masking her disbelief and forcing herself to smile, she told him she would return the next day. He then looked her over and said, in a soft voice, "Well, you can't go home wearing a ripped sweater."

He led her to his basement, where he pointed to several bags of clothes that had been left behind by Lori Frazier when she moved out. "Pick a shirt," he said. She pulled a pink top out of a bag and changed into it, leaving her ripped sweater in the basement.

He then walked her to the front door. She stepped out of the house, descended the porch steps, and began walking away, not allowing herself to relax until she was sure that he wasn't following. Her face was swollen from his punch and her neck was bruised and raw, but she was immensely thankful to be alive. When she was several houses away, she heard his voice in the darkness: "I'll see you tomorrow, right?"

She walked for a few minutes more, then stopped and began sobbing. She was overcome by feelings of relief. Whether through fortune, divine intervention, or her own force of will, she was alive. And she felt compelled to do what she could to make sure that no other woman would have to endure her experience.

CHAPTER 2

Survivors

September 23, 2009–October 19, 2009

The Rape Kit.

Typically a white box, about twelve inches long by six inches wide. Inside are envelopes, microscope slides, and plastic bags that are used to collect and store evidence from a sexual assault, including hair samples from a victim's head and pubic area, saliva and semen, blood samples, and clothing fibers.

Oral, anal, and vaginal swabs are also collected during a sexual assault examination along with skin or debris from under a victim's fingernails.

The rape kit is handled under a strict chain of custody, with each envelope and bag identified with victim information, initialed by the examiner, countersigned, and sealed. The box is then turned over to an investigating police officer who delivers it to a laboratory for analysis.

Renee Hotz, a sexual assault nurse examiner at Cleveland's University Hospitals, has processed more than a thousand rape kits. After twelve years of working with rape victims, Hotz has seen that strangulation, either with a ligature of some type or the attacker's hands, often accompanies a sexual assault.

So when Latundra "Lala" Billups came to a University Hospitals emergency room after her attack by Anthony Sowell, Hotz instantly saw the telltale signs that she had been in a fight for her life.

Before she went to the hospital, Lala had spent the night at a friend's house. She was hungry, but her throat was swollen and she was unable to swallow, so she showered and went to bed.

When she awoke the next morning, her neck felt "as if it was on fire" and her entire body ached. She had a friend drive her to the ER, where the staff decided that Hotz, the lead nurse examiner, should handle Lala's case. At the time, however, Hotz was testifying at an unrelated rape trial in downtown Cleveland. Lala was told that it could be as long as six hours before Hotz returned to the hospital.

Waiting would be difficult for Lala. She was traumatized from the attack and unsure whether she wanted to file a police report against Tone. While she wanted to prevent him from attacking other women, Lala dreaded becoming involved in the police investigation and court testimony that would likely follow his arrest. With her own record of drug-related arrests, Lala was also skeptical that police would even believe her story.

Just as she decided to leave the ER, a hospital employee asked if he could take pictures of her injuries. "Yes," she answered, resolving to follow the investigation process to the end.

Along with photos of the ligature marks on her neck, images were taken of her face, which was swollen from Tone's punches, and the puncture wounds on her hips and legs from the floor splinters.

When Hotz, 55, began her examination, she noticed that Lala's fingernails were torn and broken—an indication that she had struggled to free herself from the cord that was wrapped around her neck.

"I've even seen cases where victims have inadvertently ripped their own nails off in their efforts to remove the ligature that is being used to strangle them," Hotz says.

Not only did Lala have bruising on her neck, but Hotz could see the imprint of the electrical extension cord on her skin.

Explaining that it's typical for a victim to have pattern injuries that mirror the ligature material, Hotz says, "For example, if it was a necklace or chain, there will be impressions of the links left on their skin. In Lala's case, the imprint was so distinct that I could see the thin groove that separates the two wires in the cord."

As Hotz inspected the U-shaped ligature line, or furrow, around the front and sides of Lala's neck, she could see that there were breaks in the furrow. The breaks corresponded to where she had placed her fingers under the cord. When Hotz looked at Lala's fingers, she could see they had an impression of the ligature on them.

Like many strangulation victims, Lala had a raspy voice. Hotz notes that the rasp is a common giveaway of attack victims who are unwilling to admit that they have been strangled. "The victim may be protecting a spouse or partner, but we're not easily fooled," she says. "We can hear it in their voice."

Loss of bowel and bladder control is another sign of strangulation. Lala had soiled herself, an indication that she had been strangled to the point of unconsciousness.

Besides her physical trauma, Hotz says Lala exhibited the emotional cues of a person who has been assaulted.

"After I complete a rape examination, a police officer will sometimes ask me if the victim is being truthful," Hotz says. "I can understand that they are looking for some parameters so that they can start their investigation. In my career, I've noticed that many actual victims of rape have verbalized to me that during the attack, they stopped fighting at some point. Instinctively, they knew that if they kept fighting, it would just further incite their attacker. Although Lala initially fought her attacker, she stayed calm after she woke up from being strangled. By maintaining her composure, she deprived him of the gratification of seeing fear on her face. He lost his predatory instinct, and that's probably what saved her life."

After Hotz completed her examination, two Cleveland police officers spoke with Lala about the assault. When she told them her attacker's name was Tone and he lived on Imperial Avenue, the policemen exchanged glances.

Hotz, who noticed the exchange, would later say the cops appeared "grossly upset" when they heard Tone's name mentioned. "They obviously knew of Tone and knew that he'd assaulted other women," she says.

Lala, saying she was surprised at the officers' recognition of Tone's name, recalls, "I didn't even know his real name, so it shocked me that the cops seemed to know of him. They told me that they even knew his address. They were aware of Tone because several other women had complained that a man with that name had attacked them. I had to wonder, if the police had all that information, why hadn't they picked him up already?"

In actuality, it would take until October 27, more than a month after she was attacked, before the Cleveland Police Sex Crimes detectives would begin their investigation. Lala says she attempted to speak with detectives within days of her attack, however, she says her telephone calls were not returned. For their part, the detectives say they had difficulty locating Lala and scheduling an interview with her.

Several legal experts would later second-guess the police procedure, saying Lala's initial report, which was taken by an officer at the hospital, would have been sufficient to secure a warrant to search Tone's house.

Police officials explained later that they were afraid they would jeopardize their case if they requested a warrant before getting a detailed statement from Lala. But a Case Western Reserve University law professor discounted their concern, saying, "Without question there was probable cause for issuance of a search warrant. Any judge would have issued it."

Whether due to miscommunication or, as Lala claims, indifference by the police, the delay in investigation meant that Tone was free to attack again—this time with disastrous consequences for Shawn Morris, a fifty-one-year-old Cleveland woman. Like Lala, Shawn was lured to Tone's house by offers of drugs and companionship. And like Lala, she would find herself in a life-or-death battle.

Shawn, a tall black woman, had struggled with substance abuse problems for nearly half her life, mainly alcohol and crack cocaine. She'd had several stints in rehab. Each time, she'd managed to stay off drugs for two or three years at a time, but then she'd eventually relapse. In recent years, however, her addiction had weakened its grip. Shawn liked to say that she had gotten to the point where she was "off and on" drugs. Yet, the temptation to get high was a constant and malignant companion.

On days like October 19, 2009, when temptation became craving, she forced herself to stay busy. But even several hours of household chores didn't diminish her desire to get high. So that evening she decided to attend a Bible study session at a church in Mount Pleasant. When she arrived, she found that the session was canceled. She began walking back to her house and ran into a girlfriend, Nene, who suggested they go for a drink.

As they walked along Kinsman Avenue, Shawn and her friend passed through one of Cleveland's most drug-infested areas. For a woman who was trying to stay drug-free, Kinsman Avenue was the wrong place to be. Crack dealers and their hangers-on leaned against their cars and SUVs. Each vehicle had a T-shirt draped over its steering wheel—a sign that drugs were for sale.

Shawn and her friend met up with two more women, and the group went to a house party where Shawn satisfied her crack urge. At 3:00 in the morning, the party broke up, but Shawn wasn't eager to go home. She knew her husband, Doug, would be upset with her; she'd been gone for six hours and hadn't called home.

She'd been with Doug for eighteen years, married for eleven. At six-foot-three and 260 pounds, Doug was physically imposing yet soft-spoken and gentle. He was a homebody, and although Shawn wanted to be the same for him, she was a free spirit and often unpredictable. He'd been supportive of Shawn's drug issues over the years, but lately he had become impatient and aggravated when she relapsed.

Still in a party mood, Shawn and her friends decided to wait at a Kinsman Avenue bus stop until 5:30 A.M., when a nearby gas station opened and started selling beer. At some point in the early morning, a lanky black man stepped off a bus and approached Shawn's group to ask for a cigarette. Introducing himself as Tone, he struck up a conversation with Shawn. He told her he had served in the military and liked to cook. Shawn found him personable and also generous: when the gas station opened, he went across the street to a bank ATM, withdrew money, and then bought beer and wine for the group.

The partying continued until 7:00 in the morning, when Shawn told Tone that she was concerned her children would be waking soon to get ready for school. They would be walking to the same bus stop that she was at, and she didn't want them to see her sitting there drinking beer.

Shawn also didn't want to return to her house because she knew her husband would now be furious that she had stayed out all night. If she went home before her children left for school, they would witness an argument that was likely to escalate into a fight.

When Shawn told Tone that she needed a hangout place until her children were out of the house, he suggested they go back to his place on Imperial Avenue, about a half-hour walk from where they were.

Along the way, Tone purchased crack from a street dealer as well as a couple quarts of beer from the corner store. The two entered his house and walked up to a second-floor bedroom. As she climbed the stairs, Shawn was aware of a strong odor—like pet waste, she thought.

In the bedroom, Tone played a Temptations CD and lit incense. Tone, the perfect host, filled a crack pipe and offered Shawn the first puff. They smoked, drank, and chatted until 9:00 in the morning. She then thanked him for his hospitality and told him that she needed to get home.

When he asked her why she was leaving, she explained that she was married and that her husband would be worried about her. Tone then walked her down the stairs to the street, where a city utility crew was repairing a waterline. The morning was sunny but cold. Shawn, dressed in a gray turtleneck and lightweight burgundy sweat suit, zipped her jacket against the chill.

When she was about four houses away, she realized she didn't have her identification card. Suspecting that it had dropped out of her pants pocket while she was at Tone's, she returned to his house and rang his doorbell. He looked out his second-floor window. She had intended to yell up to him to drop her ID out of the window to her, but he motioned for her to come upstairs.

Tone met her at the side door and let her in. She stepped into the small entranceway and started climbing the steps to the second floor with Tone following. Suddenly, he fastened his arm around her neck in what she would later describe as a "military" choke hold.

His mouth close to her right ear, he instructed her to answer any of his questions with, "Yes, sir," and to follow his orders exactly. "You're not leaving here; you're not going anywhere until I say you can," he growled. "If you scream or run, I'll kill you."

She was then pushed back upstairs to the second-floor bedroom and ordered to remove her clothes. Confused and frightened, Shawn nevertheless was able to stave off the sense of panic that was enveloping her. She attempted to calm him—she'd spent fifteen years as a bank teller and prided herself on her ability to handle difficult customers. But her appeal for reason was answered by a slap across her face. He then roughly shoved her onto the bed, facedown, and began a violent and prolonged sexual assault. During the attack, he yelled, "I hate you bitches. Look at you . . . you got a husband at home and you're out in the streets."

After raping her vaginally, he tried to penetrate her anus, causing Shawn to scream. Tone then stood up from the bed and left the room. Shawn could hear him loudly closing the windows around the second floor. Then, from the living room, the music volume increased.

She realized he was preparing to kill her. Willing herself to think clearly, she saw that he hadn't closed the window in the second-floor bedroom. It was her only hope of escape. She moved quickly to the window and kicked out the screen.

Still naked, she stepped through the window opening and gripped the windowsill, planning to drop twenty feet to a narrow strip of broken pavement that ran between the side of Tone's house and the adjacent Ray's Sausage Co.

Just as she was going to release her grip to drop, Tone ran to the window and grabbed her hands. He struggled to pull her back inside, but her weight of 175 pounds was too much for him. During the tussle, she sustained several broken fingers on her left hand and a fractured right wrist.

Unable to pull her through the window, he decided instead to push her from the windowsill. Shoving against her shoulders, he broke her grip, and she plummeted to the concrete below. She was knocked unconscious, her skull fractured and eight ribs broken.

A chain-link security fence stretched across the paved area, preventing passersby from walking between Tone's house and the sausage factory. As Shawn lay in the narrow space, several neighbors peered through the fence at her. Others joined them, and soon there was a small crowd at the fence.

Minutes later, at 3:00 P.M., Donald Laster, a resident of nearby Shaker Heights, was driving past Tone's house with two friends, Leroy Bates and Vance Adams. The three men had just attended a funeral and were on their way to the deceased's family's house.

When Laster, who owned rental property on Imperial, noticed the unusual gathering near Tone's house, he stopped his Cadillac Escalade to investigate. He stepped up to the fence and saw Shawn—naked and with her face bloodied.

"She was moaning, not moving, and laying on her stomach," Laster recalled. When he saw that some of the onlookers were taking photos of her with their cell phones, Laster angrily told them to put their phones away.

Just then, Laster saw Tone, also naked, bear-walking on all fours through a patch of high weeds toward Morris. When he reached her, he bent over her with his back to the spectators.

To one onlooker, Fawcett Bess, it appeared that Tone was trying to choke Morris. He ran toward Tone and asked, "What did you do, Anthony?"

"It's cool," Tone replied. "She's my wife. We were fucking, and she fell out of the window."

"No, it's not cool—she's all bloody," Bess said.

Laster then told his friend Bates to retrieve a T-shirt from his truck. He tossed the shirt over the fence to Tone and told him to cover Shawn with it. Instead, Tone began half-carrying, half-dragging her along the concrete toward the rear of his house. Laster told him to put her down, and Sowell said, "Fuck you, this is my wife. I'll handle it."

Laster again told Tone to leave Shawn alone, threatening to "come over the fence and kick his ass" if he didn't. At that, Tone let the unconscious Shawn drop to the ground.

Suspicious of Sowell's intentions, Laster dialed 911 from his cell phone. Within five minutes, an ambulance arrived. Sowell, in the meantime, had managed to get Shawn on her feet and was walking her toward the back door of his house. Laster directed the ambulance crew toward the rear entrance. The paramedics took Shawn from Sowell and drove her to MetroHealth Medical Center in Cleveland.

In addition to the injuries to her wrist, fingers, and ribs, hospital tests showed that she had suffered a brain aneurysm. She also had the skin torn from her right leg when Tone dragged her to the rear of his house. Shawn underwent brain surgery and was heavily sedated. She was unconscious for the next three days.

She awoke on the morning of October 23. Later that day, her bedside phone rang. Answering the phone, Shawn heard Tone's voice warning her that if she told the police what happened at his house, he would kill her and her family.

Shawn then told the unit nurse that she needed to call her husband and let him know where she had been for the past three days. The nurse responded, "Oh, your husband rode in the ambulance with you when you were brought here."

Shocked, Shawn realized that it was Tone who had been in the ambulance. He'd probably been looking for an opportunity to kill her while she was unconscious, she thought. She now understood that Tone was serious about his threats. She also knew that her husband, Doug, would be unforgiving if she confessed that she had been partying at a stranger's house. She phoned Doug and told him that she had been struck by a car while crossing the street.

The paramedics who had transported Shawn to MetroHealth alerted police of the possibility that she may have been the victim of domestic violence. When police investigators questioned Shawn about her fall from the window, she initially refused to speak to them. Later, however, she allowed a detective to take a brief statement: Shawn told him that she was in Sowell's house drinking and smoking crack. While she was out on the second-floor balcony, she dropped her keys. As she reached over to pick up the keys, she lost her balance and fell off the roof.

Shawn then told police that Tone was her boyfriend. When police spoke with Tone, he repeated her story, saying, "Yes, she is my girlfriend. We were partying all day. She went off the balcony, and that's why we are here." In total, Shawn spent eight days in the hospital. Despite their skepticism about the cause of her fall and the suspicious similarity of Shawn's and Sowell's stories, police had no choice but to rule her fall as accidental.

Like he had so many other times, Tone had slipped through the cracks.

CHAPTER 3

The Smell of Dead Bodies

2007–2009

For more than two years, since the spring of 2007, the Cleveland Health Department had received numerous complaints from Imperial Avenue residents about a foul odor that had pervaded the air in their neighborhood.

Inspectors had visited Imperial on several occasions but were unable to determine the source of the smell, which one resident described as a mixture of blood and rotting meat.

On the hottest of days, the smell could be so overpowering that even residents without air-conditioning kept their windows closed. Baffled city officials quickly focused their attention on Ray's Sausage Co., a small meat-packing firm on the northwest corner of East 123rd and Imperial.

The owners, Ray Cash and his sister Renee Cash, whose father founded the business, argued that no animals were slaughtered at their facility. Suppliers delivered fresh and frozen meat to Ray's, where it was processed into sausages and other products and shipped out to stores. Furthermore, the Cashes said, there had never been a complaint in the fifty-seven years they'd been in operation.

Renee Cash was certain the smell was emanating from somewhere else in the neighborhood. "It got so bad that employees who worked in our second-floor offices kept the windows closed to keep the odor out," she says. "In the summertime, it can get hot in our building, but they preferred the heat to the smell."

Although local inspectors from the U.S. Department of Agriculture could find neither improper food handling nor disposal problems at the sausage factory, they cited Ray's Sausage for failing to "adequately control odors and vapors."

The City of Cleveland then insisted that the Cashes replace their factory's grease trap and internal plumbing, at a cost of nearly $20,000. Ray Cash spent thousands more on bleach, cleaning solvents, incense, and deodorizers. None of the measures worked. The mysterious smell continued to linger.

After the Cashes completed their costly plumbing replacement, a perplexed city inspector walked to the parking lot of the sausage factory, which was adjacent to Tone's backyard, and proclaimed that there "had to be a dead animal nearby."

Zack Reed, a Cleveland city councilman who represented the area until its redistricting, said he fielded several troubling calls about the problem in 2007. "A resident told us that it smelled like a dead person. Not dead meat, not a dead animal—a dead person," Reed recalls.

"Still, we couldn't get anyone from the city's health and building departments, the sheriff's office, or the police department to really take a thorough look at the problem," says Reed. "They just assumed it was coming from the sausage factory. But the people on the street had to live under the stench."

For Assad "Sam" Tayeh, the owner of Amira Imperial Beverage, a convenience store across the street from Ray's Sausage, the noxious odor was a mixed blessing.

During summer months, Tayeh saw a spike in sales of air fresheners and deodorizers, but he and his employees had to endure an odor that could be nearly intolerable at times.

"It was unbelievably bad, just unbelievable," Tayeh says. "The smell came in through my air conditioner vents. We put gallons of bleach and Pine-Sol in front of the vents. I got so desperate that I would stuff orange peels in my nose. My wife couldn't take it. She stopped working at the store."

While some residents chose to move away to escape the smell, most endured it—hoping it was a temporary inconvenience. Others, including Tayeh, were philosophical in their view, believing the rancid air was emblematic of the overall decay of Imperial Avenue and the surrounding Mount Pleasant neighborhood.

· · ·

Mount Pleasant, like many of Cleveland's inner-city neighborhoods, has a history that is marked by periods of prosperity and then steep decline.

Named for its attractive rolling hills and abundance of maple, oak, and birch trees, Mount Pleasant was originally settled in the 1820s by British farmers from the Isle of Mann. The area was primarily agricultural until the 1900s, when it was subdivided into home lots for generations of European immigrants who were moving east from their cramped living conditions in downtown Cleveland.

During the latter part of the nineteenth century, immigrants had come in waves from Southern and Eastern Europe, as well as parts of Asia, to work in the city's rapidly expanding steel, iron, and automobile industries. Along with its abundant labor supply, Cleveland's strategic location on Lake Erie and its network of rail lines enabled easy access to iron ore from Minnesota, coal from Appalachia, and various other raw materials used in its factories, mills, and foundries.

By 1920, Cleveland was the fifth-most populous city in the United States, with more than a quarter of its workforce employed in the vast complex of steel mills along the Cuyahoga River. The city's population included dozens of different ethnic groups who settled among others from their homelands in closely knit neighborhoods.

In Mount Pleasant, blacks had historically been a significant part of the early populace. Most had migrated from the South to work as construction laborers in the neighborhood. When their employer—a building contractor—found himself unable to pay their wages in cash, he compensated them with titles to vacant lots. Many of the workers built homes on their properties, and from the 1920s through the 1950s, Mount Pleasant was a stable, blue-collar community with one of the highest black homeownership rates in Cleveland.

Imperial Avenue, at the northern edge of Mount Pleasant, was an especially desirable address during the first half of the twentieth century. Shaded by large maple and oak trees, its well-maintained two-family colonials were occupied by teachers, doctors, and other professionals, many of them black. Boxing promoter Don King resided on the street, as did football great Jim Brown when he first joined the Browns in 1957.

Cleveland's economy was hit hard during the Great Depression, but a post–World War II industrial rebound pushed Cleveland's population to a peak of more than 900,000. Coupled with the success of the city's professional sports teams—the Indians won the 1948 World Series and the Browns dominated professional football in the 1950s—Cleveland seemed to be worthy of its business leaders' claim that it was "the best location in the nation."

Within ten years, however, the region began an irreversible slump in its auto and steel industries, which brought a host of problems to Mount Pleasant and other Cleveland neighborhoods. Factory closings and high unemployment exacerbated simmering racial unrest. Angered by de facto segregation in housing and schools, blacks rioted in the Hough and Glenville neighborhoods in the mid-1960s.

Middle-income residents had already begun their exodus to the suburbs in search of safer streets and better schools and housing, but now white flight began in earnest, leading to large population losses, corporate departures, and property deterioration. The city's deindustrialization negatively impacted tax revenues, which then led to cutbacks in community services.

In the commercial sections of Mount Pleasant, family-owned bakeries, butcher shops, and hardware stores that had existed for generations were replaced by check-cashing outlets and liquor stores. Boarded-up storefronts dotted Kinsman Avenue, the main artery in Mount Pleasant. Neighborhood conveniences such as banks, pharmacies, and dry cleaners were shuttered. At the few retail businesses that remained, metal bars covered windows and bulletproof glass separated cashiers from customers.

The residents who stayed behind in inner-city areas were those who couldn't afford to leave. Rocked by the one-two punch of poverty and a shrinking public safety net, Mount Pleasant and other largely black neighborhoods were about to suffer a new, insidious affliction: crack cocaine.

First introduced to urban areas in the early 1980s, crack quickly took root. Easy to produce and available at a price point that nearly anyone could afford, crack was a hit with buyers and sellers. The users found that they could experience an intensely pleasurable high and a respite, albeit brief, from their daily problems—all for a couple of bucks. Because the drug is highly addictive and its high lasts only fifteen minutes or so, dealers were assured of repeat business.

Crack quickly infiltrated entire neighborhoods, spurring an increase in drug-related crimes. Addicts stole or prostituted themselves to get more drugs, while gangs fought over selling rights in neighborhoods and housing projects. Cleveland's crime rate soared, with its homicide count among the highest in the nation.

While the drug's affordability—five or ten dollars a rock—was a key to its attractiveness, the social cost of its epidemic-like spread was catastrophic and enduring. Crack broke apart families—mothers left their homes for three-day drug binges, fathers died in gang shootouts or went to prison, and children were left to raise themselves or placed in foster care.

The absence of structure and adult authority had a devastating impact on school attendance. By 2005, Cleveland's public high schools had the nation's third-highest dropout rate, with less than forty percent of students graduating. Undoubtedly, many of those dropouts were lured by the street life and the prospects of easy money in the drug trade.

. . .

On Imperial Avenue, Sam Tayeh saw firsthand the calamitous impact of the crack epidemic. The influx of drugs and drug-related crime had triggered wholesale migration to the suburbs. Imperial's half-mile stretch of stately duplexes had become victim to foreclosure, vandals, and scrap metal thieves. The one-time enclave of working-class families was now a drug bazaar, with street corners and building alcoves populated by dealers, addicts, and gangbangers. It wasn't unusual for Tayeh to find empty nine-millimeter shell casings littering his parking lot when he opened his store in the morning.

Tayeh, who migrated to the United States from Palestine in 1977, purchased the convenience store from his brother in 2003. "The neighborhood was bad even then," he says. "Bad with drugs and violence. There were lots of shootings around my store, and it got worse over the years. I was starting to get nervous about being there."

After being held up at gunpoint twice and having his business broken into a half-dozen times, Tayeh installed security cameras in his parking lot. The move angered local drug dealers who believed that he planned to share his surveillance tape with police. On several occasions, the dealers destroyed the cameras with gun shots.

Tayeh considered selling the store, but with no formal education and a large family to support, he had limited employment options. While the violence in the neighborhood was disturbing to Tayeh, he says he was more troubled to see the drug culture's impact on children.

"I would see small kids outside my store begging for money so they could buy food because there wasn't any at home," he says. "One time, a mother sent her five-year-old son into my store to buy Chore Boy [a copper scrubbing pad that is commonly used as a makeshift filter in crack pipes]. Just to make sure that I knew what he wanted, his mother gave him a piece of Chore Boy to show me. I could see that it was charred—it had been used in a crack pipe. That bothered me a lot. I reported her to [Cuyahoga County] children's services."

In a disheartening twist, children sometimes exploited their parents, says Tayeh. "I saw sons selling crack to their own mothers. The sons didn't even care that their mothers were prostituting themselves to get the money to pay for the drugs."

As the neighborhood deteriorated, Tayeh saw its residents also undergoing decay. Tone, who lived nearby, was a frequent visitor to the store. When Tayeh first met him in 2005, Tone was well-dressed and friendly.

"But after three or four years, he got moody and his appearance became worse," says Tayeh. "He lost weight, and he looked dirty. He started acting weird and paranoid. We used to talk every day, but now he didn't want to talk to anyone. He would buy his Newport cigarettes and Cobra malt liquor, paying for it with coins that he had panhandled. When I saw that he had developed jerky hand motions, I knew that he had become a drug addict."

One spring morning when Tayeh was outside his store picking up litter in the parking lot, he noticed Tone standing nearby. After exchanging greetings, the two men stood for a moment looking at Imperial Avenue, which was quiet at that hour. Tone then surprised Tayeh by saying, "Someday, Sam, the whole world will know my name." Shaking his head at the cryptic comment, Tayeh returned to his sweeping.

CHAPTER 4

Resolution

October 2009

Cleveland Police Lt. Richard Durst was frustrated. Recently promoted to detective in the Sex Crimes Unit after ten years as a patrol officer, he was eager to begin work on Latundra Billups's rape complaint.

He'd been assigned the case on September 24, 2009, two days after the assault, but he'd had difficulty in reaching Latundra to schedule an interview with her. He phoned her several times and left voicemails. He even visited her house. Not finding her at home, he spoke to her mother, who told him that Latundra was a "tough one to track down."

On October 11, he spoke with Billups via telephone. Although she said she would meet Durst in his office, she was a no-show. Finally, on October 27, Latundra and Durst met at the Justice Center, a sprawling complex in downtown Cleveland that includes the Cleveland Police headquarters, the 1,800-bed county jail, and a twenty-six-story tower that houses municipal and county courtrooms.

When Latundra arrived at Durst's office, he was in the middle of a logjam of work. He asked her to wait, saying he'd be free in two hours. For a detective with a full caseload, it wasn't an unusual request. But for Latundra, who was still using drugs on a daily basis, it would be a test of her will.

"It's very difficult for a drug addict to just sit around for a couple of hours," Latundra says. "And the last place I wanted to be was at the Justice Center with all those cops walking around."

As a regular user of alcohol, marijuana, and crack cocaine for the past twenty years, Latundra had experienced numerous run-ins with the police. Over the years, she'd been arrested for a dozen offenses, including drug possession, disorderly conduct, thefts, and felonious assault. In 2002, she served a fifteen-month prison sentence for drug trafficking.

Latundra's drug abuse started in her teens, when she discovered that drinking and smoking marijuana helped her to overcome her shyness.

A self-described military brat who had spent time in a boarding school, Latundra had moved often during her childhood, with her father's Army assignments taking the family to Germany, California, Texas, Alabama, and Ohio. Although she did well academically, she recalls that she was often lonely. Latundra, who was extremely insecure as a child, says her frequent school transfers made it difficult to build friendships.

She graduated at sixteen with plans to pursue a career in social work or psychology, and eventually start a family. "I was always a daddy's girl, so I wanted to marry a soldier like him," she told friends.

Her dreams would be put on hold, though, while she indulged herself in the street life, partying with her friends nearly every day. While it would have been easy for Latundra to blame the start of her drug abuse on the bad influence of her friends, she recognized that she was using drugs to become more social. She enjoyed being the life of the party.

From marijuana and alcohol, she moved on to harder drugs. "I started smoking weed, then weed laced with crack, and then, before I knew it, I was smoking crack," she says. As she sank deeper and deeper into the grip of addiction, her drug use became reflexive and self-perpetuating—the addiction brought guilt and shame, which she salved with more drugs.

After returning to Cleveland from her 2002 prison stay, Latundra found that her felony record made it difficult to find employment. She did what she could to earn money. For a time, she collected scrap metal. Occasionally, she'd shoplift. Her inability to earn money for herself and her young children exacerbated her feelings of worthlessness and re-ignited her drug use.

"Drugs took away my problems and my feelings of inadequacy," she says. "I had to get high to ignore the realization that I wasn't a productive member of society or even of my family. I had lost everything. When I saw other women going to work, to the store, or taking care of their families, it hurt me."

Her craving for crack became the focal point and motivating force in her life. She used her monthly government assistance payments to purchase drugs—money that should have been used to buy food and clothes for her children. While she tried not to think about the impact her addiction had on her children, she clung to the belief that some day she would get cleaned up and be a good mother for them.

"I was embarrassed at what I had turned into," she says. "I wasn't raised to be a druggie and a thief. My kids would see me in the streets. They knew that their mom was a crackhead and they were ashamed of me." In 2007, her transient lifestyle prompted county social workers to remove Latundra's three youngest children from her care and place them with her mother.

"During my addiction, I never felt suicidal, but there were times I wished I was dead," Latundra says. "And this was one of those times. I experienced a lot of shame and guilt. I knew I was hurting my kids and my mother. But I tried not to think of them—and I never talked about them. The type of people who were around me back then didn't want to hear me feeling sorry for myself. I had to get tough. I had always been a sensitive, passionate person, but that wasn't going to help me to survive in the streets."

Harriet Billups, Latundra's mother, says she was saddened by the downward spiral of Latundra's life, but says she never turned her back on her. "I didn't want to give up on her; she was my daughter," Harriet explains. "But she wasn't committed to her kids; she was committed to the drugs."

By the fall of 2009, Latundra's drug use had upended her life. It wasn't uncommon for her to spend two hundred dollars a day on crack. Sometimes friends would provide a fix, but more often, she turned to prostitution.

Like many women who sell their bodies, her descent into prostitution was progressive. She began by trading sex to acquaintances for drugs. Before long, she was selling herself on the street. She was picky about her dates or "tricks" at first, but soon she was having sex with men whom she ordinarily would have found repulsive. In order to cope with the shame she felt, she learned to disassociate herself from the experience.

"I found it necessary to lower my standards and forget about my morals and values," she says. "I had always known that addicts would do all kinds of crazy things to get drugs, but I always thought there were things I would never do. I came to find out that those were just 'not yet' things: They were acts that I hadn't done 'yet.' For example, some men didn't want to wear a condom. Even though I was afraid to have unprotected sex, I wasn't going to let cash get away, whether it was ten dollars or a thousand dollars, which was entirely possible during the tax refund season. There were times when I smoked up a guy's entire income tax refund check in a weekend."

Latundra had given up control of her life to drugs. When her hunger for crack was raging, it wasn't unusual for her to be alone late at night in dangerous areas, where she risked being beaten, raped, arrested, or even killed.

"I'd walk great distances to get drugs," she says. "It was insane for me to be in certain neighborhoods at 4:00 in the morning. I wasn't oblivious to the danger, but my drug habit was so powerful that I just rationalized my behavior. I slept wherever I could, sometimes in abandoned homes that were being used as crack houses. I'd look around and I'd be in a place with no electricity or running water, no toilet paper, not even a toilet."

As an alternative to homelessness and the challenges of surviving on the streets, Latundra did what many drug-addicted women do: she found men who would provide a semblance of security in return for companionship. "We called them 'hostages,'" she says. "We'd give a man what he wants, whether it's sex, a clean house, or just friendship. And he would give us drugs and a place to stay."

In Latundra's view, Tone was neither a hostage nor a trick. "I thought he was one of the nice guys. We didn't have sex. He was just a neighbor on Imperial Avenue who invited me to his home for a few drinks. I thought I knew him. I thought he was safe. I was wrong."

As she sat in the lobby of the Justice Center on October 27, Latundra wanted nothing more than to leave and get high. The stress of being around so many cops was compounding the normal anxiety she experienced when she needed a fix.

But she recalled Tone's attack and realized she was fortunate to be alive. "I knew he was an evil person. Now I had an opportunity to make sure that what happened to me would not happen to anyone else."

When Durst finally ushered Latundra into his office to take her report, she sensed that maybe this was the reason her life had been spared.

CHAPTER 5

The Last Door

October 29, 2009

For more than a century, Luke Easter Park was a popular recreational and cultural center for the residents of the adjacent Mount Pleasant neighborhood. Originally known as Woodland Hills Park, it was renamed in 1980 in honor of Luscious "Luke" Easter, a power-hitting black first baseman for the Cleveland Indians during the early 1950s.

Easter, who was killed during a robbery in 1979, was known for his infectious smile and his towering home runs, including a 477-foot shot—the longest home run ever recorded in the old Cleveland Municipal Stadium. The park's centralized location in southeast Cleveland and its large open grounds have made it a frequent site for political rallies, concerts, and the annual black family unity day picnic.

At 6:40 P.M. on October 29, only a scattering of visitors, mostly neighborhood residents walking their dogs and the occasional jogger, were in the park when three panel vans and a black sedan wheeled into a parking area. The van doors slid open, and thirteen helmeted men in paramilitary black uniforms, high-top boots, thigh holsters, and bulletproof vests clambered out.

The men, members of the Cleveland Police SWAT team, would receive their final instructions before executing search and arrest warrants at the residence of Anthony "Tone" Sowell. Lt. Durst and another detective from the Sex Crimes Unit emerged from their sedan and joined the SWAT team.

The SWAT officers checked and rechecked their weapons and technical gear as their supervisor, Sgt. Dan Galmarini, outlined their various roles. Ultimately, the success of the night's assignment—and the safety of the men—would be Galmarini's responsibility.

Earlier that evening at SWAT headquarters, Durst had briefed the SWAT team on the layout of Sowell's house, its entry points, and a brief description of him. The plan called for SWAT to arrest Sowell or confirm that he was not in the house; then detectives would enter and search for evidence relating to the attack on Latundra Billups, including the pink sweater she left in the basement, the extension cord used to strangle her, and traces of her feces in the second-floor bedroom.

Although warrant service is a routine operation for the team—they serve 400 or so a year—the men were mindful that every situation is potentially volatile and dangerous. In Cleveland, and across the nation, the specialized skills of SWAT teams are increasingly utilized in felony warrant cases, particularly those that involve rape and other violent crimes.

"There's a safety factor whenever SWAT is deployed," says Galmarini. "We're trained to go into high-risk situations where there are guns involved. These are situations in which Sex Crimes detectives may not be comfortable. The detectives typically aren't accustomed to storming houses and conducting searches for people who may be hiding. While you can never know for sure if a person in a house has a gun, we go in expecting everyone to be armed. As SWAT members, we're always ready for violence because we're continuously training for it."

With each team member possessing an average fifteen years' SWAT experience, the men are confident in their abilities as marksmen and tacticians. Many have a military background, and nearly all have played competitive sports in high school or college. They are, in Galmarini's words: leaders who can take orders. "These guys are top-notch," he says. "They know their job well, and they enjoy the execution and satisfaction of completing a task."

At 6:50, the team piled into their vans and drove the half mile to Sowell's house. Durst parked near the front of the house, while the vans rolled to a stop just up the street. The SWAT members stepped from two of the vans and—despite the thirty pounds of body armor they were wearing—moved quickly and smoothly to the side entrance of the house. The third van carried two paramedics, who would wait outside in case they were needed.

Tonight's SWAT operation would begin with a "no-knock" entry. An officer, holding a thirty-five-pound battering ram, positioned himself at the house's side door. Richard Butler, the point man, was at his flank. The rest of the team lined up in a tight stack behind them.

At Galmarini's signal, the battering ram swung at the door, knocking it off its hinges. Butler, carrying a Benelli shotgun with a barrel-mounted flashlight, quickly entered. The others followed, their Glock nine-millimeter pistols held in two-fisted grips. Near the front of the SWAT column, an officer carried a fire extinguisher, which would be used to repel any aggressive dogs.

Butler, Wilmer Gandarilla, and four other officers climbed the grimy wooden staircase. They were tasked with arresting Sowell, who they believed was residing on the third floor. Other team members went to the basement, and the remainder would check the first and second floors. As the men entered and exited various rooms of the house, yells of "clear!" and "coming out!" could be heard.

The officers quickly swept through the first floor, where Sowell's stepmother, Segerna Sowell, had lived before she passed away in 2007. The kitchen, living room, and bedroom were orderly and clean, with Segerna's clothes still hanging in her closet, and pots and pans stacked neatly in a dish rack.

On the second floor, Galmarini and several officers entered the bedroom where Latundra said she was attacked. In the unfurnished space, they see a ripped blanket on the floor, CDs strewn about, and the feces that Latundra had mentioned in her police report.

At the same time, Butler's group has taken their first steps onto the third floor. In the messy, cramped kitchen, they see empty food containers and dirty dishes. Atop a microwave oven, a stuffed teddy bear is next to a ladies high heel shoe. They proceed down a hallway toward the bedrooms. Through his SWAT radio, Galmarini hears the men complaining about the foul smell.

The officers move stealthily along the corridor. At each doorway, an officer stands with his back to the wall, raising his gloved hand with three fingers up—signaling a three-second countdown. As the last finger disappears, two men burst into the room with gun muzzles just below eye level.

In the small bedroom where Sowell slept, dirty clothes are piled on the floor and atop the stained mattress. An open can of beer can be seen on a bedside table, along with a Bible and several pornographic DVDs. On the dresser, a spray bottle of Febreze is next to a Valentine's Day card and a box of condoms.

Butler and the others then move down the hallway toward the last door, which opens to the front area of the third floor. The smell grows in intensity as they approach the doorway. Butler turns the door knob . . . It's locked. He stands to the side while an officer swings the battering ram at the thin wooden door. As they burst into the room, the men recoil from the overpowering smell. Flashlights illuminate the space, which appears to be a sitting room or parlor. It's minimally furnished, with a small television, end table, and lamp.

Butler's attention is drawn to the floor. He points his flashlight at two dark shapes, realizing they are human bodies partially covered with black plastic.

"My first instinct was to stop and shout, 'Police, don't move!'" Butler recalled. "It took a second or two for us to realize that the people lying in front of us were deceased."

The SWAT officers wonder if Sowell himself is one of the dead. But the bodies are badly decayed and the faces are distorted and unrecognizable. A silver necklace with a clover-shaped pendant is visible on one of the bodies, while the other is wearing what appears to be a ladies' white skirt pulled up to her waist. Her ankles are wrapped with garbage bags. Cigarette butts and an empty beer can litter the floor.

As the men move about, they hear crunching sounds with each footstep. Later, they'd find dead maggots and flies caked in the treads of their boots. Meanwhile, Galmarini and several other officers had worked their way to the basement.

"Since it's common for suspects to hide under their stairs, we carefully checked that space," he says. "It was clear, but then we noticed that a section of the concrete floor had been chipped up and then covered with a mound of dirt. I looked closer and saw that a little bit of a plastic bag was protruding from under the dirt."

Just then, the officers on the third floor radioed Galmarini to come upstairs. As he climbs the steps, the unmistakable smell of rotting flesh becomes progressively stronger. A thirty-year police veteran, he's come to expect the worst when entering suspects' homes. He's learned to detach himself from the sight of families living in filthy conditions, with overflowing garbage bags, dirty diapers, weeks-old rotting food, and malnourished and neglected children and pets. But he was unprepared for the gruesome scene he encountered now.

"It was sickening to see two bodies laying side by side on the floor," Galmarini says. "I immediately suspected there was violence involved because they seemed purposely positioned. I knew I had to get everyone out of the room so that we could secure the area and preserve any evidence for the crime scene investigators and homicide detectives."

Backing out of the room into the hallway, he noticed several rolled-up towels that had apparently been pushed against the bottom of the door to keep the stench of decomposition from seeping out.

"We've all smelled dead bodies at their worst, in the heat of the summer," Galmarini says. "But the smell in that bedroom was just awful. The odor clung to us. Later, we all had to wash our clothes to get the smell out."

After securing additional search warrants for other areas of the house, homicide detectives arrive and are briefed about the third-floor bodies by Galmarini. He also tells them about the suspicious mound of dirt in the basement.

"Since we found two dead bodies upstairs, my antennas were up that there could have been other bodies," he says. "It was even possible that there was someone alive and tied up somewhere in the house."

Within a half hour, yellow police tape would be wrapped around the perimeter of Sowell's property and Imperial Avenue would be clogged by police vehicles, coroner's vans, and TV news trucks.

．．．

Across the street from Sowell's house, neighbors and curiosity seekers gathered in small groups watching the flurry of police activity. The cluster of people includes longtime Imperial Avenue resident Debbie Madison. The fifty-three-year-old had been napping when her son awakened her at 8:00 P.M. to tell her that dead bodies had been found in Anthony Sowell's house.

Madison left her house and joined the onlookers. When she sees coroner's investigators remove two shrouded bodies from the house, she is concerned that one of them is Sowell.

The thought that Sowell might be dead saddens her. During their casual neighborhood encounters, he had always been polite and helpful. On several occasions, she'd seen him mowing the lawns of his elderly neighbors, and he'd once repaired a leaking kitchen faucet in Madison's house. One afternoon when Madison, a single parent, was trimming shrubbery in her front yard, Sowell offered to assist. While working alongside her, he told her about his heart problems, even lifting his shirt to show her the scar from his pacemaker surgery.

Madison realized that she didn't know much about Sowell's personal life. She knew that he had served in the Marines and that he was dating a woman named Lori. "My impression was that they were happy together," she says. "I'd see them walking around the neighborhood together."

Madison then remembered that Sowell's sister, Tressa Garrison, and her children lived several blocks away on East 130th Street. Sowell had mentioned how close he was to his nieces and nephews, so Madison decided to drive to Tressa's house to gently break the news to her that her brother might be dead.

When she arrived and knocked on the door, Sowell's nephew Ja'Ovvoni Garrison answered. From the porch, Madison looked past Ja'Ovvoni and into the house. She was startled to see Sowell nonchalantly sitting on a couch holding a video game controller. *As if he doesn't have a care in the world,* she thought.

"At first, I was shocked to see him alive," she recalls. "I just looked at him and thought, 'If two dead people are in your house, why aren't you one of them?'"

Madison's instinct was to immediately return to Imperial Avenue and inform the police of Sowell's whereabouts. But when Sowell stepped onto the porch to talk to her, she found herself telling him that dead bodies had been discovered in his house.

"I wanted to get away from there, but I guess I just wasn't streetwise or slick enough to find a way to talk myself off that porch," she says. "I still couldn't comprehend that he was capable of murder. This was a man who sat on his porch and made small talk with people as they walked by his house. He would share his food with neighbors. I tried to tell myself that maybe the people they'd found in his house had died by accident. Like, maybe they had fallen and hit their heads against a coffee table."

But when Madison told Sowell about the bodies in his house, he became agitated and seemed as if he wanted to flee. She then offered to drive him back to his house so that he could speak with police. When he seemed reluctant, she said firmly, "I feel that you need to tell the police what is going on."

At that, Sowell began moving toward her car. Although Madison was still unsure that he was in some way responsible for the dead bodies, she was afraid to be alone with him. She suggested that his nephew ride with them, but Sowell told him to stay.

As Sowell was getting inside of Madison's car, he looked at her and said softly, "It's all going to come out now."

Confused, Madison asked, "What's going to come out, Tony?"

"That girl made me do it," he replied.

Madison assumed he was referring to Lori, but she didn't question him. They drove in silence to his house.

"It was very tense being in the car with him," she recalls. "I was thinking that when we got to the corner of East 123rd and Imperial, I would be so relieved to get him out of my car."

However, at the sight of the police barricades, Sowell became nervous and asked Madison to turn around and drive him back to his sister's house.

Madison returned him to Tressa's. After she watched him enter the house, she began her trip back to Imperial Avenue.

As she drove, she was overcome by the realization that she had been alone in her car with a killer. "I was in shock," she says. "My knees were shaking so bad that I could barely drive. I just screamed all the way back home. I just couldn't believe that this had just happened."

When Madison returned to her home, she told her son and several neighbors that Sowell had seemed to admit that he had killed the two people found in his house. Despite an Imperial Avenue neighbor trying to dissuade them from informing the police, Madison's son and a friend disclosed Sowell's whereabouts to a uniformed officer.

Within minutes, Madison, her son, and his friend were in a police car traveling back to Tressa's house. Cleveland Homicide Detective Melvin Smith was driving behind them. At the house, Smith spoke with Tressa and Ja'Ovvoni, who said Sowell had left on foot just ten minutes earlier. After getting a description of what he was wearing—dark pants, brown or black hooded jacket, and a black cable cap—the officers took Madison and the others home.

As crime scene investigators combed Sowell's house, police began organizing a manhunt. The search for Sowell, which focused on the many abandoned buildings and empty homes in Mount Pleasant, would involve the U.S. Marshals Service and scores of regional law enforcement officers.

· · ·

Madison was unable to able to sleep that night. "After the police took my report and dropped me off, I was so frightened that I told my daughter to turn on every light in the house," she says. "It was surreal to know that a killer had been living across the street from me. It was like something out of a horror movie."

CHAPTER 6

A Bigger Situation

October 29, 2009

While studying journalism at Norfolk State University, Stan Donaldson didn't envision that his career path would ever include a stint on the police beat. His interest lay in writing issue-oriented stories that were intended to spur community discussion. "Putting it out there and hoping it lands well," he would say about his journalistic agenda.

However, in 2009, as a general assignment reporter for the *Plain Dealer,* Cleveland's daily newspaper, Donaldson was assigned to the nighttime police beat. He soon discovered that he enjoyed being out in the neighborhoods covering breaking news and digging for the truths behind the "official stories" offered by law enforcement and governmental agencies.

Not only was he drawn to the fast-paced excitement of the cops beat, but he also found gratification in humanizing crime stories and exploring the impact of violence and drugs on the inner city.

Working the police beat at a big-city daily requires a singular combination of tact, aggressiveness, and writing skill. Effective police reporters are able to maintain mutually respectful relationships with sources while at times also pressing them for information.

Donaldson, a soft-spoken black reporter, had a knack for gleaning answers from police brass, prosecutors, and the coroner's office—sources who are customarily tight-lipped.

On any other night, Donaldson would have looked forward to catching a tip or a police broadcast and being a first responder to a shooting, armed robbery, or drug bust. But tonight, he was hoping for a quiet work shift. He would be off duty in a couple of hours and then on his way to Detroit to spend the weekend with his fiancée, who was attending medical school there.

Donaldson was twenty-nine and had worked as a reporter at the *Detroit Free Press* before coming to the *Plain Dealer*. He was looking forward to catching a Pistons game with old friends during his visit. In fact, he hoped to make it to Detroit—a three-hour drive—in time to have a beer before the bars closed.

At 8:00 P.M., he was on call at his apartment. He had just finished packing his suitcase when he received a phone call from the *Plain Dealer* newsroom. Two decomposing bodies had been found in the attic of a house on Imperial Avenue. According to the sketchy information provided by his editor, it appeared that the victims may have been an elderly couple.

"I figured I'd get to the scene, get my information, type it up, and I'd be on the road to Detroit in no time," Donaldson recalls.

But when he arrived at Imperial Avenue and saw law enforcement vehicles and TV trucks parked crookedly along the street, he sensed the story was more involved than police had initially indicated.

"As I walked toward the house, I heard a lady screaming and moaning from across the street," he says. "From what I could hear, she seemed to be saying that a friend of hers had been found in the house. That seemed odd to me. Her emotional reaction didn't really fit with what the police had said about the situation. I remember that the police spokesperson downplayed the lady's crying and said it had nothing to do with what was going in the house."

Flipping open the cover of his reporter's notebook, Donaldson began jotting down the basic facts of the story. He had a couple of hours of work ahead of him, but he was confident that he could file his story and make it to Detroit for last call.

. . .

Cleveland Police homicide detectives Melvin Smith and his partner, Lem Griffin, arrived at Sowell's house at 8:00 P.M. Slipping surgical masks on their faces, they did a walk-through of the lower floors and then climbed to the third-floor sitting room to view the bodies. The masks offered scant protection against the smell of death. Smith, a police officer since 1987, would later say the odor was "horrendous."

Due to the bodies' advanced decomposition, their race and gender were indeterminate to the detectives. Smith noted that plastic bags covered the legs of one of the bodies. Nearby was a clump of hair and a white-handled steak knife. The windows were covered by black plastic and a flat-bladed shovel was on the floor.

. . .

Down the hallway, in a bedroom, Smith finds a Social Security document and an Ohio food stamp card issued to a woman: Telacia Fortson. On a chair, women's panties are draped over prescription medicine bottles. Piled atop the dresser are random items of women's jewelry, including gold hoop earrings, bracelets, and an orange necklace.

. . .

Dr. Frank Miller III, the Cuyahoga County coroner, arrives at the house shortly after the detectives. His large staff includes seven forensic pathologists and a team of investigators, but it's his custom to personally respond to homicide scenes involving multiple victims.

Miller, tall and bulky with receding blond hair and wire-rimmed glasses, appears younger than his forty-one years. He speaks briefly with homicide detectives and then lumbers upstairs to view the two bodies in the sitting room. A forensic pathologist who has conducted more than 2,300 autopsies during his thirteen-year career, Miller seems undisturbed by the rancid smell in the house.

Recalling his team's actions that day, Miller says, "We removed the visible bodies from the third floor and then we took a look at the suspicious area under the stairs in the basement. We realized that if someone had taken the time to bury a body there, then we probably were going to have a bigger problem. My feeling from the outset was that this situation was going to get worse. I knew that we were going to have to search the entire property very carefully for other bodies."

. . .

As police investigators and coroner's officials prepare their preliminary reports, Crime Scene Unit detective Kristine Rayburn takes hundreds of digital images throughout the house. Shadowing other CSU detectives, Rayburn photographically documents the evidence that they collect, tag, and package. In the basement—an unkempt space with aqua-blue walls and rat droppings on the floor—Rayburn's images show broken furniture and soiled mattresses piled next to large garbage bags filled with women's clothing.

In Sowell's third-floor bedroom, Rayburn takes photos of a bare mattress covered by employment agency paperwork. On the bedside stand is a stack of movie DVDs, including *Night of the Living Dead*.

Photos of the second floor show a sparsely furnished area with just a chair and a rug in one bedroom. In a closet, the only item is a Winnie the Pooh lunchbox.

CHAPTER 7

Positive Hits

October 30, 2009

The local media, relying primarily on information from a police spokesperson, break the story that two decomposing bodies have been found in a duplex on the city's southeast side.

The news media reports that police found the two bodies when they went to arrest the home's resident, Anthony Sowell, fifty, for an attack that occurred there on September 22. Sowell, a registered sex offender who had served a fifteen-year prison sentence for an attempted rape in 1989, was not at home and was currently being sought.

Calling him "dangerous," police asked for the public's help in locating Sowell, described as six feet tall and 155 pounds, wearing eyeglasses and possibly a moustache or beard. Sowell's last known occupation was scrapping—collecting and selling metal and other waste material. Police alerted scrap yards and metal recycling facilities to be on the lookout for him.

. . .

While reporters are digging through court records and police files for background information about Sowell, forensic investigators comb his house for evidence. They focus initially on the suspicious mound of dirt under the basement stairs. After removing a layer of dirt, they discover a partially decomposed body. The body, which is wrapped in duct tape, appears to be female. Her wrists are bound with twine.

The discovery of a third body triggers a more intensive search. An FBI cadaver dog, specially trained to recognize the scent of decomposing human flesh, is brought to the house and immediately leads its handler upstairs to the third-floor sitting room.

The dog sniffed at a section of patched wall only a few feet away from where the first two bodies were found. To the investigators, it was apparent that the wall had been cut open and then repaired. After pulling away the drywall, detectives and the coroner's team discover a crawl space. They peer inside and see a pile of dirt, similar in consistency and volume to the pile they had found in the basement. A stuffed trash bag had been set in front of the dirt, blocking access to the crawl space.

"We had to move the black bag out of the way to get a closer look at the mound of dirt," says Coroner Miller. "To my embarrassment, that black bag contained a body."

Then, after scooping away handfuls of dirt, the investigators discover another body—the fifth so far.

"After finding the third body in the basement, I was pretty convinced that this was a strange case. And now I was certain," Miller says. "You don't get too many people who keep decomposed bodies in their homes. Generally, I've only seen these scenarios when people are illegally trying to collect social security benefits from a dead person or when an elderly parent is taking care of a disabled child. In cases where the elderly parent is the caregiver and they die, the child sometimes just can't get it together to notify the authorities about their parent's death."

But this situation was macabre from the start, says Miller, explaining, "We were seeing all kinds of burial methods—bodies were wrapped in blankets and plastic garbage bags and left lying out on the floor, while others were packaged in bags and covered with dirt. In the basement, someone had taken a lot of effort to wrap the body in duct tape. It was also odd that someone had bothered to carry dirt all the way upstairs to cover the body in the crawl space."

When the cadaver dog didn't indicate a "positive hit" in any other parts of the house, she was taken outside to Sowell's backyard. The dog quickly moved to an area near the house's back steps, sniffing excitedly at a patch of dirt that appeared to have been recently disturbed. After carefully excavating a two-foot layer of dirt, investigators found a decomposed body wrapped in clear plastic. Its gender indeterminate, the body had a phone charger cord wrapped around its neck and a strip of cloth binding its wrists.

. . .

Of the six bodies that had been found in Sowell's house and backyard, Miller identified two as black females. Although the race and gender of the other bodies are not immediately discernible, evidence showed that at least four were strangled. Some still had some form of ligature —rope, electrical cord, or wire—around their necks. In several cases, the wrists and ankles of the victims had been bound with twine or shoelaces.

Because the bodies are in varying stages of decomposition, Miller faces difficulty in identifying the victims and determining when they died. He urges the biological relatives of people who have been reported missing, particularly around the Imperial Avenue area, to provide DNA samples to help with identification.

. . .

For assistance in determining a timeline for the victims' deaths, Miller turns to Joe Keiper, a self-described "bug guy." Keiper, the curator of invertebrate zoology at the Cleveland Museum of Natural History, is one of only a couple dozen scientists in the United States with extensive experience in forensic entomology. Put simply, his expertise is determining the species and age of bugs found on a corpse. With that information, Keiper can help police estimate when death occurred.

Keiper explains to news reporters that the distinctive odor of a decomposing body attracts dozens of different types of flies and beetles. The first responders are typically blowflies, whose sense of smell is so acute they can detect death from more than a mile away. ("A bug's sense of smell puts a bloodhound's to shame," Keiper says.)

Blowflies can colonize a body quickly after death, depositing hundreds of eggs in nostrils, eyes, ears, mouths, and other orifices. Within a day, the eggs hatch into larvae—or maggots—that feast on rotting flesh. Maggots are thorough and efficient eaters, equipped with hook-like appendages that enable them to break through the skin surface. Once they've burrowed into the body, they secrete digestive juices on the dead tissue, creating a liquid that is sucked back up by the maggot.

For law enforcement purposes, blowfly maggots can be particularly useful evidence because they tend to grow at predictable rates—depending on environmental temperature, fly species, and other variables. Generally speaking, the larger the maggot, the older it is. By collecting and studying the largest maggots from a victim, Keiper can judge the postmortem interval—the period between death and the body's discovery.

. . .

It's Friday evening and news of the discoveries has spread. Across the street from Sowell's house, clusters of people line the sidewalk and tree lawns watching wordlessly as coroner's technicians and police haul body bags and evidence from the house. The spectators include family members and friends of Cleveland women and teens who have been reported missing. They hold photos of their loved ones, hoping that they won't be found in the house. Others seem resigned that their children, parents, and siblings are among the victims.

An impromptu memorial of balloons, prayer cards, and photos of missing people has been erected against the brick wall of an Imperial Avenue restaurant. The sidewalk is crowded with flowers and stuffed animals, left there by neighborhood residents, community activists, and visitors from throughout Northeast Ohio who have traveled to Imperial Avenue to mourn, share their anger and fear, or just satisfy their curiosity.

. . .

At 8:30 in the evening, police halt their search for more bodies. Cleveland Police spokesperson Lt. Thomas Stacho said investigators would resume the next morning, combing the house and yard "inch by inch, foot by foot."

Meanwhile, the hunt for Sowell intensified, with Cleveland Police and the U.S. Marshals Northern Ohio Violent Fugitive Task Force canvassing the Mount Pleasant area. "Sowell is the most wanted man in Cleveland right now," Stacho said.

For Latundra Billups, the at-large Sowell was particularly fearsome because he had threatened to kill her if she told police that he attacked her. Sex Crimes detective Richard Durst said police gave weight to his threat. Durst explained: "Sowell knew where Latundra lived, and we knew what he was capable of, so we had to find her a 'safe house' until he was in custody. The Sowell case quickly became very high level, involving the FBI and the Department of Homeland Security."

Crime Stoppers and the U.S. Marshals Service offered $12,000 in rewards for information leading to Sowell's arrest. Like many metal scrappers, Sowell targeted foreclosed and abandoned houses in his neighborhood, pilfering aluminum siding and copper plumbing and wiring. Police know that Sowell was familiar with the locations of numerous vacant houses. If he decided to hide in one, it would be difficult to find him.

Nevertheless, U.S. Marshal Pete Elliot was confident that Sowell would be apprehended. "We will turn every stone until we find him," Elliot announces.

Elliot's confidence was intended to ease the concerns of the Mount Pleasant community. But whatever relief the residents experienced quickly turned to anger when they learned that Cuyahoga County sheriff's deputies had been at Sowell's house on the morning of September 22, a month before the discovery of the six bodies—and just hours before he tried to kill Latundra Billups in a second-floor bedroom.

News reports revealed Sowell's status as a sex offender and his pattern of vicious crimes. The community learned that he had moved to 12205 Imperial Avenue in the summer of 2005, after serving a fifteen-year prison sentence for choking and sexually assaulting a twenty-one-year-old pregnant woman.

He rented the third floor of the house, which was owned by his stepmother Segerna Sowell, who had lived in the house with Anthony's father, Thomas Sowell Sr., until his death in 2003. Segerna lived on the first floor of the house, but she moved to a nursing home a month after Anthony's arrival.

When he was released from prison in 2005, Sowell was classified as a "sexually oriented" offender, the least restrictive of the three categories in effect in Ohio at the time.

Sowell's low-risk classification was due, in part, to the results of a psychological evaluation he underwent shortly before his prison release. The evaluation, which was intended to determine his likelihood of committing another sexual assault, concluded that he was "unlikely to reoffend."

Per his status as a low-risk offender, Sowell was required to report his address to the Cuyahoga County Sheriff's Office just once a year for ten years. He was also not required to notify his neighbors of his sex offender background.

Several years later, in 2006, Sowell's offender status changed with the passage of the Adam Walsh Child Safety and Protection Act. The new federal law established a national sex offender registry and a uniform system of classifying offenders.

Sowell was reclassified as a Tier Three offender, the most serious category. He was required to check in with the sheriff's office every ninety days, and he was subject to surprise at-home visits.

On September 2, 2009, Sowell checked in with the sheriff's office, as required.

On September 22, deputies made an unannounced "knock and talk" visit to Sowell to verify that he had not moved from his Imperial Avenue address. He met the deputies at his side door and chatted amiably with them. They left—unaware that bodies were stashed throughout his house and in his yard.

Later that same day, Sowell brutally attacked Billups, choking her until she passed out. Then, on October 19, Sowell raped Shawn Morris, who eventually escaped by jumping from a second-floor window of his house.

Community activists complained that if sheriff's deputies had conducted an in-house investigation, the dead bodies on Sowell's third floor and basement would have been discovered—and other women would have been spared from sexual attacks and even death.

But a sheriff's office investigator explained that without an arrest or search warrant, the deputies had no authority to enter Sowell's home. "For four years, that man was compliant," the investigator said. "He came in when he was told to, and he never varied. There was no reason to look at him for not complying with the sex offender law."

Sowell's neighbors joined the chorus of angry voices. They were upset that they were never told that a sex offender was living among them.

The sheriff's investigator explained that a peculiarity in the law enabled Sowell to "fall through a crack." Because he was already living on Imperial Avenue when he was reclassified as a Tier Three sex offender, he wasn't required to notify his neighbors that he was an offender. "Once an offender moves to a new address, then there would be notification," she said.

. . .

In Detroit, where he's visiting his fiancée, *Plain Dealer* reporter Stan Donaldson reads online accounts of the Sowell case. As more bodies are discovered and bits of Sowell's background are revealed, Donaldson realizes that he wants to cover the story.

"Of course, everybody wanted to report on a situation that involved a makeshift tomb," Donaldson says. "National news organizations were coming out of the woodwork. Out-of-state journalists and writers from Cleveland who had never even been to the Mount Pleasant neighborhood wanted to be part of this story. But I knew the neighborhood and the people. I knew I had to be involved."

CHAPTER 8

Capture

Halloween 2009

It's Halloween and a serial killer is on the run in Mount Pleasant.

At noon, Cleveland Police Chief Michael McGrath assures nervous parents that it's safe to trick-or-treat in the neighborhood. But he advises parents to escort their children and make sure they stay in groups.

In about six hours, the costumed youngsters will share sidewalks and front porches with nearly a hundred law enforcement officers who are now in their second day of a door-to-door manhunt.

Spearheading the hunt is Sgt. Ronald Ross, a member of the vice unit in the Cleveland Police Department's Fourth District, an area notorious for its high crime rate.

A twenty-year veteran, Ross received the assignment the previous night. "I was on duty and I got a call from our deputy chief, Ed Tomba. He asked me what time my shift ended," Ross recalls. "I was scheduled to leave at 9:00 P.M., but when the deputy chief is on the phone, I know I'm going home late."

Tomba told Ross that police brass and city officials wanted Sowell in custody before the trick-or-treaters began making their rounds on Halloween night.

"We live in a society of TV and movies, and they didn't want anyone turning the night into a Michael Myers thing," explains Ross, referencing the fictional villain from the *Halloween* horror movies. "It would have been mad chaos," he adds. A street cop for most of his career, Ross was instrumental in forming the CPD's Gang Impact Squad in late 2007. In its first six months, the undercover unit confiscated dozens of guns from gang members and arrested more than three hundred people for violent crimes and weapons and narcotics violations. The squad also had a key role in solving several high-profile gang killings, including the torching death of a twenty-five-year-old man.

"The deputy chief thought I had done a good job of finding shooters when I was in the gang unit," Ross says. "I know the streets; and he knew that he could count on me to find Sowell quickly. Basically, he just told me to do my thing."

Ross, along with detectives Robert McKay, Farid Alim, and Luther Roddy, equipped themselves with shotguns and bulletproof vests. Knowing that Sowell would be on the lookout for police vehicles, the men piled into unmarked cars—two in an undercover van and the other two in a sedan.

"We hit the streets and started knocking on doors," Ross says. "There was no other way we could have handled it. All the modern technology that we have now is great, but ultimately we have to go right back to old-fashioned police work. So we beat the bushes. We probably searched a hundred houses that night. We checked the homes of his relatives and his known associates, and we even checked an old childhood home of his."

Other police officers suggested that Ross monitor the bus and train stations for Sowell, who didn't own a car. But Ross was certain that Sowell would be found in Mount Pleasant.

"Sowell was a guy of the neighborhood, and I figured he was going to stay here because he was comfortable here," Ross says. "I told my guys that we were going to catch him walking down the street and it was going to be a nondramatic capture."

That night, Cleveland Police received hundreds of tips about Sowell's whereabouts. "It seemed that every time someone saw a curtain move in a house, they called us," Ross says. "As a scrapper, Sowell knew all the abandoned houses in the neighborhood. We broke padlocks off doors and searched the houses that we thought he might be in." By 3:00 in the morning, the men were tired and losing their edge. Ross told them to grab some sleep and be ready to resume the search at 6:00 A.M. "We needed to be sharp. There were risks involved in searching every nook and cranny of empty houses. We knew that Sowell was in a position where he had nothing to lose."

When the team regrouped, they spent the next several hours checking scrap yards that Sowell was known to frequent, suspecting that he may show up in need of quick money.

. . .

At noon, a light rain fell as Cleveland resident Joe Veal was driving on East 102nd Street about a mile from Imperial Avenue. Through water-streaked windows, Veal noticed a man walking on the sidewalk who seemed to match the description of Anthony Sowell that he'd seen on news reports. The man was wearing a backpack and a hoodie and was hunched against the rain, but Veal was certain enough of his identity that he drove to the Fourth District police station.

Veal saw two patrol officers outside the station and told them that he thought he spotted Sowell. "Follow me," he said, leading them to East 102nd near Mount Auburn Avenue. The hooded figure was still there. The officers approached him and told him that he resembled Sowell.

"I know I look like him, but I'm not Sowell," the man said. "You guys already stopped me last night. You checked me out and let me go."

One of the officers, patrolman Charles Locke, pulled the man's sweatshirt hood down to get a better look at his face. "He told us his name was Anthony Williams," Locke recalls. "He kept telling us we had the wrong guy."

Locke and his partner were unsure whether they'd found Sowell, but they weren't taking chances. The officers told him to get on the ground and handcuffed him. They searched his backpack and found a box cutter, an empty wallet, and a piece of carpet.

Minutes later, Sgt. Ross was radioed and told to meet Locke and his partner at East 102nd and Mount Auburn. "We pulled up, and I saw a guy who resembled Sowell sitting in the back of their police car," Ross said.

"But he didn't really look like the pictures that I had of Sowell. In the pictures, it appeared that he had a scar on his face. However, that could have been a scratch that had healed over. There was also some weight fluctuation between the suspect and the description I had."

When trying to identify someone, Ross said he focuses on the person's ears and eyes because they rarely change over time, unlike other facial features. But as he examined the man in the patrol car, Ross still wasn't positive that it was Sowell.

"But he was cool as a cucumber—kept saying he was Anthony Williams and that we had the wrong guy," said Ross. "I said to him, 'It's definitely too close to call on this one. I have a handheld fingerprint machine in my office. I'm going check you on it real quick. If you're not the guy we're looking for, we'll take you wherever you need to go and send you on your way.'"

Ross and the other officers drove him to a mobile command unit that was set up near the Imperial Avenue crime scene. Just as Ross was about to check his fingerprints, the man blurted out, "I'm Anthony."

"Anthony who?" asked a detective.

"Anthony Sowell. I'm the guy you're looking for."

He then dropped to his knees, sweating profusely, "as if someone had poured a bucket of water over him," Ross recalls. "We all looked at each other like, 'Wow! We just busted one of the biggest serial killers in Cleveland history.'"

Ross read Sowell his Miranda rights and asked him if he needed medical assistance. Still on the floor, Sowell said he "didn't want any help" and that he "just wanted to die."

Ross then radioed deputy chief Tomba that Sowell was in custody. He was told to transport Sowell to police headquarters for interrogation by detectives from the Sex Crimes and Homicide units.

As they transported Sowell, recalled Ross, he listened to police officers on their patrol car radios "going nuts" over Sowell's capture. "It was surreal," he said. "It felt good to know that we did a good job. That's what me and my guys do. We're out on the streets every day giving one hundred percent. But when you catch someone like Sowell, it's very satisfying."

During the trip to downtown Cleveland, Ross and Sowell made small talk. At one point, Sowell said he was "glad it's over." Ross then asked Sowell if the five bodies in the house were all that would be found. "I think so," said Sowell.

Ross then asked, "What about outside?"

"Oh, those, too," Sowell answered.

Ross and the other officers in the car glanced at each other. "We noticed that he answered the question in the plural, which got us concerned because at that point only one body had been found in the backyard. We didn't talk much more until we got to police headquarters. Sowell then told us that he 'wasn't a bad guy; he just needed some help.' Then he asked for a cup of coffee and a cigarette."

. . .

For more than eight hours, detectives interview Sowell. At times, he seems close to taking responsibility for the deaths of the six people found at his house, telling detectives that he had experienced surreal dreams and nightmares in which he hurt women by wrapping his hands around their necks.

At the beginning of the taped interrogation, which occurred October 31 and November 2, detectives coax Sowell to be forthcoming about his role in the crimes, offering supportive comments as well as coffee, cigarettes, and fast-food meals.

"I don't know . . . But I'm trying to help you," Sowell says when he is asked specific questions about the bodies found in his house. "It's more complicated than you think."

When detectives push Sowell for details, he becomes irritated and rubs his face or bends over to fidget with his shoelaces. He says he doesn't remember the names or physical descriptions of the victims. "Understand, you guys are badgering me and I'm racking my brain," he complains, his voice a gravely baritone. "Maybe a thought is coming . . . and I'm trying to say something . . . but you interrupt."

Sowell then leans back and says, "I can't describe nobody. I cannot do it . . . But I'm trying to."

The Sex Crimes detectives had started the interrogation by focusing on the rape allegation made against Sowell by Latundra Billups in September.

Sowell admits that he knows Latundra—whom he calls Lala—from the Mount Pleasant neighborhood, but he says that their sexual relations were consensual and that they had "hooked up" a couple of times. He says that Lala was a drug user who would occasionally come to his house when she was hungry or needed a place to sleep.

Sometimes she would strip down to her panties and walk around his house. "That was the hustle game," he explains. "That was to try and get me to buy her drugs."

Sowell says that on September 22—the day of the alleged attack—he purchased forty dollars of crack for her and then they walked back to his house. He tells detectives that Lala was into kinky sex and asked him to whip her with an extension cord. He says he refused, telling her, "You got to be out of your mind."

According to Sowell, he and Lala had "regular sex" and then she left his house unharmed after changing into a shirt that she took from a bag of clothes in his basement.

In her police report, Lala said that Sowell offered her a shirt because he had ripped her sweater when he attacked her. Detectives now ask Sowell what would have prompted Lala to change her shirt at his house. He is unable to provide an explanation. When asked why Lala would accuse him of raping and strangling her, Sowell attributes it to vindictiveness, saying, "She's just bitter because I told her I wouldn't buy her any more drugs . . . She said she was going to get me."

Sowell is then handed off to the homicide detectives, who begin their questioning by asking him about the living arrangements at his house. He explains that he generally stays on the third floor. However, his stepmother has been hospitalized, so he sometimes stays on the first floor, which was her living space. Once detectives have established that Sowell is the only resident of the house, they press him to explain why there were bodies on the third floor and in his basement.

"Hey, Tone, this is really, really important," a detective says. "This next fifteen minutes might be the most important fifteen minutes of your life. What we're looking for is for you to be honest with us . . . Now you know we have been to your home . . . "

"Okay. What, what, what?" says a clearly perplexed Sowell, repeatedly rubbing his hand over his bald head.

"Upstairs on the third floor where you stay, we saw . . . we found . . . some folks up there. So what happened up there on that third floor?"

Sowell leans forward in his chair, bouncing his heels against the floor. "I just hate what they did—what they do to me. I'm a nice guy. I feed them, and they steal and treat you like shit. They forget about you. My head . . . I don't know what's wrong with me," he says, his voice trailing off.

A detective tells Sowell that he notices some anger in his words. He then asks Sowell when he first lost control of his temper.

"After me and my girlfriend broke up, I guess," Sowell replies. He tells the detectives that he began hearing a voice in his head that told him to do bad things. The voice's name was Arnie, he says, explaining that it gave him instructions to "rape those girls and shit." Sowell, now rambling, continues: "People don't give a fuck about nothing, nobody . . . even when you help them. I don't know what happened, but I know it had something to do with my last girlfriend."

He then becomes agitated, confiding to the detectives that he felt used and discarded by his ex-girlfriend, Lori Frazier, who had struggled with a longtime drug addiction. Sowell says he worked ten-hour days as a machine operator at a rubber molding factory to provide for her every need. When she was arrested for a drug offense, he walked an hour and a half from his home to the Justice Center in downtown Cleveland to visit her in jail. He made that trip three times a week, he tells the detectives.

"I walked so that I could save a little money and put it on her [jail commissary] account," he says. "She never knew I walked down there. Then I had to turn around and walk an hour and a half back home."

Sowell tells the detectives that when Frazier resolved to kick her addiction, he helped her every step of the way, encouraging her to enroll in drug abuse programs and appearing as a character reference for her at several court hearings. Frazier eventually did become sober, he says. But shortly afterwards, she left him, saying she needed a healthier environment. Confiding in the detectives as if they are his therapists, he says he was heartbroken and angry about losing her. He says he felt like she had taken advantage of him and then abandoned him.

Calling the breakup "traumatic, very traumatic," Sowell says Frazier betrayed him. "I was with her all the time and I did everything for her . . . I helped her and then when she got better, she just didn't give a fuck."

A detective shifts the discussion from Frazier, telling Sowell that many of his neighbors have said he was a good guy who was always willing to offer a helping hand.

Sowell reacts positively; his posture relaxes and a thin smile appears. "It's like every time I go out my door, somebody needs this, somebody needs that," he says. "I cut their grass, I fix their pipes. I don't mind that . . . because that's what neighbors are supposed to do. They try to pay me and I was like, 'No, don't pay me.'"

"You fixed your neighbor's sink," a detective says approvingly.

"She told you that?" Sowell asks.

"Yeah, I will tell you what. She didn't forget that."

"Yeah, I fixed her sink," he says, smiling.

"People love you, Tony . . . A lot of people value you. I know right now, you think that you are some evil person . . . I don't believe that to be true, not from what I talk to other people about. You are valued."

"She told you I fixed her sink? Yeah, I did that," Sowell says.

"Yeah, that was important to her."

"I know everybody is going to make me out to be evil, but I'm one of the best . . . "

In a soothing tone, the detective then prods Sowell. "And you loved your girlfriend . . . you didn't want to hurt her . . . maybe you take that anger out on some other people, huh? . . . Tony, what was it about the folks we found in your house that pissed you off?"

Sowell admits that he occasionally took his anger out on women, particularly those whose drug abuse and irresponsible lifestyles reminded him of Frazier's. He complained that Frazier didn't spend time with her four children, all of whom lived with their relatives.

Frazier would sometimes disappear for days at a time on drug sprees, says Sowell. "And her kids used to call asking, 'Have you seen my mommy? Is my mommy there?'"

Sowell says he tried to reason with Frazier, telling her, "How do you think I feel when your kids call here two or three days straight . . . and I don't know where their mommy is? If something happens to you, how am I going to be able to face them? I'm supposed to be your man and everything, but then I let something happen to you?"

Detectives then shift gears, asking Sowell where he typically meets women. He says he meets women in his neighborhood, sometimes as they walk past his house on the way to the beverage store. He then offers a lengthy, sometimes contradictory, explanation of his relationships with women.

While he says that he knows that women are "hustlers" who are out to get what they can, he says it's his nature to help them, to give them food, clothes, and money. He tells the detectives that he used to give hamburgers and buns to a young woman in his neighborhood. "She hadn't ate in three days and her boyfriend had left her," he says. But he also decried the way women treated him, saying they didn't appreciate his kindness.

Sowell says it wasn't uncommon for women to proposition him for drugs. While partying with women at his house, he concedes that he sometimes lost his temper. "One thing that always made me mad was if they had kids," he says. "That's a big thing in my head . . . I'd say to them, 'Why aren't you with your kids? You'd rather be doing this than be with your kids? You are all mothers!'"

Visibly upset, his voice rising, Sowell abruptly mentions his own mother, saying, "She still today never told me she loved me . . . never . . . never in her life . . . it's hard to explain."

"Now I think I get you," a detective says. "Tone, these women, they were hurting their children and their families by the lifestyle they were leading."

"Using people, tricking them, robbing them, lying," Sowell says. "Take your money . . . take your watch . . . snatch and they're gone."

When he felt betrayed and taken advantage of, says Sowell, the anger set in and he began hearing a "voice" that told him to "hate and punish." Whatever occurred next was a "blur," he says.

Detectives ask Sowell how he punished the women.

"Would you slap them and beat them with your fists?"

"I don't think it was nothing like that," Sowell answers.

"Would you choke them? Would you stab them? What do you think it was, Tone?"

"I don't know . . . I think I just choked them," he says in a low voice.

After a few more questions about what he did to the women, Sowell says, "They were strangled. That's all I can tell you."

"So you strangled them?"

"I think it was with my hands . . . That's all I can tell you," he answers. "I don't remember using [a rope or piece of clothing] to strangle the women. . . . But maybe I did. I'm just saying they were all strangled."

Detectives then become firm with Sowell, asking him how many bodies police could expect to find in his home. "I just don't remember," he says. "It's like there's two of me or something. I just don't know. That part of me is missing. It's like it's not real . . . like it never happened. I can't explain it to you."

Sowell says he sometimes experienced blackouts when he was with women. When he emerged from a blackout, the woman would be gone from his house, leaving him confused about what happened to her. "Reminded me of my girl, that's the best I can tell you. It was like everything's cool, she was spending the night or something. [And the next morning] I'd be like, 'Damn, where'd you go?'"

Sowell says his mind was a "blank" when he was with the women in his house. It was like a dream, he says. "And then when I wake up, everything is okay."

He confesses to having experienced the surreal dreams or "blackouts" that lasted between ten and fifteen times.

Detectives press him for the names of the women he was with. Sowell says he can't remember their names, but he says he might be able to recognize their faces if police showed him photographs.

"But they were females?" the detectives ask.

"Yes," Sowell says.

"All black females?"

"Yes," says Sowell, adding that they were all adults. No children were involved, he says.

Sowell is insistent that he can't remember the victims' identities or even whether they were ever really in his house.

"The bodies in your house, there's no way you can avoid. . . ," a detective presses. "You know those dreams came true. You know those weren't false dreams? There's nothing you can say . . . And you even admit the bodies were there."

"I've told you the same thing over and over. You ain't been listening to me," yells Sowell. "I don't remember actually killing nobody."

The detectives become increasingly frustrated with Sowell as he continues to deny knowing there were bodies on the third floor or in the basement of his house. Expressing skepticism, they tell Sowell that even if he experienced a dream episode while strangling the women, he couldn't have been oblivious of the bodies.

One of the detectives leans in toward Sowell and says, "There's no way you didn't know about the bodies. With six bodies, you couldn't have forgotten about killing them all. The dream ended as soon as you hauled that dirt up there and put it on top of a damn body."

They remind him that someone had taken considerable effort to wrap the bodies in plastic and carry dirt from outside to the third floor and the basement. They add that someone had also stuffed clothes against the bottom of the sitting room door to prevent the stench of decomposition from leaking out of the room.

"Didn't the bad smell in the house bother you?" Sowell is asked.

He shrugs and says he was aware of an odor, but says he considered it no worse than the smell of a dog. Sowell also acknowledges that he became frightened one day when he saw that his sandals were bloodstained. "I liked to wear my sandals around the house," he says. "And when I went to get them, I thought, 'Oh, I must've stepped in some blood or something.'"

The detectives take a break, telling Sowell they are frustrated by his lack of cooperation. They leave the room and then return with a bag of food from McDonald's. Sowell chews on French fries while saying again and again that he didn't know there were bodies on the third floor of his house. He then tells the detectives that he was forbidden from opening the door to his third-floor sitting room.

"Who told you not to go into that room?" he is asked.

"The voice in my head told me," answers Sowell. "I was told that the room was off-limits . . . I was scared to go in there."

He was asked if his fear stemmed from the fact that two decomposing bodies were laying on the floor of the sitting room.

"Probably," he says.

The detectives continue to press for an explanation of how bodies ended up in his house and backyard, but Sowell repeatedly says, "I don't know."

"I can't believe this, man," a detective shouts. Then he asks, rhetorically: "How does dirt get in your house on the third floor in a crawlspace on top of a body? You say you don't know . . . How did the dirt get downstairs, in the basement under the second-step stairwell on top of a body? You say you don't know . . . How did the body get in your backyard? Again, you say you don't know."

Sowell howls and clamps his hands against his face. "I don't care what you believe," he says. "I don't care what you believe . . . Then fuck it . . . I'm telling you the best I can."

Suddenly, he seems to comprehend the enormity of the crimes he is accused of. Elbows on his knees, rocking back and forth, he says, "My life is over."

. . .

At one point during the detectives' rigorous questioning, Sowell virtually admits to killing the women found in his house. Although he insists that he doesn't "remember actually killing anyone," he says, "I guess I did that" when detectives challenge him to explain how bodies ended up on his third floor.

Head bowed, staring at a spot on the floor, he says, "It had to be me."

A detective then describes the body that was buried under a pile of dirt in his basement, asking, "Why would the arms and hands be bound?"

Sowell rubs the top of his head. "I guess I did that, too," he says.

"Why would you say that?" asks the detective.

"Because nobody else could have did it."

"With the dreams you say you're having, would you say that you're capable of that?"

"I guess I am," Sowell answers.

. . .

Night falls outside of the Justice Center window and Sowell is visibly fatigued. He leans forward in his chair, his elbows on his knees, his hands clasped. He takes long pauses before answering questions and, at times, wipes tears from his eyes.

The detectives plead with Sowell to help them identify the six victims.

They ask him for the names of the women or descriptions of the clothing and jewelry they were wearing when they were in his house.

"I'm trying, but I don't remember names," he says. Attempting to jog his memory, detectives show Sowell a diagram of his house marked with the various spots where victims were found. Sowell points to several of the locations, offering general descriptions of the corresponding victims such as their height and what they were wearing when he met them.

They then show him a series of pictures of women who have been reported missing. He adamantly denies recognizing any of the faces. At one point, he shouts that he is done talking and demands that he be returned to his jail cell.

Appealing to his manhood, his belief in God, and his sense of honor as a former U.S. Marine, the detectives tell him: "The families of these women are hurting. They need closure. What if you thought that your daughter was in that house? You'd want to know, wouldn't you?"

Sowell agrees, but says, "I'm trying to give you what I can . . . But I have no memory. I'm not thinking reality from fantasy."

In softer tones, the detectives assure Sowell that they are not judging him. "We don't judge nobody, okay? We know that something triggered you to do this . . . But whatever you did, we know you got honor. What's that saying? 'Once a Marine, always a Marine' . . . You're a Marine until the day you die. You need to do the right thing. We just want you to forget about yourself right now and think about helping these families."

Softly, Sowell says, "I can't help them."

CHAPTER 9

An Insatiable Appetite

November 3, 2009

Police detectives and coroner's personnel clamber over mounds of dirt and kneel beside trenches in Anthony Sowell's backyard. Shielded from public view by a large blue tarp, the investigators have unearthed new horrors.

Earlier in the day, after a trio of cadaver dogs sniffed and pawed at a section of freshly tilled dirt in the rear of the yard, police brought a backhoe and dump truck to the scene.

Coroner Frank Miller supervised the backhoe operator as he carefully peeled back thin layers of soil until the edge of a black plastic bag was spotted. Miller and his team then took over the digging, using small shovels and rakes. In the shallow pit, they saw what appeared to be a skeletal human arm. Whisking clumps of dirt away, they reveal a partially mummified body, its hands tied above its head, ankles bound with cable wire, and a knotted cloth wrapped around its neck.

After the discovery of a seventh body, investigators decided to excavate the entire backyard. "We did a total grid search, digging up every part of the yard that wasn't paved," Miller says.

As darkness falls, a heated tent is erected in the backyard so crews can work into the night. Under the glare of spotlights, the forensics team finds four more bodies in the yard, which now resembles an archaeological dig site. The workers, clad in protective jumpsuits and plastic gloves, slide tarps under the bodies and gently lift them from their shallow graves. Most are partially clothed and so badly decomposed that their gender is not immediately discernible.

Television stations and newspapers learn about the ghoulish burying grounds, igniting a frenzy of media attention. A dozen TV satellite vans are now parked along Imperial Avenue, which has been barricaded at both ends by fire trucks.

By 8:00 P.M., the street in front of Sowell's house is crowded with camera crews, neighborhood residents, families of missing victims, and concerned and curious people from throughout Cleveland.

A second, larger, tarp has been strung around Sowell's backyard to hide the forensic workers from the newshounds. But the reporters and camera crews are able to circumvent the privacy measure by persuading neighbors to allow them access to the upper floors of their houses. From their perches, the camera operators transmit live images of the excavation activity to TV stations, cable news channels, and online news sites.

"And then the hovering news helicopters arrived," Miller says. "They quickly became a nuisance. The police department eventually had to ban helicopters from the area."

Meanwhile, inside Sowell's house, investigators are doggedly hunting for evidence. Police had suspended their search for the past two days, awaiting the issuance of a comprehensive search warrant that gave them permission to take apart the house "brick by brick if necessary," said a police spokesperson.

Now, in the cluttered, musty basement, a detective is picking through piles of household items and clothing. In a far corner, he spots a pink plastic bucket that has punctures and gouges around its rim. Inside the bucket is a paper bag. Opening the bag, he is startled to see a human skull.

To Miller, the skull didn't seem to have been manually dismembered. He suspects that through natural decay, the victim's head just separated from its body. Since there was dirt and gravel in the bucket, he says it's probable that the intact body had been buried in the backyard at one time.

"It may have been buried too shallow and the head began to show because of rain erosion or an animal digging it up," Miller theorizes. "Maybe the killer saw that his work was showing and decided to dig it up and move it."

Miller assesses the punctures on the bucket, concluding that they are bite marks, perhaps from a dog or large vermin.

Investigators stop their search efforts around 9:00 P.M., planning to resume in the morning. The forensic team carries evidence bags from the house to their vans, walking briskly through the gauntlet of scoop-hungry reporters.

The victim count is now at eleven, making 12205 Imperial Avenue among the deadliest crime scenes in Cleveland history. Police Chief McGrath tells reporters that all measures will be taken to make sure there are no undiscovered bodies in Sowell's house, including dismantling walls and floors if necessary.

"It appears that this man had an insatiable appetite that he had to fill," says McGrath. Addressing concerns that Sowell may have dumped victims elsewhere in his neighborhood, the top cop assures Clevelanders that police are checking for bodies in all vacant homes within a half mile of Imperial Avenue.

The large congregation of neighbors, commiserators, and curiosity seekers that had filled Imperial Avenue has dwindled to about thirty. Relatives of missing women are watching anxiously, wondering if their loved ones are among the victims. Spontaneously, the family members join hands with one another, praying aloud for the unidentified victims.

. . .

TV stations and cable news shows interrupt regular programming to announce that the Imperial Avenue death toll is now at eleven.

Miller discloses to the media that the killer or killers had wrapped and taped all of the victims in different ways. "Most had their wrists and ankles bound with wire or shoelaces or rope," he says. "Seven had a ligature around their neck. We've also seen that there is a variety to the ligatures, including belts, coaxial cable, cloth, and extension cords."

When asked his reaction to the scope of the serial killings, Miller says he was initially shocked by the discovery of the first six victims. "And I was certainly not expecting that we would find five more. Clearly, this situation is out of the norm. Whether this [killer] is sociopathic or psychopathic or has dissociated from any kind of conscious, moral, or superego control, there is—to put it in layman's terms—definitely something wrong with this."

News services disseminate information about the Imperial Avenue horrors and Anthony Sowell to a worldwide audience. The public learns that Sowell is a Cleveland native born in 1959 to working-class parents. His mother, Claudia, worked as a dry cleaner presser and his father, Thomas Sowell, was a jack-of-all-trades construction worker prone to drinking and a nomadic lifestyle. Thomas moved away when Anthony was an infant, leaving Claudia to raise him and his maternal half sister Tressa.

Former schoolmates and neighbors recall that young Sowell had a small circle of friends, but he was quiet and considered "different," which led to occasional teasing and bullying by other children. He attended Shaw High School in East Cleveland, but he didn't have enough credits to graduate with the rest of his senior class. In January 1978, shortly after he had impregnated his girlfriend Twyla Austin, the eighteen-year-old Sowell joined the U.S. Marine Corps. Eight months later, Austin gave birth to Sowell's daughter, Julie.

Sowell spent his eight-year enlistment at military bases in North Carolina, California, and Japan, primarily working as an electrician and also as a cook. While stationed in North Carolina, he married a fellow Marine, who told friends that she married Sowell to prevent him from "drinking himself to death."

By all accounts, Sowell was an exemplary Marine, although his military record was blemished when he went AWOL for two months, leading to a demotion in rank. He eventually regained his rank and was a sergeant when he was honorably discharged in 1985. His wife divorced him shortly after he left the Marines.

Sowell returned to the East Cleveland area and spent the next five years adrift, working at various menial jobs and drinking heavily. According to some sources, he was also using and selling crack cocaine.

In 1989, he was accused of kidnapping and repeatedly raping a twenty-one-year-old woman in the East Cleveland house that he shared with his mother, grandmother, and numerous relatives. The victim, Melvette Sockwell, who was pregnant at the time, says Sowell bound, gagged, and held her hostage in his third-floor bedroom. Sockwell was able to escape by wriggling through a dormer window onto the roof after Sowell, who had been drinking, fell asleep.

Sowell was arrested and charged with kidnapping and rape. Freed on bond, he failed to show up for his court hearing. While police searched for him, a thirty-one-year-old Cleveland Heights woman, also pregnant, said Sowell brutally raped her. When she refused to cooperate with police, the investigation was dropped.

In the Sockwell case, Sowell pleaded guilty to attempted rape and was sentenced to fifteen years in prison. While incarcerated, he worked as a cook, electrician, and food server. Sowell earned his GED and completed several programs, including drug awareness, anger management, and an

Alcoholics Anonymous treatment program. However, despite his request to attend sex offender treatment, he was not admitted to the program. He was reportedly denied entry because he refused to admit that he had committed a sex crime.

. . .

The coroner's office announces that the six bodies found on October 29 and 30 are females and were all victims of homicide. Spokesman Powell Caesar says at least five of the victims had been strangled. Two of the victims were black, but the race of the others has not yet been determined due to advanced decomposition. None of the six victims has been identified.

Now, with the discovery of four more bodies and a skull, all in various stages of decay, the coroner's staff is stretched to their limits. Noting the tremendous scope of work involved in identifying eleven people and performing eleven autopsies, Miller says, "It's very rare to find this many bodies at once. It's a bad day in Cuyahoga County."

Saying that forensic pathologists will rely heavily on DNA matching to identify the victims, he appeals to biological relatives of missing women to provide DNA samples, a process that involves swabbing the inside of a person's cheek to collect buccal cells.

Miller says that samples from a mother or child of a missing person are typically most helpful in matching genetic markers. Technicians will then compare the swabs of relatives with DNA that has been extracted from victims' teeth and long bones such as the humerus and femur.

Caesar says it hasn't been determined how long the bodies were at Sowell's. "They could have been there anywhere from weeks to months to years," he says, adding that some of the bodies may have been in the house or yard since 2005, which coincides with Sowell's release from prison.

Miller says the severe decomposition of some victims will make it impossible to determine when they died. Although he says he is hopeful that all eleven will be identified, he cautions, "There's a possibility that we may not be able to identify everyone."

Police urge friends and family of missing people to bring biographical information and photographs to Cleveland's Fourth District police station or to a temporary command post that has been set up near Sowell's house.

. . .

As the victim count rises on Imperial Avenue, so do the tempers of Sowell's neighbors and the relatives of missing women, who say that Cleveland police and city officials were indifferent to their concerns.

The people who live near Sowell's home question why cops, firefighters, health inspectors, and a raft of local authorities failed to pinpoint the source of the stench that plagued the neighborhood for several years.

Residents reported the foul odor to health and building department departments as early as 2007, but inspectors repeatedly said they could find no cause. Eventually, the blame settled on a nearby meat-packing plant. But the smell persisted even after the owners of Ray's Sausage Co. replaced their sewers and plumbing systems.

The nightmare on Imperial Avenue continues to unravel, with neighbors not only wondering if more bodies are entombed in Sowell's house, but also expressing bewilderment that the killing spree carried on for so long without detection. The news that some of the victims may have lain dead since 2005 has galvanized the community's anger at the police department for its inconsistency in investigating missing persons. Family members wait anxiously to learn whether their loved ones will be identified as Imperial Avenue victims.

Reports surface that at least two women who are currently missing had lived near Anthony Sowell. Janice Webb disappeared in June 2009 and Nancy Cobbs was last seen in April 2009. Cobbs's daughter, Audrey Williams, tearfully tells a TV reporter, "I hope that my mother is not one of the victims and I hope she comes home."

Several other missing Cleveland women were reportedly last spotted near Sowell's house. Telacia Fortson, a thirty-one-year-old mother of three, went missing on May 31, 2009. Her mother, Inez Fortson, tells reporters, "The last time I saw her, she kissed me on the forehead and said 'I'll see you next week.' But I never heard from her again."

And the family of Michelle Mason says she was last seen one block away from Sowell's house when she vanished in October 2008.

The families join a growing number of community activists and Mount Pleasant religious leaders who are voicing complaints about the police department's perceived disinterest—and even unwillingness—to take reports about missing adults, particularly those who live in the inner city.

The Cleveland Police respond strongly to insinuations that they shrug off missing persons reports. Spokesperson Lt. Thomas Stacho says in a press conference that police prioritize their search efforts on juveniles and adults who are elderly, ill, or endangered. The police department averages between 1,500 and 2,500 missing persons reports a year, with the vast majority of those reports involving runaway youths.

Missing adults are somewhat of a conundrum for law enforcement agencies because they can legally leave home without informing anyone, explains Stacho. "Adults are adults. They can choose not to go home. We talk to family members to try to determine where they suspect the missing person might be. But if there's no indication of foul play or wrongdoing and no further leads, there's not much we can do."

. . .

When news outlets around the world carry stories about Clevelanders' frustrations in getting police to investigate disappearances of their family members, Chief McGrath steps to the defense of his department, saying, "Police will not be surprised if nobody filed missing persons reports on some of these people."

To the family of Tonia Carmichael, McGrath's pronouncement is grating. Carmichael's daughters and mother say they repeatedly pleaded with police for help in finding Tonia after she vanished in November 2008.

A resident of the Cleveland suburb of Warrensville Heights, Tonia, a fifty-two-year-old black woman, had struggled with a drug addiction for years and was known to hang out near Sowell's house. Although she occasionally would be away from home for several days at a time, she stayed in regular contact with her family. So when she hadn't been heard from in three weeks and she failed to pick up two paychecks from her employer, Tonia's mother, Barbara Carmichael, was afraid that something had happened to her.

Barbara, a seventy-one-year-old retired nurse, attempted to file a missing persons report on December 2, 2008, at the Warrensville Heights police station, where officers were aware of Tonia's drug use. "They refused to take the report on her," Barbara says. "The officers belittled it and made jokes. They told me to go home and wait awhile because as soon as her drugs ran out, she'd turn up."

The police officers' advice would prove tragically prophetic: a year later, Tonia did turn up—buried in the backyard of Anthony Sowell's house. A cord from a cell phone charger was wrapped around her neck, and her hands were bound behind her back.

At a press conference on November 4, 2009, Cleveland police and the county coroner's office announce that Tonia had been positively identified as one of the eleven Imperial Avenue victims. Miller said that Tonia—the first of the eleven to be identified—had been strangled. Her nude body was found in a shallow grave along with three small paper bags containing human bones.

Sobbing, Barbara Carmichael tells media representatives that it had been agony not knowing what had happened to Tonia. "I expected the worst when I heard about those bodies in there," she says. "I knew that my baby could be one of them. It's what we had feared the most."

Barbara was only seventeen when she gave birth to Tonia, her second child, in 1956. She divorced Tonia's father soon afterwards. Raising Tonia and her brother, Donnie, in a tough Cleveland neighborhood, Barbara cautioned her children about the dangers of the street, while making sure they understood the importance of hard work and the value of education.

Tonia was a "very smart, happy child" who earned good grades in school and participated in 4-H and other activities. But at age sixteen, she became pregnant with her first child, Markiesha, and dropped out of high school. In 1976, Tonia's twenty-one-year-old brother, Donnie, was killed—the victim of an armed robbery. The next year, Tonia had a daughter, Donnita, and then a son, Jonathan. Tonia didn't marry any of her children's fathers, choosing to raise them herself.

She earned her high school equivalency degree and attended community college, where she took business and psychology courses. She worked at several jobs to support her family, including as a medical secretary, restaurant server, and barmaid.

Tonia's neighbors recall that she was fiercely protective of her young children. In the late 1980s, when crack cocaine began saturating Cleveland neighborhoods, Tonia was known to shoo drug dealers away from the sidewalk in front of her three-bedroom home.

Despite her antidrug stance, Tonia herself became ensnared in the grip of addiction. Some family members blame one of Tonia's boyfriends for hooking her on crack, while others say she began using drugs to help her cope with the death of her father.

No matter the reason, her drug use spun out of control by 1997. She lost her job, her home was foreclosed, and the county's department of children's services took Jonathan, then 12, from her because she left him alone for days at a time while she binged on drugs.

Tonia's addiction led to numerous drug-related crimes, including possession, theft, and soliciting. In her desperation to feed her hunger for crack, she stole her mother's car and pilfered money from her children. After a prison stint in 2003 for drug and theft offenses, she emerged clean. But she soon resumed her crack use.

On November 10, 2008, Tonia asked her mother for twenty dollars, explaining that she needed to have her truck door repaired. Although Barbara was concerned that Tonia would use the money for drugs, she consented. The next day, when Tonia hadn't returned home, Barbara and her grandchildren began searching nearby neighborhoods. There was no sign of her or her pickup truck.

Family members tirelessly canvassed Mount Pleasant for her. They posted hundreds of "missing" flyers on utility poles and in storefront windows.

Weeks later, Barbara spotted Tonia's truck—its door repaired—as she was driving near East 118th and Kinsman Road, only four blocks from Sowell's house. Soon afterwards, she learned that Tonia hadn't picked up her paychecks at work.

Barbara approached Warrensville Heights police on December 2, 2008, to report Tonia missing. While she says police didn't pursue Tonia's disappearance because of her drug history, Warrensville Police Chief Frank Bova says records show that his detectives conducted searches for Tonia on December 4, December 23, February 9, and February 10, including checks at several houses, bars, and motels.

According to police reports, detectives also interviewed the man who repaired Tonia's truck. He said Tonia told him that she was going to run a few errands and then she planned on "having some fun."

Nevertheless, Tonia's family insists their efforts to report Tonia missing were stymied by Warrensville Heights police. In frustration, they tried to file a missing persons report at Cleveland's Fourth District police station, which is close to where Tonia's truck was found. However, according to Barbara, a Fourth District police officer said he could not take the report on Tonia because she was not a resident of Cleveland.

"What upset me so bad . . . is that the Fourth District would not take the report even though she disappeared right around the corner from them, and we found the car there," said Donnita during a TV interview. "And at the Warrensville Heights police station, they made jokes [such as] 'Oh, go home, she'll show up by Christmas, after the drugs are all gone.' When the [Warrensville police] officer wouldn't take the report, I went back up and demanded to see the officer in charge. That's the only way I got her reported missing."

Law enforcement officials in Warrensville Heights and Cleveland both say they followed correct procedures. "We take these cases seriously," said Stacho, the Cleveland police spokesman, noting that Tonia's family was turned back to Warrensville police because she was last seen in their city.

Unmoved by their explanations, Donnita says the police weren't interested in looking for her mother because they had stereotyped her as a black inner-city female who used drugs. "People forgot about her," she says. "Just because she was a drug user doesn't mean she isn't a person. They dropped the ball."

When the horrific news broke about the unidentified bodies at 12205 Imperial Avenue, Barbara's intuition told her that Tonia had been found. Two days later, the coroner's office told Barbara that her DNA was a match for the sample taken from Tonia's remains.

Markiesha Carmichael-Jacobs tells Cleveland news reporters that her mother's death has left a sense of profound emptiness. "We're still going to talk about her. We're still going to remember her throughout the day, but it's still hard not being able to touch her."

Tonia's autopsy was performed by Dr. Elizabeth Balraj, who stated in her report: "Miss Carmichael's height is fifty-nine inches and the weight of her remains is seventy-eight pounds. Her body was wrapped in clear plastic material and covered in mud and dirt. There is advanced postmortem decomposition and her facial features are not visible. Numerous maggots infest the body. A Kyocera cell phone charger cord is wrapped tightly around her neck. Hands are bound at the wrist and tied tightly behind her body with cloth fabric. She is wearing the following rings on her fingers: a metal ring with a blue stone with multicolor flecks; and a metal ring with purple stones . . . Miss Tonia Celeste Carmichael came to her death as the result of asphyxia by cervical compression due to ligature strangulation . . . The manner of death was homicide."

CHAPTER 10

Survival: Gladys Wade

November 4, 2009

With the Imperial Avenue death toll at eleven, reporters and correspondents from national and international news media have brought attention to the hardscrabble neighborhood. The street is lined with TV trucks while camera operators and reporters compete for space on the clogged sidewalks.

The atypical nature of the case—the crime, the victims, and the suspected killer were all discovered simultaneously—has the mainstream media, bloggers, and the public hungering for information. However, Cleveland Police are reluctant to release details, for fear of tainting their investigation.

Some police sources say they expect the body count to rise, noting that law enforcement agencies in California and North Carolina—two places Sowell lived during his Marine Corps service—are investigating unsolved murders during the time he lived in their states.

The dearth of information has frustrated the local community and exacerbated the media's interest in the gruesome murders and Anthony Sowell, who is now known worldwide as "the Cleveland Strangler."

· · ·

At his home in suburban Cleveland, Sam Tayeh, the owner of Amira Imperial Beverage, watches evening news reports of the serial killings and Sowell's arrest. While Tayeh is stunned that eleven bodies are found within a hundred feet of his store, he is not shocked to learn that Sowell is involved.

Released from prison in the summer of 2005, Sowell moved to Imperial Avenue and was a frequent visitor to Tayeh's store. After 2006, Sowell began purchasing boxes of garbage bags, specifically extra-strength, heavy-duty bags. When Tayeh once asked him why he needed so many bags, Sowell said he was "cleaning around his house."

Tayeh now understands, with chilling clarity, what the bags were used for. He also remembers a day when Sowell wandered around the store, frustrated that he couldn't find electrical extension cords.

Now, Tayeh stares at his television and thinks back to the spring afternoon several years ago when Sowell predicted his own infamy: "Someday, Sam, the whole world will know my name," he'd said.

Tayeh sits in silence, realizing that it's likely that many of the Imperial Avenue victims were women whom he knew—neighborhood residents who had shopped at his store.

. . .

Cleveland resident Gladys Wade is also watching news accounts of the Imperial Avenue murders. The forty-one-year-old survived a brutal assault by Sowell a year earlier. She is transfixed by the televised images of Sowell's face, frightened by the memory of how close she came to being one of his victims.

The day after Sowell's capture, U.S. Marshals visited Gladys's home to question her about her experience. Local news reporters, tracing Sowell's lengthy history of violence against women, have also learned about Gladys's incident. Gladys tells them that she is haunted not only by the attack but also by the indifference shown by police detectives assigned to her case.

Recounting the details of her attack, Gladys says she had spent the afternoon of December 8, 2008, visiting her sister in Mount Pleasant. Before boarding a bus for home at 5:30 P.M., she stopped at Amira Imperial Beverage to purchase a Molson Ice and a pack of Newport 100s. She was dressed for cold weather, wearing a heavy coat, turtleneck sweater, jeans, and long john underwear. She was also carrying a bag of clothes that she had brought from her sister's house. She placed the beer and cigarettes in the bag.

She left the beverage store and began walking toward her bus stop when Sowell approached her. "Merry Christmas," he said. "How about coming back to my place and having a beer?"

She smiled at the stranger, saying, "No thanks, I already have a beer. But Merry Christmas to you also." She walked past him, pulling her coat tight.

Suddenly, she felt her shoulder grabbed from behind. She was spun around and punched in the side of her face. She crumpled to the sidewalk and blacked out. When she regained consciousness, Gladys found herself being dragged by her coat collar up a driveway. She struggled, but the collar was pulled tight against her neck, essentially strangling her. She lapsed in and out of consciousness as she was pulled inside his house and up to the third-floor living room, where she blacked out again.

Gladys awoke to an eerie scene. She was on the floor beside a Christmas tree. The only illumination in the room came from the tree's garish multi-colored light bulbs. Taking stock of her physical condition, she found that her coat and sweater had been removed, her back and legs ached from being dragged up the steps, and her face was bloodied and beginning to swell.

Still wobbly from Sowell's punch, she crawled on her hands and knees to the living room door. The door was locked. Afraid and angry, Gladys screamed. Sowell burst into the room and punched her several times.

"Scream all you want," he told her. "Nobody will hear you. You better get ready to die."

Crying now, she pleaded with him to let her go.

"Bitch, take off your pants!" he yelled, his face contorted in rage. She screamed again and he dove on top of her. She rolled away, getting to her feet and running through the doorway. At the top of the stairs, he tackled her and their momentum sent them both tumbling down the steps. At the second-floor landing, he maneuvered on top of her, but she rolled him off and stood up.

In the pitch-black stairway, she was disoriented. Feeling dizzy and attempting to gain her balance, she thrust her hand against the door that led to the second-floor living area. She heard glass break and felt a searing pain in her right thumb. Later, she'd learn that she had pushed her hand through the pane of glass in the door.

She then began inching forward in the darkness, unsure where the steps were. He clutched her legs, knocking her off balance, and they skidded down to the first-floor landing. They both got to their feet. She reached for the door handle that led outside, but he spun her against the wall and pressed his thumbs tightly into her neck.

Through clenched teeth, he said, "I'm going to kill you." He was slight of build, but his grip was vise-tight. Struggling for breath, Wade raked his face with her nails, trying to gouge his eyes. He recoiled in pain, releasing his grip. Wade was able to wriggle away.

She reached for the door, but he grabbed her again, fastening his hands around her neck. To Gladys, Sowell now appeared demonic. "His eyes were glowing," she recalls, "like the devil had possessed him."

He leaned his weight against her, squeezing her neck. Fighting for breath, Wade tried to pry his fingers from her throat, but his grip was secure.

She realized that she was seconds away from unconsciousness. As her strength ebbed, she thought, "Oh my God, is this how I'm going to go out? I can't die like this."

With a final effort, she reached toward his crotch, grabbing his testicles through his pants. "I squeezed and twisted as hard as I could," she recalls. He screamed and doubled over. Gladys pulled the door open and bolted from the house.

She ran toward a small group of men who were standing on the sidewalk near Sowell's driveway. Cradling her lacerated right thumb with her left hand, she told them she had been attacked and pleaded for help.

Just then, Sowell walked up with Gladys's coat in his hand. "Don't listen to this bitch," he laughed. "She tried to steal my watch." Gladys protested, but the men turned away, ignoring her.

"I just started crying," she recalls. "I was in this circle of people, screaming that this man had attacked me, and nobody would hear me."

Sowell, playing to the onlookers, warned Gladys to stay out of the neighborhood. Bleeding and desperate to get away from him, Gladys ran across Imperial Avenue and into Bess Pizza, a small carryout restaurant. She asked employees to dial 911 for her.

When no one responded, Gladys held up her injured right thumb and pleaded for assistance. The store manager offered her a towel for her hand, telling her that she needed to leave because she was dripping blood on the restaurant floor.

"From my appearance and the condition I was in, I guess they figured I was just a crackhead," Gladys says.

The manager guided Gladys toward the door, saying, "We don't want to have anything to do with this. There's a pay phone outside the building that you can use."

Just then, Sowell stepped inside the restaurant and tossed Gladys's coat at her. She hurried from the restaurant, running for at least a dozen blocks.

"I was traumatized . . . cold . . . in pain . . . and exhausted," she says. "I wanted to just lie down, but I was afraid that he was following me, so I kept running. And then, finally, I saw a police cruiser."

Cleveland police officers Kevin Walker and Angel Serra Jr. saw her waving and stopped. According to their report, Gladys told them that Sowell had "punched and choked her and tried to rip her clothes off." Walker observed that she was bleeding from her hand and had scratches on her neck. She told him that she was afraid that Sowell would find her and kill her.

The officers radioed for an ambulance, waiting with Gladys until it arrived. She was transported to the local University Hospitals emergency room, where she received twelve stitches in her thumb. Photos were taken of the bruises and lacerations on Gladys's neck, face, and legs. Her finger-nails were clipped to check for traces of Sowell's skin and blood. Nurses collected her clothing, noting that the zipper on her pants was broken.

While she was being treated, Gladys told two police officers the location of Sowell's house and that they would likely find her blood smeared on the steps and walls between the first and second floors. The officers went to investigate. Because they didn't have a search warrant, they couldn't enter the house—they could only look inside through the windows. From a side window, they saw what appeared to be blood in the locations that Gladys had described. They also noticed that the snow around the entrance of Sowell's house seemed to suggest a struggle took place.

The next day, Gladys met with Sex Crimes detective Georgia Hussein to give her statement. She told Hussein what Sowell was wearing during the attack and that he would probably have numerous scratches on his face from their fight. She also said she had left her turtleneck sweater and other clothes in Sowell's house.

A search warrant was issued, and Officers Walker and Serra went to Sowell's house. They found Gladys's turtleneck and also a bucket contain-ing shards of glass and another item of her clothing. They arrested Sowell on suspicion of attempted rape and attempted murder.

But two days later, authorities released Sowell without filing criminal charges against him. In explanation, Cleveland Chief Prosecutor Victor Perez said there was "insufficient evidence" to sustain charges.

When pressed by the news media at the time, Perez conceded that charges were not filed, in part, because he found notes on the case that indicated a detective in the Sex Crimes Unit did not believe that Gladys was "credible."

For Gladys, the news of Sowell's release was devastating. "The woman detective I spoke to didn't take me seriously at all," Gladys said. "Sowell told police that I robbed him and that I assaulted him. And evidently his story was somehow more powerful than mine. It was like a slap to my face."

Gladys was unable to convince the Sex Crimes detectives of Sowell's brutality. But she knew that the prosecutors and the police were making a grave error.

"They claimed there were 'no visible signs' of injuries, but the police officers and nurses at the hospital and the employees at Bess Pizza saw me bleeding," she said. "The police never bothered to check that Sowell was a registered sex offender or that he had been recently released from prison. They didn't check it out because they knew that I had been arrested for drugs in the past and I was out on bail for an assault case. To the prosecutors and police, I was just a crackhead. . . . I was a nobody."

. . .

At various times in her adult life, Gladys struggled with what she admits was a "pretty bad" drug problem. "There were years when I was smoking as much crack as I could get," she said. "Paying for it by panhandling, begging, shoplifting, and anything else I needed to do."

Gladys's path to addiction was circuitous and unexpected. Born in Cleveland to hardworking parents, she was musically inclined, played sports, and did well in school. Her parents split up when Gladys was nine, but her father remained a strong presence in her life.

From a young age, Gladys was drawn to music. Encouraged by her uncle Jimmy Garrett, a Motown Records musician and the music director for The Supremes, Gladys sang and played flute. She graduated from Shaw High School in East Cleveland, where she was a member of the nationally recognized marching band.

Gladys earned a music scholarship to Central State University, traveling throughout the United States and Europe with the school's concert band. Consistently on the Dean's List, she was on her way toward achieving her dream of becoming a classical musician.

But with only five class credits left to complete her bachelor's degree in music education, Gladys left Central State. Her decision was spurred, in part, by a messy breakup with her college boyfriend.

She moved to nearby Dayton, Ohio, took a job as a nursing assistant, and began dating a man who introduced her to drugs.

"I was young, innocent, and not street-smart," she says. "I should have realized that he was bad for me from the start. It seemed like I was always missing money. One day, he got me drunk and pulled a crack pipe from under the mattress. He asked me to try it and I did. Crack was fun, at first. But it became very demanding, and then it became a sickness. He got me hooked and I lost my job. Then he started selling me to the drug boys. I was his ticket to getting drugs."

Gladys was eventually able to extricate herself from her boyfriend and return to her family in Cleveland. She kicked her drug addiction and started working as a nurse's aide and part-time music tutor. But after aggravating a back injury she had incurred in a car accident in the mid-1980s, she found herself in chronic pain and unable to work. Over the next several years, she had bouts of dependency on painkillers, which led to several arrests for drug abuse.

In the early 2000s, Gladys became reacquainted with old friends who had gotten caught up in the drug lifestyle. She relapsed and within months had lost her apartment and was living on the streets.

"I just got caught out in the mist," she said. "I was homeless and strung out real bad. I was always wondering if I would survive from one night to the next, but I didn't want to go home to my family because I didn't want to be judged. I didn't need that guilt on top of what I was going through."

Gladys was adrift on the streets until Thanksgiving Eve 2003, when she met Leander Thomas in a chance encounter. The two soon became a couple, sharing an apartment in East Cleveland. Over the next five years, with Thomas providing a stable influence, Gladys was off the streets and sober.

Gladys and Thomas enjoyed a relatively trouble-free relationship until July 2008, when they were involved in an altercation with a custodian at their apartment complex. Both Gladys and Thomas were charged with assault and released on bond to await their hearings.

On December 8 at noon, Gladys said good-bye to Thomas and left home to visit her sister. Six hours later, she would find herself in a fight for her life with Anthony Sowell. When prosecutors decided not to bring charges against Sowell—despite Gladys's visible injuries—she was bitter and depressed.

Three days later, her boyfriend took a plea deal in the assault case and began serving a two-year prison sentence. Gladys was placed on probation for her role in the incident.

"Without Leander around to take care of me, I just felt lost. It wasn't long before I relapsed again," she said. "It was wintertime and I was back on the streets, shuffling between crack houses and sleeping in rat-infested abandoned buildings and bus stops. Sometimes, I would walk all night because I couldn't find a safe place to sleep. It's scary living on the streets—it's a dangerous life. But with Sowell on the loose, I was terrified every day. If he found me, I knew that he'd try to kill me."

On October 31, 2009, when Gladys learned that Sowell had been arrested, she says she went into shock. "It took me four days before I cried.

Then I started to feel guilty. I felt like I should have been more assertive to the police about my experience with Sowell. I could see in his eyes that he was a heartless killer. I knew that I couldn't possibly have been his first victim. I was also dead certain that there were going to be more victims if he wasn't arrested . . . many more."

Tragically, Gladys was correct. According to police and coroner's findings, it's likely that six women died in Sowell's house after her attack on December 8, 2008.

CHAPTER II

Six-Million-Dollar Man

November 4, 2009

CLEVELAND—A judge ordered Anthony Sowell to be held without bond this morning on five counts of aggravated murder in an ongoing investigation into the discovery of at least 10 bodies in his house and yard on Imperial Avenue. Cleveland Municipal Court Judge Ronald Adrine said that in his 28 years on the bench, "This is the most serious set of allegations I have ever seen."

Assistant County Prosecutor Brian Murphy said, "The state believes that Sowell is an incredibly dangerous threat to the public, not only in Cleveland, but beyond the city's limits." Murphy said that Sowell is facing the death penalty. Sowell's public defender, Kathleen DeMetz, asked that a bond be set, noting that he has a pacemaker for a heart condition.

—the *Plain Dealer,* November 4, 2009

Media coverage is intense as Sowell is arraigned in municipal court on charges that he killed five women whose decomposed remains were found in his house and yard on October 29 and October 30. All of the women, each identified as "Jane Doe" in the November 4 arraignment documents, were strangled.

Wrists and ankles shackled, Sowell shuffles into the courtroom clad in a blue paper jumpsuit that is typically worn by inmates who are considered suicide risks. A phalanx of sheriff's deputies and corrections officers surround him, while others are stationed in the court hallways and the building lobby.

Sowell stands motionless, speaking only once, after Judge Adrine asks him if he is unable to afford an attorney and needs court-appointed counsel. "That's correct, sir," answers Sowell, in a whisper. Adrine then turns the case over to the Cuyahoga County grand jury and Sowell is returned to the Justice Center jail, where he has been held in solitary confinement since his arrest on October 31.

Police believe that he is also responsible for the murders of the other six victims found in and around his home, says Deputy Police Chief Ed Tomba, who tells reporters that in his twenty-four years in law enforcement, he has "never seen anything like" the death scene he viewed in Sowell's house. Tomba says that police will continue their investigation before filing additional charges.

Two days later, on November 6, 2009, Sowell appears in Cuyahoga County Court, where a judge sets his bond at five million dollars.

. . .

The coroner's office releases the autopsy reports for the eleven victims. All were black females. Seven were strangled with a variety of ligatures, which were seemingly chosen randomly and impulsively. Ligatures included a cell phone charger cord, a shoulder strap from a briefcase, coaxial cable, a shoelace, and a green belt with a metal buckle. Most of the victims still had the ligatures wrapped around their necks when they were found.

An eighth victim was strangled by the killer's hands. Two other bodies and the skull found in the basement were so decomposed that pathologists couldn't determine the exact causes of death, but autopsies showed that all three died of homicidal violence. Due to the advanced decay of the eleven victims, no evidence of sexual assault was discernible, says coroner Frank Miller.

The coroner's reports revealed a shocking glimpse at the horrors the women must have endured in their final hours. They were all partially clothed; several were nude from the waist down. Most were gagged, with rags or socks stuffed in their mouths or their own shirts wrapped around their faces. Their hands were tied above their heads or bound tightly behind their backs. Ankles were tied together with rope, wire, socks, and shoelaces.

Tonia Carmichael, whose body was found in a shallow grave in Sowell's backyard, has been identified so far. Unable to identify the decomposed bodies through fingerprints and visual recognition, the coroner's office attempts to determine the identities of the victims by matching their DNA with DNA samples collected from relatives of black women who have gone missing in Cleveland.

"Without DNA, it's going to be very hard to find out who these people are," says Miller. "We have DNA [from the victims] ready to compare, but now we just need to get more people to submit DNA samples."

The most reliable DNA matches come from nuclear DNA, which is found in the nucleus of cells and contains genetic material from both parents. But nuclear DNA can't typically be extracted from bodies that are decomposed and skeletonized, like those found at Sowell's. In these cases, forensic experts can attempt to create a genetic profile from mitochondrial DNA, which is more resilient—although somewhat less reliable—than nuclear DNA. Even corpses that are severely decayed contain mitochondrial DNA, or mtDNA, in hair follicles, bones, and teeth.

Since mitochondrial DNA is inherited along maternal lines, mtDNA samples are taken from the mothers, grandmothers, and children of the dead women. A mother passes on mtDNA to her sons, but the sons can't pass it down to their children, Miller explains.

He says his staff's "arduous" task in identifying the dead women is all the more challenging because only a half-dozen people have come to the coroner's office to provide DNA test samples. Clevelanders' unwillingness to give DNA likely stems from their fear that police will use their samples to link them to other crime cases.

Despite public assurances from the coroner that DNA samples will not be shared with police, Stanley Miller, the head of the NAACP in Cleveland, voices the concerns of the black community.

"People are very reluctant because they don't trust the establishment," he says. "They don't trust the police, and they are not very apt to give up something like DNA that can match you to anyone, anytime, forever. That's an issue."

City leaders, police officials, and black pastors jointly address the dilemma, emphasizing the responsibility of family members to help the coroner's office identify the Imperial Avenue victims.

Frank Miller says that people who are still hesitant to provide DNA samples should consider supplying dental records of missing persons, which can be just as helpful as DNA. He urges family members to contact his office with the names of dentists who may have treated their loved ones.

. . .

Six-year-old Christen Fortson barely knew his mother, Telacia. Shortly after she gave birth to him in April 2003, the Cuyahoga County Department of Children and Family Services began the process of removing him from her custody. Case workers were concerned about Telacia's history of drug offenses, her four suicide attempts, her lack of permanent residence, and her failure to complete drug treatment programs.

In a 2003 report, a social worker wrote: "Mother has engaged in acts of domestic violence . . . child at risk." Noting that Christen's father's identity is "unknown," the report stated that Telacia lacked the parenting skills to care for her child. Christen was taken from her and placed with a family friend.

In 2004 and 2006, Telacia gave birth to daughters who were also removed from her custody. Telacia told friends that she was devastated over the loss of her children, whose names she had proudly tattooed on her arm.

Telacia had struggled with substance abuse for years, but crack cocaine had overtaken her life. Shuttling through a series of short-lived, abusive relationships with men, she stayed in city shelters, on the streets, and occasionally with her adoptive mother, Inez Fortson, in East Cleveland.

Inez had been a divorced mother of two sons in 1978 when she spotted Telacia playing happily with other foster children at an adoption picnic. Inez says she had always wanted a daughter. When she saw Telacia, then age nine, she felt an instant connection to her. Telacia had been placed in the county's foster care system three years earlier, after being removed from her parents' custody.

Inez, a county employee, provided a loving atmosphere for Telacia, but the little girl struggled to overcome her feelings of abandonment. After spending her earliest years shuffling from one foster family to another, she seemed to struggle to find her sense of belonging.

Telacia was a quick learner and showed an aptitude for writing poetry, arranging flowers, and styling hair. In her teen years, however, she became rebellious and reckless. She began experimenting with drugs at fourteen. She ran away from home repeatedly and was arrested several times for criminal damaging and assault. She was sent to a residential treatment facility, where she earned her high school equivalency diploma.

In the early 2000s, she became involved in a stormy relationship with Terrance Minor, an ex-convict who was sixteen years her senior. She had her daughters, Telacia and Talia, with Minor, who obtained custody of the children because of her drug use and instability. Minor says he was saddened and angered by Telacia's inability to change her lifestyle. Afraid that she would negatively influence the children, he told her to stay away from his house.

"If she called, I'd hang up on her," Minor says. "But she would occasionally walk past my house, hoping to see the girls playing outside in the yard. The kids loved her, so she knew that I would let her visit them for a while."

In 2008, Telacia was sent to prison for seven months for stealing money from Minor. She emerged and immediately resumed her crack use. She stayed with Inez infrequently over the next several months, but she maintained fairly regular contact with Minor.

On June 3, 2009, she visited Inez, bringing a bag of groceries for her. She stayed for a while to clean the house and cook dinner, then left. "We were on good terms at that point in time," Inez says. "I had the feeling that she was really trying to get her life on track."

It would be the last time Inez would see her.

As the weeks went on and Minor didn't hear from Telacia, he became worried. "I had a gut feeling something was wrong," he recalls. "For a while, she had been coming around to braid the girls' hair, but now her pattern was broken."

Minor reported his concerns to Inez, who called East Cleveland police in July to report her daughter missing. Inez checked area hospitals, the county morgue, and nearby police departments, but no one had information on Telacia.

On Halloween 2009, after the arrest of Anthony Sowell, Inez received a telephone call from a man who knew that Telacia was missing. He told Inez that he remembered giving Telacia a ride to Sowell's neighborhood. Police took a report from Inez and asked her to bring one of Telacia's children to the coroner's office to provide a DNA sample.

On November 5, 2009, Inez and six-year-old Christen sat in a coroner's examining room. A technician brushed a cotton-tipped swab against the inside of Christen's cheek. The next day, Inez learned that Christen's DNA was a match. Her daughter was one of Sowell's victims.

Telacia's body, lying on the floor next to another, had been found by the SWAT team in the third-floor sitting room. According to her autopsy report, her remains weighed only forty-six pounds. She was wearing a sleeveless shirt and was naked from the waist down. She was also wearing a ring and a necklace with a clover-shaped silver pendant that had embedded into her chest. A white-handled kitchen knife was beside her body.

"The left arm is extended over the head and the right arm is flexed in front of the chest," her autopsy report stated. "The body is clothed from the waist up in a sleeveless light-colored shirt which is bunched around the upper chest. A cloth ligature is around the neck."

Noting that the cause of death was asphyxia by cervical compression, a forensic pathologist would later explain that the blood vessels in Telacia's neck were constricted, stopping blood flow to her brain. Death would have occurred within three to five minutes.

. . .

It had been over a year since Latanya Irby, 26, had spoken with her sister, Tishana Culver. The two had lived together on Imperial Avenue, only a few doors away from Anthony Sowell. So when bodies were discovered in Sowell's house on October 29, Irby thought it possible that Tishana would call to discuss the shocking news about their neighbor.

"But then I had a dream that she was dead," Irby says.

Seven days later, her fears were realized when she learned that the remains of her older sister's body were found in a trash bag that had been stuffed in a crawl space on Sowell's third floor.

Tishana, 31, had been strangled, apparently with a four-foot length of fabric that was found near her mummified body. Her collarbone had been broken and her wrists were bound with cloth. She was wearing a brown shirt and brown pants.

Tishana had worked as a nursing assistant and a beautician, says her mother, Yvonne Williams-McNeill, who described her daughter as a troubled woman with a good heart. Tishana had been estranged from her family since March 2008, primarily due to her drug abuse. Her family never reported Tishana as a missing person because they thought she was staying with her boyfriend in Akron, about thirty minutes away.

"I thought that's where she was all the time," Williams-McNeill says. "I didn't know for sure where she was, but I prayed for her. Wherever she was, she was in God's hands."

Tishana was an A student who didn't have many problems growing up, according to her mother. Her father was Sam Culver Jr., who has a long criminal record. He left Williams-McNeill when their daughter was just an infant.

In her sophomore year of high school, she became pregnant with her first child. She would eventually have "at least" five children, says her mother, although a relative says Tishana may have had as many as eight children with several different fathers. All of her children were taken from her and raised by Williams-McNeill and other family members.

After graduation from high school, Tishana began smoking marijuana and crack. Irby says her drug use escalated after the death of her boyfriend, Marcus Johnson, whom she was planning to marry. Johnson was found shot in the head in 1998 in a Cleveland park, a gun on the ground next to him. The coroner's office ruled his death a suicide.

"She loved Marcus. His death devastated her," says Irby. "She checked herself into a treatment facility and was diagnosed as bipolar and depressed."

Irby says Tishana was helped by medication, but then she began a string of abusive relationships. In 2001, she hooked up with Carl Johnson (no relation to Marcus), who shared a crack addiction with her. The relationship would last seven turbulent years. "They had a lot of altercations, including physical fights," Irby says, adding that her sister, who stood five feet tall, was feisty and had often got into fights with boys and girls in school.

On several occasions, Tishana and Carl attempted to kick drugs—with limited success. When money was tight, Tishana traded her body for crack. In a *Plain Dealer* interview, Carl said he hated that Tishana was prostituting herself, but it didn't stop him from smoking the crack she brought home.

"Addiction is a sickness, and I'm not proud of anything I did," Carl said. "Whenever she put that red lipstick on, I knew what it meant . . . Unless I tied her down, there was no way I could stop her. I hated to watch the person I love hop in and out of cars."

Tishana accumulated a string of criminal offenses, mainly for drug use and soliciting. In 2005, she was sent to prison for eighteen months after she attacked Carl. The couple had three children together, including one who was born to Tishana while she was incarcerated.

After being released from prison, Tishana left Carl and moved into Irby's house on Imperial Avenue. But soon her sister and mother learned she was on the streets trading sex for drugs. Afraid that Tishana's children would see their mother prostituting herself, Irby asked her to leave the neighborhood.

Shortly after bodies were discovered in Sowell's house, police officers canvassed the Imperial Avenue neighborhood with his photo, asking residents if they had information about him. Irby told police that she remembered Sowell from the nearby Amira Imperial Beverage store.

Irby recalled buying a lottery ticket and noticing that Sowell was hanging around, "checking out" everyone in the store. "He didn't talk to me," Irby said. "But I felt his presence staring at me."

On November 5, Tishana was the third Imperial Avenue victim identified. The coroner's office did not ask her family to submit a DNA sample because Culver's DNA was already in the CODIS system, a nationwide database of criminal offenders.

Over the next week, seven more victims would be identified. Nearly all were crack addicted, alienated to some degree from their families, and existing on the margins of society. They were captive to drug cravings that had led them to the streets and finally to 12205 Imperial Avenue.

- Nancy Cobbs, a grandmother of five who lived near Sowell, was identified on November 6. Nancy, 43, had been working in construction when she went missing in April 2009.
- Crystal Dozier, 38, left behind seven children and four grandchildren. Crystal, who was thirteen when she had her first child, was last seen in May 2007. She was identified on November 7.
- Amelda "Amy" Hunter, 47, was a bookworm who enjoyed reading Charles Dickens. A cousin of Crystal Dozier's, Amy became pregnant by one of her schoolteachers when she was fourteen. Her remains were identified on November 7.
- Michelle Mason, 45, was last seen on October 4, 2008. The mother of two was HIV positive and suffered from bipolar disorder.
- Janice Webb was 48 when she went missing in June 2009. Along with several of her sisters, Janice fell victim to the crack epidemic that hit urban areas in the late 1980s. She left behind one son. She was identified on November 9.
- Kim Yvette Smith, who was nicknamed Candy, was last seen on January 17, 2009. The only victim who had no children, she was an artist and an accomplished singer. Candy, 44, was the ninth victim identified.

- Leshanda Long, 25, was the youngest of the eleven victims. Born to a crack-addicted mother, Leshanda was thirteen when she first became pregnant. She had three children by the time she was eighteen. Her skull was found wrapped in paper in a bucket in Sowell's basement. DNA tests confirmed her identity on November 11. The rest of her body was not recovered.

The last victim identified was Diane Turner, 38. Missing since September 2009, her decomposed body was found in the third-floor sitting room by SWAT officers. Diane's remains weren't identified until December 4 because the coroner's office had difficulty locating her family members. She had five children; all were removed from her custody by county authorities.

Miller credits his staff for their around-the-clock efforts in identifying the eleven victims. Working with police, the coroner's office had constructed a database that included dozens of black women who had been reported missing in Cleveland. From that pool of missing persons, they relied on police tip lines and family members who provided DNA samples.

"We were able to hit all eleven victims with just sixty DNA reference samples," Miller says, adding that it was quite fortunate that most of the victims were from a focused area in the Cleveland Police Department's Fourth District.

"It's also fortunate that they were all discovered in a local burial ground," he says. "This case is not as difficult as one involving an interstate trucker, for example, who kills people in different cities. The eleven victims in Cleveland weren't transported from anywhere, and they all appear to have been killed in Sowell's house."

. . .

On November 13, 2009, amid heavy security, Sowell was brought to court and arraigned on counts of attempted murder, felonious assault, and rape in connection with the September 22, 2009, sexual assault of Latundra Billups. The Billups attack ultimately led to Sowell's arrest and the discovery of eleven bodies in and around his home.

Cuyahoga County Judge John P. O'Donnell added another million dollars to Sowell's existing five million dollar bond and remanded him to the county jail. He also ordered Sowell to submit a blood sample for an HIV test.

Gayle Williams, assistant county prosecutor, told the court that Billups remains very fearful and is concerned for her safety.

"She was only breaths away from becoming another victim of Mr. Sowell," Williams said.

. . .

The next day, homicide detectives and FBI technicians were at Sowell's house to conduct thermal-imaging tests. The FBI used the X-ray technology to peer inside walls and other voids to make sure there were no more bodies hidden in the house.

Police also supervised building inspectors as they searched for sections of walls that may have been cut open and then dry-walled. In Sowell's backyard, crews resumed digging in hopes of finding the remainder of Leshanda Long's body.

. . .

Word soon spreads of the renewed police activity at Sowell's. Families of the eleven victims and leaders of the black community stage an impromptu rally on Imperial Avenue, questioning how police could have missed the pattern of disappearances among Cleveland's black women.

In response, police officials say they did not detect a pattern. "If we had, we would have followed up on it," says a spokesman.

The family of Michelle Mason does not agree that police did everything possible to find her after she was reported missing in 2008. Mary Mason, Michelle's sister, says that Sowell could have been apprehended sooner if police had shown more interest in listening to citizens' complaints about their missing loved ones.

Saying that police seem not to care about inner-city women who have criminal records and histories of drug abuse, Mason tells reporters, "Shouldn't the police have noticed that we had so many black women missing before this?"

Nevertheless, Cleveland Police say their records indicate they fully investigated the disappearance of Michelle, who was found strangled and buried in Sowell's backyard.

Along with accusations that police ignored missing persons reports, activists demand that police explain why Sowell was released from custody after being accused of attacking Gladys Wade in December 2008. Despite finding blood and other evidence in his house that seemed to back Gladys's claim, a Sex Crimes detective found Gladys's story to be "not credible." Over Gladys's protestations, city prosecutors declined to press charges and sent Sowell home.

"If they would have believed me, more women wouldn't have lost their lives," Gladys says.

Police now dispute Gladys's version of events, saying that she did not cooperate with detectives who were attempting to follow up on her report.

The community is also troubled by news that Sowell was visited at home by two county sheriff's deputies on September 22, 2009, just hours before he attacked Latundra Billups. The routine check was part of the reporting requirements imposed on sex offenders such as Sowell.

The deputies confirmed that Sowell was living at his listed address, but they did not enter the residence, per standard policy. They also did not report noticing any unusual smells—despite complaints from neighbors about the stench wafting from the charnel house that Sowell called home.

Several hours after the deputies' visit, Sowell raped and tried to kill Latundra in an empty second-floor bedroom. Latundra reported the brutal crime to police, who waited more than a month to execute a search warrant at Sowell's. A police spokesman explained that it took thirty-six days from the time of the initial report to execution of the warrant because detectives couldn't find Latundra to interview her.

While the search warrant was in process, Shawn Morris was attacked by Sowell on October 20. Shawn says she and Sowell were partying, when he inexplicably punched her and told her he was going to kill her. She escaped by jumping out a second-floor window. Shawn did not cooperate with detectives who attempted to question her about the incident.

At a press conference, Police Chief McGrath says there was never any reason to suspect Sowell of murder. He explains, "Over the last three years, including the call we just had on October 20, there was only one other call to that address."

He noted that Sowell's history shows a propensity to prey on people who were close to him. "He had a specific motive," McGrath said. "His victims that we know about met him on the street, and he got them to his house. I have to believe all these victims voluntarily went to the residence."

Indeed, police reports and court records show that Sowell was adept at initiating conversations with women in his neighborhood, usually by offering them alcohol and drugs.

. . .

On December 1, 2009, a Cuyahoga County grand jury indicted Sowell on eighty-five counts related to the deaths of the eleven women found in his house and buried in his yard. Tellingly, the indictment included attempted rape and attempted murder charges stemming from the attack on Gladys Wade a year earlier.

McGrath sidestepped reporters' questions about the initial handling of Gladys's case, saying that new evidence about the attack had been discovered in the past year. He added that county prosecutor Bill Mason had made the decision to include the Wade incident in the indictment.

Calling Sowell a "monster," Mason said he preyed on women who were homeless, living alone, and had drug or alcohol addictions. "After luring them inside his home, he tormented them, threatened them, and assaulted them. He murdered eleven of them," said Mason.

Sowell's charges include eleven counts of aggravated murder with a "mass murder specification," meaning multiple people were killed in a similar fashion.

. . .

The Cleveland Police Department secures a search warrant to retrieve DNA from Sowell. A police press release states that Sowell's sample will be compared against DNA from cold case crimes across the United States to determine whether he is a suspect in other criminal matters.

Cleveland Police also announce plans to work with the FBI's Behavioral Analysis Unit. A key focus of the unit is profiling serial killers. An FBI spokesman says investigators are retracing Sowell's life back more than thirty years to his service in the U.S. Marines from 1978 to 1985. Of special interest are unsolved crimes around the bases where Sowell was stationed, including Parris Island, South Carolina; Cherry Point, North Carolina; Okinawa, Japan; and Camp Pendleton, California.

And in Coronado, California, near Camp Pendleton, Police Chief Louis Scanlon announced that a woman contacted his department after seeing Sowell's face on TV. The woman said she was certain that Sowell had raped her in 1979.

Meanwhile, Sowell is held on a six-million-dollar bond in the Cuyahoga County Corrections Center. A corrections official tells reporters that Sowell is locked in solitary confinement to protect him from other inmates who are friends or relatives of his victims and may have revenge on their minds.

Noting that Sowell has declined visitation requests, the official says that he receives more mail than most inmates. "A lot of people want to see his soul," he explains. "Many people want to be his friend or pen pal. Everyone seems to be curious about who Anthony Sowell is."

CHAPTER 12

"Psycho"

1959–1978

Eleven-year-old Anthony Edward Sowell watches silently as his niece is stripped naked and tied to a stairway banister. Standing motionless next to his family members, he is transfixed by the sight of his mother, Claudia Garrison, mercilessly whipping the ten-year-old girl with the cord from an electric iron.

The girl's shrieks of pain mingle with Garrison's shouts and curses, echoing throughout the large house. Garrison continues lashing the girl with long, practiced strokes, even after her thighs, buttocks, and chest are dotted with blood.

The girl, Leona Davis, and her twin sister, Ramona, are beaten nearly every day. Eventually, both girls would run away from home to escape the punishment.

"Home" is a sage-green three-story residence at 1878 Page Avenue in East Cleveland. Garrison purchased the house in 1969, shortly after the death of her daughter, Patricia Davis, the mother of Leona, Ramona, and five other children.

The Davis children shared the ten-room house with Garrison, her four children, and her mother, Irene Justice. The household was conspicuously absent of father figures. Anthony's father, Thomas Sowell Sr., left Garrison shortly after Anthony's birth on August 15, 1959. The elder Sowell, known as a carouser, was incarcerated throughout much of the 1960s and 1970s. He was married several times and fathered five children, four of whom were considerably older than Anthony.

In the late 1990s, Thomas Sowell Sr. married Segerna Henderson and the couple settled into the first floor of a large duplex at 12205 Imperial Avenue that had been owned by Thomas's father.

Neighborhood residents and Sam Tayeh, the owner of the nearby beverage store, said that Segerna had a positive, calming influence on her husband. Although his drinking days were now seemingly behind him, Thomas Sr. occasionally displayed a lewd sense of humor. Tayeh recalls that Thomas Sr. once brought a grotesquely large dildo into his store, waving it in front of customers.

"My father was a colorful character," says Thomas Sowell Jr., one of Anthony's three half brothers, all born to Virginia Ogletree. "He'd always been a philanderer who lived by his wits. He was in and out of jail a lot when I was young. From what I heard about him, he was an old-school dude. Some people say he was a safecracker; others say he was a check-kiter."

During Thomas Sr.'s first stint in prison, Ogletree divorced him. "But she never said anything bad about him to us kids," says the younger Thomas, who managed a municipal forestry department until his retirement several years ago. "She always made us understand that no matter how he lived his life, he was our dad and he deserved our respect."

When Anthony was two years old, his father introduced him to his half siblings. "One day, he just brought him over to our house and said, 'This is your brother,'" recalls Thomas. "We were surprised that he had found the time to have another kid. My dad had been in prison for years. We just shook our heads and said to him: 'Okay dude, how did you find the time while you were doing time?'"

Due to the age difference between Anthony and his half brothers, a close relationship never developed.

"We were older and basically doing our own thing," Thomas says. "I guess we just didn't have time for him." However, Thomas's older brother, Allan Sowell, made an effort to interact with Anthony, despite their sixteen-year age difference.

"My dad had asked me to look out for Anthony," Allan says. "So when Anthony was eight or nine, I took him to a Cleveland Indians baseball game. I remember that he was a good kid, with an infectious smile and a nice personality. We had a big brother relationship, but I was already raising a family, so I was pretty busy. I just didn't have a lot of time for him and we lost contact."

Allan, a retired social worker, spent the latter part of his career investigating allegations of child abuse and neglect. He was sixteen when he first met his father, Thomas Sowell Sr. "My dad was a rolling stone, a womanizer. He was a drinker for a time," Allan says. "He knew he couldn't be around for Anthony. I think he was worried about him and wanted me to stay involved with him."

Claudia Garrison's other three children: Tressa Garrison, Owen Davis, and Patricia Davis, also had absentee fathers. Patricia herself was the single parent of seven children, most of whom never knew their fathers.

Garrison, strong-willed and independent, worked several jobs concurrently, including dry cleaner presser and steel mill laborer. Because she was rarely at home, she was insistent that her children become self-sufficient at an early age.

By the age of five, Sowell was accustomed to coming home from school with a key around his neck to an empty house. Garrison was also eccentric about her identity, using several first names, including Gertrude (her preference) as well as Mickey and Nicky.

Despite the seeming lack of parental influence in his life, young Sowell appeared to be well-adjusted and studious. "He was the kindest child you wanted to deal with. He was always very respectable," recalls Katie Tabb, a Page Avenue neighbor.

His sixth-grade teacher, Cathy Whelan, describes Sowell as a "quiet and nice young boy who came to school to learn—not to fool around."

In junior high science class, Sowell was an enthusiastic student who took a special interest in electricity, recalls Cary Seidman, his instructor. Seidman also taught Sowell the basics of chess, which would become a lifelong interest for him.

But inside the walls of his house, Sowell's education took a much darker turn. He often witnessed his grandmother and mother impulsively and brutally beat his nephews and nieces, particularly Leona, Ramona, and their brother Jesse Darnell Hatcher.

Before moving to Page Avenue, Patricia's family lived in a series of rental homes, rarely for more than three or four months at a time. "We moved so often that it became a blur," Leona recalls. "We were in and out of schools so quickly that we didn't really get a chance to make friends."

Patricia, who was seventeen years older than Anthony, suffered from a congenital heart condition and respiratory ailments. She gave birth to five of her children before the age of eighteen, many of whom had birth defects. Although doctors warned her that pregnancy could be life-threatening to her and her unborn babies, she continued to have children, including conjoined twins.

Unable to hold steady employment due to her health, Patricia took occasional housekeeping jobs, sometimes driving the children with her to homes and offices, where they would wait in the car for several hours while she worked.

When health and economic conditions were particularly dismal for Patricia, she would move her family into Claudia's home. But a quarrel would inevitably erupt between the two women, and Patricia would storm out, children in tow. "Sometimes, we'd sleep in the car until we found an apartment to live in," Leona recalls.

While living with Claudia, the Davis children would, on occasion, be slapped or spanked by Claudia and Irene for breaking house rules. But in 1969, when twenty-nine-year-old Patricia died during a bronchial asthma attack, her children were placed under Claudia's authoritarian care. Leona and Ramona would later bitterly recall that Claudia did not have a funeral service for Patricia. "We weren't even allowed to express our grief over losing our mother," Leona says.

Along with custody of the seven children, Claudia became the recipient of their Social Security payments and other public assistance benefits, which she used to purchase the nearly 4,000-square-foot Page Avenue house.

Set on elevated terrain, with a gabled portico, dual chimneys, and a third-floor dormer window, the spacious house stood in imposing contrast to the more modest homes on the street.

"It was fun when we first moved to Page Avenue," Leona says. "We would slide down the stairway banister and climb the cherry tree in the yard. The rules were strict: We had a lot of chores and we weren't allowed to have friends visit us or have birthday parties. But we liked living there—for the first month or so."

Under the sole governance of Claudia and her mother, the children were expected to perform hours of chores to exacting standards—or face harsh punishment.

"Claudia would beat us for the slightest of reasons, such as leaving a dirty dish in the sink or because the dog made a mess in the house," Leona says. "We had to walk on pins and needles to stay out of her way, but the punishment still became an everyday thing."

Describing the whippings, Leona says that Claudia would first order her to take all her clothes off. "Even at age ten, I had developed breasts, so the boys in the house would gather around and stare at me while I was standing there butt-naked," she says. "Then Claudia would tie my arms to a stair railing so that I couldn't jump out of the way. She'd grab whatever was handy—a cord, belt, stick, or a switch—and start hitting me. The whippings would last until she got tired. Ramona would get beat the same way, on the front of her body and back."

Leona recalls that Anthony was nearly always present for their whippings, sometimes watching stone-faced and, at other times, laughing. Occasionally, his half brother Owen, who was sixteen years older than Anthony, would look on also.

Jesse Hatcher, five years younger than his sisters Leona and Ramona, would also endure years of punishment in the Page Avenue home. In his case, Claudia would bring him to the living room and instruct him to remove his underwear. Bent over a chair, he was lashed across his legs and buttocks with a belt or cord until blood appeared.

"For a while, it happened nearly every day," says Jesse, adding that the scars on his legs were so prominent that he was embarrassed to wear shorts in gym class.

Beatings would occur at all hours. On nights when Garrison worked late, she'd wake up the children to administer punishment. "It was psycho," says Ramona.

Irene Justice was also physically abusive, says Leona, recalling, "Here was this elderly, overweight lady who could barely walk, but she would still hit us in the head with her cane."

No less a taskmaster than her daughter, Irene Justice would command the Davis children each Thursday to remove all items from the kitchen cabinets and pantry and then thoroughly clean the interior surfaces.

On holidays, particularly religious celebrations such as Christmas and Easter, Claudia and Irene—both habitual churchgoers—were particularly insistent that the house be in spotless condition.

"Holidays were just horrible," says Leona. "Great-grandmother Irene would make us clean all night long. While the younger kids were cleaning, the older kids would have to stay up late cooking."

Any shortcomings—perceived or real—would result in a beating. On some occasions, the punishment occurred for no apparent disciplinary reason.

"I think Claudia just didn't like me, maybe because she sensed that I wouldn't take her guff, no matter how much she whipped me," Leona says. "Eventually, Ramona, Jesse, and I turned the beatings into kind of a game to see who wouldn't cry when we got beat up."

Leona also thinks she and her twin were singled out for beatings because they were darker-complected than the other children. "I think that Claudia just didn't like dark-skinned kids," Leona says. "Sometimes, she would scream from downstairs, 'Tell them black twins to get down here. It's time for a beating.' Our brothers and sisters were light-skinned, so they were spared."

Claudia's own children were also spared from the systematic beatings. The Davis twins say they can't recall Anthony or Tressa Garrison or their siblings ever being abused.

While Anthony may have escaped Claudia's wrath at home, his shy demeanor and slight build attracted attention from schoolyard bullies at Kirk Junior High School in East Cleveland.

"He always seemed to be an easy guy to pick on; he was an easy mark," says Cavana Faithwalker, who attended junior high with Anthony in the early 1970s. Faithwalker, a poet, artist, and staff member at the Cleveland Museum of Art, remembers Anthony in those years as "very, very quiet and docile."

Schoolmates constantly teased Anthony, focusing on his lack of girlfriends and his assumed sexual inexperience. In reaction, Anthony sometimes feigned a tough-guy persona.

Faithwalker recalled an incident on a basketball court when a group of teens were taunting Anthony about being a virgin and questioning his manhood. Sowell erupted and tried to fight a much bigger boy.

"He threw a basketball at the guy. Fortunately for Anthony, another kid stepped in and cooled things off," Faithwalker said. "Anthony tried to be a hard-ass and a badass, which everyone does at that age. But it seemed to me that he was not up for that game. It wasn't his thing. He was no fighter, but the guy he blew up on was. Anthony was basically just a quiet and introspective person. He should have just sat back and been a nice guy."

. . .

For Leona, Ramona, Jesse, and, to a lesser extent, their sister Monica, the most evident consequences of their beatings was an accumulation of scar tissue and a spate of misconduct in school. Leona recalls that several teachers noticed the welts on her arms and back and suspected that her school behavior was related to abuse she was experiencing at home. So when she was disruptive in class, her teachers declined to report her misbehavior to the school administrators or to Claudia.

"They would just put me in the coatroom all the day," says Leona. "The teachers were looking out for me. They knew if they reported me to the principal, Claudia would be notified and I would get a whipping when I went home."

While she found sympathy and a semblance of protection at school, Leona was desperate to escape the abusive environment at Claudia's house. She ran away several times, but she was always taken back home.

After one particularly severe beating, Leona fled barefoot from the house, wearing only her pajamas. She was soon spotted by a passing police car and taken into custody. Leona refused to tell the police her address and phone number, despite their promises to not take her home.

"They told me they just wanted to call my family and tell everyone that I was safe," Leona says. "So I gave them the phone number at home. But the police called county social services and they told Claudia where I was."

Although Leona told a social worker about her abuse, pleading with her to remove her from Claudia's house, she was taken home by the police. When the police arrived, Claudia denied beating Leona, telling the officers that the girl was lying. Within seconds of the officers departing, Claudia struck Leona in the head with a high heel shoe, the spiked heel embedding in her forehead.

As Leona lay sobbing on the floor, blood seeping from her forehead, Claudia told her to "go take a shower and clean up."

Overcome by feelings of hopelessness and despair, Leona contemplated shooting Claudia and Irene. The women stored several loaded handguns in a second-floor closet. Leona took one out while no one was at home and practiced shooting it out of a bedroom window. "But when the gun went off, it nearly knocked me off my feet," says Leona. "It scared me and I realized that I wasn't a killer."

A month later, Leona took an overdose of pills that she found in Irene's medicine cabinet. She was taken to a hospital emergency room and then returned home to a whipping. Several weeks later, in hopes of being remanded to a juvenile facility, she started a fire in Claudia's bedroom.

The plan worked. After confessing her involvement to the responding firefighters, court officials committed her to a residential mental health center.

"I felt safe there. I was locked up and nobody could hurt me," she said. "I had been tired of the abuse, the beatings, and the running away. I left Page Avenue when I was twelve years old and I never went back."

. . .

While Tressa Garrison, Anthony's half sister, agrees the beatings of the Davis children were severe, even to the point of drawing blood, her recollections differ from Leona's in several respects.

Tressa, who is seven years younger than Anthony, says it was her grandmother Irene Justice who administered whippings—not her mother Claudia.

"It was Miss Justice who was the disciplinarian in the house," says Tressa. "My mother was hardly ever home. She was at work all the time."

In Tressa's recollections, the Davis twins were mischief-makers who acted out and threatened other kids in school. "When one got in trouble, the other would follow," she says. "The school would call home all the time to report about them. Leona even tried to set our house on fire. My grandmother tried to get help for them, but she couldn't afford it. Her bills were too high. The water bill alone for the house was about $600 a month."

Saying Leona and Ramona likely forgot who their punisher was, Tressa explains, "When people grow up, they actually forget a lot of things. I know I forget stuff."

Tressa's own childhood was not without turbulence. At age eleven, she became pregnant—the result of a sexual assault. Unhappy that her mother forced her to have an abortion, Tressa ran away from home. Eventually, she was sent to a juvenile detention center, where she stayed off and on until she was eighteen.

Although Tressa admits that she was not subjected to the same disciplinary measures as the Davis children, she says she was struck by her grandmother's cane on several occasions. And her mother once threw a shoe at her, bruising her eye socket.

Tressa concedes that her mother was prone to anger, especially if the house wasn't cleaned or she caught a child stealing. "But she didn't enjoy whipping people," she says. "My grandmother was the beater. My mom worked hard and expected her house to be clean—no ifs, ands, or buts. If it wasn't clean, she got mad. I don't blame her. Sure, there were a few times when my mother got mad enough to hit the children. She had to whip Jesse Hatcher once because he stole money from my grandmother."

Anthony was not entirely exempt from Claudia's anger, says Tressa, recalling an incident in which he failed to complete a household task.

"Anthony didn't get his work done around the house," Tressa says. "He went to boxing practice instead. He came home and was tossing a baseball around in the front yard. My mom drove down the street, knowing that he didn't do his work. When she pulled in the driveway, he ran up to her window to say hello. But she punched him in the face. He started crying and said, 'Mom, you broke my nose.' She just said, 'I don't give a fuck.'"

. . .

Years later, a social worker, Lori James-Townes, would speak with Tressa about Anthony's childhood environment. As James-Townes sat in Tressa's living room and discussed the frequent beatings in the Page Avenue home, she could hear Claudia softly crying from her bed in an adjoining room.

"Claudia was very ill, hooked up to an oxygen tank, and not coherent, but she somehow understood what we were talking about," says James-Townes. "Every now and then, I could hear Claudia make a comment. When I mentioned to Tressa that Anthony said he remembered being awakened at night by Claudia and beaten with an extension cord because the kitchen wasn't clean, Claudia corroborated his story. From the other room, she told me that she 'beat all of the children because she didn't know who was responsible.' I also heard her mumble something about whipping Anthony on another occasion because she thought he stole from her."

James-Townes says she then pointed out the likelihood that Anthony lived in constant fear that he would be woken up, tied to a banister, and whipped. "Claudia then began crying uncontrollably," James-Townes says. "I then finished my conversation with Tressa and walked over to say good-bye to Claudia. She said to me, 'I hope you didn't hear anything too bad that would make you feel bad about me.'"

Claudia's final statement "came out of the blue" and reminded her of a "deathbed confession," says James-Townes. "Perhaps Claudia needed to unburden the guilt she felt for administering beatings four decades earlier. It seemed that something was haunting her and weighing on her spirit. Maybe she felt better getting it off her chest."

Calling 1878 Page Avenue a "houseful of craziness," James-Townes says that Anthony and the other children were exposed to multiple risk factors, including emotional and physical abuse, religious fundamentalism, and a rigid rules system. The long-term impact, she says, is that nearly all of the children who grew up in Claudia's house are afflicted with a mental illness or substance abuse problem. Several have been institutionalized.

When the Davis children moved into the Page Avenue house, it stressed Claudia and Irene. They reacted by subjecting the children to a high level of abandonment and domestic violence, which traumatized young Anthony and had a "catastrophic, horrific cumulative effect on his development," she explains. "In general, child abuse of the kind experienced by Anthony is the biggest contributing factor for adult criminal behavior."

James-Townes also cites the high number of teenage pregnancies among Anthony's siblings, saying, "The women in his family have said the only use they have for men is to father babies. They can't hold onto their men or have functional relationships."

In that milieu, Anthony did not learn how to form healthy bonds with women, she says. "He didn't experience any physical touching or a bonding process while growing up. Later in life, when women would approach him, he would put his hands up. He had a hard time being intimate. He didn't like when women made the first move on him."

CHAPTER 13

The Honor Man

1978–1985

Several months after turning eighteen, the bashful, introspective young man whose social awkwardness made him the target of schoolyard bullies abruptly left his mother's home for Marine Corps boot camp.

The reasons for Sowell's enlistment seem complex, divergent, and unrelated to any sense of patriotism or duty. Prior to joining the USMC, Sowell had signed recruitment paperwork with the U.S. Army. Just before finalizing his Army enlistment, he opted to become a Marine.

Years later, during a courtroom interview by his attorney, Sowell was asked why he switched military branches. He said, "I heard the Marines were tougher."

Prodded to explain why he wanted to go the more difficult route, Sowell said that he had "a point to prove." He went on to say that it was important for him to show "that I can do it. I was constantly kind of put down and stuff."

"Were you picked on in school?" asked his attorney.

"Sometimes," Sowell said.

"Why would kids pick on you?"

"Because I was quiet and all to myself sometimes and avoided . . . I just wasn't used to really associating with a lot of kids from the slums."

"So you joined the Marines to prove a point?"

"Yes," said Sowell.

"To whom are you going to prove it?"

"My mother."

Later in the interview, Sowell was asked if his mother was affectionate toward him. "Never," he answered, explaining that his mother was not a nurturing woman and that she had never hugged him or told him she loved him. He also described the numerous "whuppings" he and other children received from Claudia and his grandmother in the Page Avenue house.

"Did you get to a point, Anthony, where you wanted to get out of that house?" the attorney asked.

"Yes . . . I just wanted to escape."

"How did you escape?"

"I joined the Marines."

Several years later, Sowell would disclose to a relative that he decided to enlist in the Marines after his mother told him that he wasn't "tough enough or smart enough" for the Army. Sowell, according to the relative, felt driven to show his mother that not only did he have the right stuff for the Army but that he could succeed in the "tougher" Marine Corps.

Along with fleeing the dysfunction of 1878 Page Avenue and "proving a point" to bullies and his mother, the Marine Corps offered an alternative to Sowell's limited employment options. He had attended East Cleveland's Shaw High School, but he dropped out in twelfth grade after he learned he didn't have enough credits to graduate. Without a high school diploma, Sowell's job prospects were dim.

Sowell may have had yet another reason to leave East Cleveland: he had just made his seventeen-year-old girlfriend pregnant.

Twyla Austin first met Sowell in 1977, when she was a junior at Shaw High School. Austin, whose family had recently moved to the Cleveland area from Atlantic City, New Jersey, says she was walking home after school one day when Sowell asked if he could walk with her. Saying he "seemed nice," Austin started a relationship with Sowell.

Austin recalls that Sowell spent much of his free time boxing for the police athletic league in those years. "He treated me fine," she says. "He was working and he had money, so we would go to movies and stuff. He didn't own a car, so we mostly hung out at his house."

Describing the roomy Page Avenue residence as a "mini-mansion," Austin says the couple spent most of their time in the first-floor den watching TV. She says she remembers Irene Justice "whacking" the Davis children with her cane on several occasions, but she doesn't have memories of Claudia yelling at the children, nor does she remember anyone, including Anthony, complaining about being hit or abused by her.

She also says that Claudia (who insisted that Austin call her Gertrude) was a hoarder with an inordinate fondness for old evening gowns. Although Claudia rarely socialized, she owned dozens of long formal dresses that had been dry-cleaned and stored in clear plastic bags.

According to Austin, Sowell offered no particular reason for joining the Marines. "He didn't say, 'I'm going to escape my horrible family' or anything like that," she says.

While Austin says Sowell was not aware that she was pregnant when he left for the Marines, other sources say that Sowell did know—and might have even had doubts that he was the child's father. "He found out I was pregnant when he was in boot camp," Austin says. "He was happy about the news. There was no drama."

As to Sowell's stated desire to join the Marines to "prove a point" to his childhood bullies, Austin says she doesn't recall him saying he was picked on when he was younger.

No matter what compelled him to enlist, Sowell reported to the Marine Corps Recruit Depot at Parris Island, South Carolina, on January 24, 1978.

. . .

The Marine Corps trumpets its boot camp as the most challenging basic training program of any of the U.S. military services. With more than seventy training days crammed into a twelve-week period, the grueling process requires a high level of physical fitness as well as the ability to memorize and learn a substantial amount of information. Just as important, the recruits are judged on their ability to exemplify traditional Marine values of honor, integrity, and leadership.

Seemingly against all odds, Sowell—the bullied, docile high school dropout—thrived in boot camp. Upon completion of basic training, Sowell was named Honor Graduate of his seventy-member class. As the top performer of his group, he was the only recruit to be automatically promoted from private to private first class.

"That's a big deal," says Walter Bansley III, a former Marine and a military lawyer in Connecticut. "As the honor man of his boot camp, he must have greatly impressed his officers. In general, he would have had to be really physically fit, very respectful, orderly, and clean. The Marines pride themselves on being the best of the best, so he had to endure a lot of pressure in boot camp. That would have required tip-top shape and a really outstanding military bearing."

When asked about Sowell's improbable achievement, Bansley theorizes: "He obviously had some screwed-up, dysfunctional family background. When he got to the Marines, he found a place he liked. In the Marine Corps, he finally had a family and he responded well to it."

After basic training, Pfc. Sowell reported to North Carolina's Camp Lejeune for three weeks of combat training. He'd already learned basic choke holds and hand-to-hand fighting skills in boot camp; now he would continue training to become "not only an elite warrior but also a noble one," according to USMC recruiting material.

At Camp Lejeune, Sowell would learn how to disable and kill using his bare hands as well as improvised weapons of opportunity. He became proficient in blood chokes—a category of choke holds that involve the application of pressure to the carotid artery, which then stops the flow of oxygen-rich blood to the brain.

As compared to air chokes, which are used to block breathing, blood chokes (often called strangles) are considered a superior killing technique. Strangling—either by hand or ligature—can take as little as eight to thirteen seconds to incapacitate a person, while an air choke can take several minutes.

Combat training was followed by a month of instruction on electrical wiring. Sowell was then assigned to Marine Corps Air Station Cherry Point in Havelock, North Carolina, as an electrician.

In September 1978, eight months after Sowell enlisted, Austin gave birth to a daughter, Julie. She says that Sowell sent money and bought gifts for the baby, but the couple didn't pursue a relationship. "We were both young and dating other people at that time," Austin explains.

Sowell spent five of his seven years in the Marines at Cherry Point, living in a secluded trailer park for part of that time. He also served assignments at Camp Pendleton in California and Camp Butler in Okinawa, Japan.

While at Cherry Point, Sowell married a fellow Marine, Kim Yvette Lawson, in September 1981. Sowell and Lawson had met while both were deployed in Okinawa.

Lawson, a California native, told her family that she married the twenty-two-year-old Sowell to keep him from drinking himself out of the Marines.

"He was drinking heavily," says Lawson's mother, Norma Lawson. "Kim felt sorry for him and wanted to help him. She didn't want him to get a dishonorable discharge."

Sowell would later say that Kim understood him—and handled him—better than anyone he had ever known. "I don't know . . . We just had that connection," he says.

Alluding to intimacy issues that he blames on a childhood devoid of affection, he says, "Things were tough for me when I grew up. My mom never showed me that she cared about me. Kim was able to help me with those problems."

Sowell also says that Kim was instrumental in helping him recover from a potentially catastrophic incident in 1982 when a radiator hose exploded in his face. On that night, according to Sowell, he had driven to a fellow Marine's going-away party. On the way home, his car overheated. He opened the hood and noticed the radiator hose was hissing. He twisted the hose to check its connection and it blew apart, spraying him with boiling radiator coolant.

"I didn't have a chance to close my eyes, so the [fluid] just went straight into my eyes and face," Sowell recounted. He suffered second- and third-degree burns to his skin and damage to his corneas that left him blind.

His sister, Tressa, and daughter, Julie, then four years old, happened to be visiting at the time. In Tressa's case, the trip to North Carolina was of a punitive purpose. She'd been regularly skipping school and staying out all night, so Claudia sent her to live with her brother.

"But Tressa was only fifteen and I didn't want her and Julie to have to watch me deal with my injuries, so I sent them home," Sowell said.

His eyes bandaged and unsure if he'd ever see again, Sowell relied on Kim to care for him. Three months later, doctors removed the bandages and Sowell was able to see.

Kim filed for divorce from Sowell in 1985, on the day she was discharged from the Marines. She would die thirteen years later at a steel mill in Pittsburg, California. A steel roll handler with only two months on the job, Kim, 37, was killed when a 500-pound metal block became dislodged and fell on her throat.

· · ·

Sowell's military career—although meritorious—was slightly blemished. During his Okinawa deployment, he was knocked down from sergeant to corporal after "an alcohol-related incident with a military police officer," according to Marine Corps records that were reviewed by Bansley.

"Apparently, he was out drunk one night with a lance corporal and he got in a beef with an MP," Bansley says. "As a sergeant, he shouldn't have been out with a lance corporal anyhow, but this was Sowell's only thing of a disciplinary nature. It happens to a lot to people who are stationed overseas. That's why the Marine Corps tries not to keep them there for more than a year."

Nevertheless, says Bansley, Sowell was a "really good" Marine until that incident. "In cases like these, the Corps usually requires an individual to get alcohol counseling, but it looks like they dropped the ball on this one." Sowell's records also indicate that he went AWOL for several months at one point, but Bansley downplayed the significance of the incident, noting that Sowell had regained his rank of sergeant by the time he was honorably discharged on January 15, 1985.

Sowell departed the Marine Corps with a chest full of ribbons and praise, including a rifle sharpshooter award, good conduct medal, sea service deployment ribbon, a certificate of commendation, a meritorious mast, and three letters of appreciation from the U.S. government.

"It's pretty clear that if he would have stayed in the Corps and stayed on track, he could have made it a good career," Bansley says.

While Sowell presented the image of a model Marine—a respectful, well-trained "elite warrior"—his military record doesn't reflect the dark secrets he left on Okinawa.

In the notorious red-light district of Okinawa City, which is known to U.S. military personnel as "Hooker Hill," Sgt. Sowell indulged his twisted sexual fantasies.

Several sources, including a prison friend and a Marine who served with Sowell, say that he targeted women who worked as entertainers—strippers and prostitutes—in the district's many nightclubs.

Perhaps Sowell's interest in the bar workers, most of whom were recruited from the Philippines, seemed no different than that of countless other U.S. overseas servicemen who have been stuck with the label "oversexed, overpaid, and over here" since World War II.

But Sowell's fascination with the petite, almond-eyed women went beyond simple sexual pleasure. He was acting out deviant fantasies that included bondage, choking, and domination.

"Sowell told me that whenever he would go out on leave from his base, he would find strippers—young, poor girls who would agree to have sex with him for a couple of dollars," says Roosevelt Lloyd, who befriended Sowell in the late 1990s when both were incarcerated. "Once he got a girl back to her hotel room, he could do whatever he wanted to her. He was a U.S. Marine officer, so she felt she had to comply. This is probably when he first started acting out his fantasy package."

Sowell spent many of his weekends in Hooker Hill nightclubs during the year he was stationed in Japan. Painted in garish candy-colored themes, with pink and blue neon signage, the bars were packed with partying servicemen—mostly Marines—and the sultry Filipinas who were working hard to attract their interest and then their money.

"He had his way with these foreign women for the whole time he was in Okinawa," says the fifty-five-year-old Lloyd. "He tied some of the girls to a chair and then put a rope around their necks. That was his version of sex—but it went way beyond sex and into anger."

A Marine who partied in Okinawa with Sowell says his activities with the women became increasingly bizarre. "He liked to talk about how he choked and strangled them," he says. "My opinion is that he probably abused women while he was on leave in Okinawa. But since he didn't kill any of them—to my knowledge—no one knew what he was up to. He just strangled them as a domination thing. And then he went back to the base as if everything was normal."

Lloyd, who works as a machine operator in Cleveland, says he is not so sure that Sowell didn't leave any victims in Okinawa. "He told me about having sex with the bar girls, but he didn't tell me much about the deviance. He would never say, 'Oh, by the way, I also strangled a few of them.' But a mutual friend who was in the Marines with Sowell has told me some bad things happened over there. It wouldn't surprise me if Sowell had killed a few strippers while he was overseas."

Lloyd says that Sowell's Marine Corps training would have made him a particularly capable predator. "The Marines taught him all these great standards: How to walk, talk, hold open doors, how to be polite, and how to be a gentleman. As a Marine, he also became an expert in how to observe, how to survive, how to kill, and how to get rid of evidence when you kill. He took his military training and he used it for his own deviant purposes."

CHAPTER 14

Back on the Block

January 15, 1985–September 20, 1990

Seven years after leaving East Cleveland to join the Marine Corps, Anthony Sowell reentered civilian life. In military parlance, he was "back on the block."

Sowell's block—East Cleveland—had changed considerably since he'd been away. The city had been on a slow economic decline since the start of Northeast Ohio's industrial contraction in the 1960s. But now the community that was once home to nineteenth-century industrialists such as John D. Rockefeller, the Standard Oil founder and world's first billionaire, was blighted and corrupt.

So-called "white flight" had resulted in a population that was ninety percent black, with more than a third of the city's residents living below the federal poverty level and thirty percent of its households led by an unmarried woman. Two of its elected officials were charged with theft in office in 1985, while the city's water and sewer funds were found to have deficits in excess of two million dollars. Three years later, the Ohio State Auditor declared a fiscal emergency in East Cleveland.

On its hard-knock streets, a skeleton crew of police officers responded only to high-priority calls. East Cleveland, like many areas of neighboring Cleveland, had been polluted by crack cocaine, cheap and powerfully addictive. Crack addicts were willing to steal, sell, or barter nearly anything to get high. The crime rate soared and entire neighborhoods were overrun by drug dealers.

Like his hometown, Sowell had also been in steady decline. Beginning his Marine Corps service as a spit-shined, squared-away Honor Graduate of his boot camp class, he had become a predator, using his weekend leaves in Okinawa to covertly indulge his deviant desires with an unknown number of bar girls.

Sowell, now 25, was exchanging his regimented military life for the chaotic environment of East Cleveland. He'd returned to the large house at 1878 Page Avenue, which was now a sort of enclave within an area of the city that had become a virtual drug supermarket, where violent crime was an everyday occurrence.

Like many returning servicemen, Sowell struggled to acclimate to the civilian world, which must have seemed disorganized and disorderly in comparison to the intense discipline of the Marine Corps. In his bedroom, he was fastidious about the placement and cleanliness of his belongings.

Sowell shared a third-floor bedroom with his nephew, Jesse Darnell Hatcher, for several months in 1985. Hatcher recalls that ex-Marine Sowell was "very particular" about his bedding and clothes. "He was more calm and quiet than he'd been before he went into the service," Hatcher says. "But nobody was allowed to mess with his stuff. Everything was rolled up military-style. If anyone touched it, he would get very upset."

Sowell's sister, Tressa Garrison, and Twyla Austin, the mother of his daughter, Julie (who was seven at the time), also recall that he seemed prone to anger when he returned.

"He was stern and very direct when he came out of the service," Tressa says. "He'd lost his playfulness. You can see the change in people after they leave the Marines. They don't seem to have a soft spot anymore. It's almost like Anthony was meaner."

Tressa herself admits to anger issues and a tendency toward depression. A mother of nine children by four men, she has been arrested several times for domestic violence and unashamedly says she has a firm hand with her children—and their fathers.

Her relationships with men have been typically volatile and unstable. She describes one incident in which she was charged with assault: "The father of [several of] my kids hit me. I was big, fat, and pregnant, and he slapped me and pushed me into the wall. There was even an imprint where my head hit the wall. I picked up a skillet and hit him in the face with it. I wanted to break his nose."

She says she put another husband "out" because he stole money from his own children.

Tressa, who has been arrested for grand theft, child neglect, and disorderly conduct, was investigated by county social workers in the mid-

1980s after a report that she disciplined her daughter by picking her up by her neck.

Describing herself as a former cocaine user, Tressa says she first started using the drug in her teens. "I was a head barmaid by the time I was age sixteen," she says. "On nights when I had to work late shifts, I snorted coke for an energy boost."

But in 1988, when she realized that she had a drug problem, she attempted to enter rehab. "I asked my kid's father if he would babysit for me while I was getting treatment," Tressa says. "He said he wouldn't, so I kicked drugs cold turkey. I was twenty-two then and I've been sober ever since."

. . .

Shortly after Sowell returned from the Marines, Austin and Julie moved into the Page Avenue home, although she says her relationship with Sowell was no more than a friendship. In fact, relations between the two were tense since she had filed court motions complaining that he was behind on his child support payments. Sowell was also unhappy that Austin had—without explanation—refused to list him as Julie's father on her birth certificate.

Sowell's domestic problems with Austin were compounded by his recent divorce from his wife of four years, Kim Yvette Lawson, a woman, he said, "who cared about him more than any other woman he'd ever known."

Sowell was either unable or unwilling to find legitimate employment in the years following his Marine service. It's likely that he supported himself by selling drugs from the Page Avenue house, according to comments made in later years by Tressa.

Beset by family problems and anxious about his future, Sowell drank heavily. He would later tell a psychologist that he had at least six drinks nearly every day during the latter half of the 1980s. On some days, he started drinking early in the morning and would occasionally black out.

He also admitted that he became more aggressive while drinking. Sowell's problems with aggression and alcohol abuse are reflected in his post-Marines police record: He was convicted of domestic violence in 1988 (the victim is not identified in police records) and spent a week in jail. In that same year, he was arrested for possession of drugs.

Sowell also faced charges at various times for disorderly conduct, driving while intoxicated, criminal trespassing, and public drunkenness. Early in 1989, he was arrested for aggravated burglary, but the case was dropped when police failed to find enough evidence to charge him.

. . .

Since returning home in 1985, Sowell had persistently engaged in petty criminal acts, mainly alcohol-related. However, on July 22, 1989, he erupted in a sadistic assault that surpassed the sexual deviance he unleashed in Okinawa.

The incident began in the predawn hours at a drug-infested motel in East Cleveland. Several patrol cars had arrived at the motel to investigate a complaint. The police activity attracted the attention of twenty-one-year-old Melvette Sockwell, who was waiting for her boyfriend to return to their room. To Sockwell, it looked like a drug raid was underway.

According to a police report, Sockwell, who was pregnant, had a history of drug use and was worried about the possibility of being arrested. Sowell was also at the motel. Noticing Sockwell's nervousness, Sowell lured her into his car by saying that her boyfriend had asked him to take her to his house until the officers left. Sowell then drove Sockwell to his nearby Page Avenue home.

Sockwell disputes the police report, saying that she actually met Sowell after her car broke down on Euclid Avenue and he stopped to offer assistance. "He said he would drive me to his house and let me use his telephone," she explains.

No matter which story is accurate, Sockwell and Sowell arrived at his house shortly about (6:15 A.M.) and walked to the rear door.

"It was still dark and there was a big black tree in the backyard that was casting spooky shadows," recalls Sockwell. "It was almost like a warning or omen for me."

Because Sowell was a stranger to her, Sockwell was hesitant about entering the house. But once inside, her concerns eased when she saw toys and children's clothing.

"Let's go upstairs," Sowell told her, taking her hand.

"He told me to tiptoe on the stairs so that we didn't wake up his sister Tressa," Sockwell says.

On the third floor, which Sockwell remembers as well-kept and clean, she asked Sowell if she could use his telephone.

"Up until that point, Anthony seemed like he was okay," says Sockwell. "But then he shut the door and locked it in a way that frightened me. He closed the bedroom window and told me to sit down. Then he came from behind me with a long knife. He pulled a big suitcase into the middle of the room and said, 'I don't think I need to tell you what's going to happen now.'"

Sockwell says she began to take her clothes off, believing that if she complied, she'd survive. "I was three months pregnant, so I thought that he might show some mercy," she says. "But he threw me on the bed, choked me, and raped me . . . again and again."

At the culmination of each assault, Sowell ordered Sockwell to wash up in his bathroom and then put her clothes back on. "He kept saying he was sorry, but then he repeated the whole thing—each time telling me to take my clothes off and raping me again. After a while, I started crying and he stuffed a towel in my mouth. He then performed oral sex on me, which surprised me because he didn't know me at all and that's such an intimate act."

During one of the assaults, Sockwell realized that Sowell was attempting anal sex with her.

Although frightened, she was able to rebuff him by calmly explaining that she'd had an episiotomy a year earlier.

"I told him I would hemorrhage and get blood on him," she says. "I realized that my best chance for surviving would be if I tried to stay composed and not panic or scream."

As the hours passed and the attack continued, day turned into night and back to day. Sockwell says that after she had been in his bedroom for fifteen hours or so, her stomach began growling from hunger. Sowell heard the rumbling and told her, "You might as well say your prayers because I'm going to feed you, then I'm going to kill you." He then tied a rag around her mouth, bound her wrists with a necktie, and tightened a belt around her ankles.

"But first," he said, "I'm going to get some rest." Then Sowell, who had been drinking heavily, dozed off.

When Sockwell was certain that Sowell was sleeping, she began inching off the bed. "I didn't think I could get through the door without waking him, so I wiggled on the floor towards the window," she says. "My hands were tied behind my back, so I had to use my head to nudge the window sash up. The whole time I was trying to get the window open, I was looking at the knife beside him. I knew if he woke up, he would kill me."

When the dormer window was open enough for her to fit her body through, she slid herself headfirst over the windowsill and onto the steep roof, some twenty-five feet above the ground. "I could have fallen off the roof, but I didn't care. He told me he was going to kill me, and I believed him."

With her feet wedged into the gutter, Sockwell sat on the roof and scanned the street for people. "I saw two elderly ladies getting into a car. I shook my head back and forth and tried to yell through my gag at them, but I wasn't sure that they saw me."

Just then, her arms were gripped tightly from behind. She felt herself being dragged through the window and back into the bedroom.

Thinking it was Sowell, Sockwell was terrified. In actuality, her muffled yelling had awakened Tressa, who was now glaring at her.

Sockwell recalls that Tressa grudgingly removed the restraints from her wrists and ankles.

"When I told her what I had been through, she got angry and said, 'Well, why didn't you just scream for help?' She acted as if I was lying about everything just because I didn't scream," says Sockwell. "I wanted to slap her. She had to know that if I had screamed, he would have killed me."

Although Sockwell, while on the roof, hadn't been certain that the elderly women had heard her distress cries, police and fire crews were soon at the house. The police officers walked upstairs and roused the still-slumbering Sowell.

Sockwell recalls that she was stunned by Sowell's reaction to seeing uniformed officers standing over him. "He just casually rolled over on his side and said, 'I'm going back to sleep.'"

Sockwell was transported to University Hospitals, where she was examined and her injuries photographed. Sobbing, she told police that Sowell had choked her so hard that she felt her body tingling. "I thought I was going to die," she stated in her report.

Sowell was arrested and indicted by the county grand jury on multiple counts of rape and kidnapping. He was released on bond, but he failed to show up for his court hearing. On December 8, 1989, the court issued an arrest warrant.

Eight months later, while a fugitive, Sowell was accused of another rape. In this case, a pregnant thirty-one-year-old woman said she was attacked while drinking with Sowell on June 24, 1990, in a Cleveland house.

The woman was sitting beside Sowell on a love seat, according to police, when he suddenly began choking her. Screaming obscenities, he described the sex acts he was going to perform. He then told her that "she was his bitch, and she had better learn to like it."

Wrapping his hands around her neck, he pulled her upstairs, where she was raped orally, anally, and vaginally.

The woman begged him to stop—telling him she was pregnant—but he continued the attack, even ordering her to say, "Yes, sir, I like it."

Sowell fell asleep, enabling the woman to escape and report the attack to police. Sowell was still asleep when officers came to the house at 8:00 A.M. They arrested him but were forced to drop the charges when the woman would not cooperate with investigators.

However, police now had Sowell in custody for the 1989 Sockwell rape case. After plea-bargaining with prosecutors, Sowell agrees to plead guilty to a lesser charge of attempted rape.

On September 12, 1990, he is sentenced to five to fifteen years in prison. Sowell, now 31—a relatively late age for a prison first-timer—is taken to the Lorain Correctional Institution.

Melvette Sockwell did not attend Sowell's court hearings or his sentencing in 1990. "I just couldn't handle seeing him," she said. "I stayed drunk for four months after the attack. It's the only way I could handle the severe anxiety that I was feeling every night."

Sockwell told police at the time of her attack that she was certain that Sowell had brutalized other women. "It was the way that he kept telling me he was sorry—repeating it over and over," she says. "It was like he knew that he was doing something terrible, but he was unable to stop himself from doing it."

CHAPTER 15

Model Prisoner

1990–2005

Less than five years after leaving the fierce structure and hierarchy of the Marine Corps, Sowell was again in an environment that demanded obedience and conformity.

And just as he'd adapted well to the uniformity of the Marines, he acclimated smoothly to the grinding monotony of incarceration. In prison-speak, Sowell "knew how to do time."

Incarcerated from 1990 to 2005, Sowell served his sentence in four different Ohio penitentiaries. Prison records show that he was rarely in trouble while behind bars. He had no major rules violations and just four warnings for minor infractions.

"Anthony Sowell likes structure," says Roosevelt Lloyd, who shared close quarters with him for seven years and knew his mind-set perhaps better than anyone. "As long as there is a set of rules, he is in his comfort zone. That's a key part of his personality."

Prison, at its most fundamental, is about order. And Sowell has sought order his entire life, says Lloyd. "That's why he was such a good fit in the military and in prison. Marine training is all about keeping things in their place—everything must be accounted for. In prison, Anthony would know exactly where his possessions belonged. He would know immediately if something had been moved or taken."

Social worker Lori James-Townes says it's not surprising that Sowell—the model Marine—was also a model prisoner. Sowell likely found solace within the confines of the military and the locked units of prison, she says, explaining, "He grew up in an unpredictable and chaotic household where there were no boundaries. So the structured environment of prison reduces Anthony's anxiety. He is hyper-vigilant, so it's important for him to be in control. He needs structured situations."

While Sowell's fastidious nature and seemingly compulsive adherence to order may have put him out of sync with street life, Lloyd says those character traits are looked upon favorably by the prison staff.

"You have 1,500 to 1,800 people in an average-sized corrections facility, so that's a lot of different attitudes and personalities for the guards to deal with," he explains. "In any facility, the rules and regulations are the structure that provides the boundaries between the inmates and guards. Every prison has red lines on the floor that are not to be crossed. You need an okay from a captain or lieutenant to cross them. Some inmates go with the flow and others don't. Anthony worked within the boundaries and stayed inside the red lines, so the staff members knew that he was not a disciplinary problem or an escape risk.

"Everybody who knew him—the guards, warden, kitchen staff—gave him high praise for his manners and work ethic. He did everything that was required of a good prisoner. That type of a prisoner is appreciated by the administration because they know they can hold him accountable. They can leave him in their office alone and he's not going to steal anything—like most prisoners would. Anthony had that kind of accountability; he had doors opened to him."

Sowell held a variety of jobs in prison, including yard maintenance worker, assembler, electrician, and food service prep cook, where he worked with Lloyd. For several years, he also worked in the dining hall as a line server, a position that appealed to his natural disposition as a detached observer.

Lloyd—noting that Sowell was "perfect" in his role as a food handler—says that he preferred to deal with the prison population from behind a counter.

"In the dining hall, Sowell would rather serve 1,500 inmates than be among 1,500 inmates," he says. "And then after he served them, he tried to avoid them. He didn't want to get in a situation where he would have to fight. He knew there are certain things you don't do in prison: You don't borrow, loan, steal, gamble, associate with gang members, or tell anyone why you're in prison. If you get involved in those situations, you're going to get in fights. You can't even borrow a pack of cigarettes from certain people in prison because they are going to ask for two packs in return. If you're a hustler and you fail to pay someone back, you better have someone backing you or you're going to get punked out, stabbed, or even killed. Sowell understood that when you're in prison, you're only in prison for one reason: To get out."

Lloyd, who was incarcerated from 1988 to 2009, first met Sowell in the mid-1990s at Grafton Correctional Institution. They were bunkmates in a dormitory-style housing unit. The two began their friendship playing basketball against each other.

"My first impression of him was that he was very competitive, he had a smart look about him, and he was pretty strong, physically," Lloyd recalls. "We ended up being friends and respecting each other because we were both stand-up guys back then. At that time, I didn't know what he was locked up for. He could have been a terrorist or a bad check-writer. You don't know who you'll end up being friends with in prison and you don't ask someone what their crimes were. What you see are a man's habits and whether he has respect and courtesy. In prison, you see the real person; you see everything but his crime."

The two friends shared more in common than a love of basketball and mutual respect: both Sowell and Lloyd were imprisoned for sex crimes and both were first-time offenders who had been sent to maximum security facilities.

"I'd never been incarcerated before; I never knew what prison was like," Lloyd says. "When you go straight from the street to hard time like we did, your entire demeanor changes. You know you're not playing kid games. It's life or death in there. You're thrown into a subculture that's the lowest of the low, so you have to show no fear; no weakness. If you come in with a macho, strong attitude, you need to go where the tough guys are. And those guys are usually in the weight room. If you can lift 300 or 400 pounds, you'll have eight to ten guys looking out for you. If you can't hang with the tough guys, you need to find another way to survive."

While Lloyd, whose heavily muscled torso belies his fifty-five years, stayed busy in the prison weight room, Sowell's record shows that he was an active participant in courses aimed at controlling his temper and curbing his substance abuse. His classes included "Living Without Violence," "Cage Your Rage," and "Positive Personal Change." He also attended two twelve-step Alcoholics Anonymous programs: "Adult Children of Alcoholics" and "Drug Awareness Prevention."

In addition, Sowell earned his high school education in prison, taking his GED examination at Grafton and passing with flying colors.

Sowell's prison résumé, however, is conspicuously missing sex offender therapy. Records show that he signed up for a sex offender treatment program in 1993 but was denied admission. The reason for his denial, according to a prison spokesperson, is that Sowell refused to admit he had committed sex offenses.

If Sowell would have acknowledged his sex crimes and subsequently completed offender therapy, it's likely he could have been considered for early parole from prison. But Lloyd says Sowell faced a dangerous catch-22. If he admitted that he was a sex offender, he would have been a marked man in prison.

"Sex offenders are number one on the list of hated people in prison," Lloyd says. "Prisoners are even more likely to accept a murderer. They can rationalize it by saying that the murder could have been an act of passion. But when it comes to sex offenses, inmates just don't understand the crimes. They don't know why it happens."

Sowell was well aware of the consequences faced by inmates who exposed themselves as sex offenders. He knew they were called perverts by other inmates and that they were attacked on the basketball court.

"Sowell also knew that his personal attitude is that he would have to hurt anyone who confronted him," Lloyd says. "As a Marine, he was trained to deal severely with anyone who was a threat."

To avoid the certainty of fights and the potential for disciplinary action, Sowell would have had to go into protective custody if he exposed himself as a sex offender. In protective custody, he'd be isolated from other inmates, but he'd also lose many of his freedoms and rights, including access to educational programs and prison jobs.

James-Townes, who is based in Maryland and consults throughout the United States on criminal justice issues, laments the conundrum of sex offenders who seek therapy in prison.

While she says it's important that offenders take full responsibility for their crimes, she notes, "Once sex offenders are subjected to that label, they are absolutely at a higher risk for assault or murder by other inmates. If they are considered weak, they can be subjected to constantly doing sexual favors for stronger inmates. In prison, Anthony Sowell was housed in a big dorm-type area with 300 inmates. They typically lock those doors at night. I'm sure men get assaulted all the time."

Lloyd, in contrast to Sowell, was able to participate in sex offender therapy program with no fear of backlash from his fellow prisoners. Lloyd completed a two-year program at Madison Correctional Institution, which houses Ohio's Sex Offender Risk Reduction Center (SORRC). The SORCC was launched in 1995 in response to a dramatic increase in the population of sex offenders in state prisons.

"The way Madison is set up, there are a lot of sex offenders, so it doesn't matter if you are exposed or not," Lloyd says. "If you are there, everyone pretty much assumes what your crime is."

After graduation from SORRC, inmates are typically sent to general population in other institutions. In Lloyd's case, he was transferred to Grafton, where Sowell spent the last nine years of his sentence. Prison records don't conclusively show whether Sowell was provided an opportunity to participate in SORRC.

But Sowell's decision to deny his sex offenses while at Grafton is understandable, says Lloyd, explaining that Sowell would have become a pariah. "He confided in me about his past, but it was pretty easy for him to keep it a secret from everyone else. Nowadays, inmates have access to the Internet in prison. They can find out everyone else's business. They will then spread the word throughout the prison. But back in the days when Anthony and I first got to prison, an inmate's crimes were hush-hush. Nobody would know what we did unless we told them ourselves."

. . .

Despite Sowell's good behavior in prison, the state's parole board consistently denied him early release. Parole officials cited the "serious nature of his offense" in turning down his requests. Sockwell joined with the county prosecutor in voicing opposition to his release each time it was considered. Sowell would serve his maximum sentence of fifteen years.

Although Sowell's violent crime was noted as the primary reason for his parole denial, Lloyd says Sowell privately blamed his mother Claudia Garrison. The parole board, when considering a request, takes into account the candidate's prospects for a stable home life outside of prison. Claudia, however, wouldn't commit to providing her son with a home to return to.

"He was definitely angry at his mother," Lloyd says. "They were constantly fighting and at each other's throats; they never seemed to get along. But even though she wouldn't send him money or a food package while he was in prison, he rarely said anything bad about her. He even tried to say that it was his grandmother who did all the whipping when he grew up. But every once in a while, he would slip and call his mother a 'bitch.'"

Lloyd can't recall Sowell ever mentioning his father, who passed away in 2004 before Sowell was released. "His sister Tressa would send him a little money, a little food. She visited him one time; so did a couple of other family members. But he never had any visits from friends in all the years I knew him."

Sowell, the "stand-up guy," got along well with inmates and corrections officers, yet his prison friendships were limited to a chess buddy, a staff member who occasionally allowed him special privileges, and Lloyd.

"He didn't let people get close to him," Lloyd says. "We were 'bunkies' for a long time, so we got pretty tight. We talked a lot about our plans when we got out. Anthony wanted to get his GI loan reestablished, buy a car, and get a home of his own. He was planning to stay in the food industry. He was a pretty creative cook in prison—he had to be because of the limited ingredients that were available in the kitchen."

When Sowell was about a month away from his release date, he learned from family members that his stepmother, Segerna Sowell, was being defrauded by her nephew, who lived in her home at 12205 Imperial Avenue.

"Word got down to him in the joint that his nephew was ripping off his stepmom's Social Security payments," Lloyd says. "So now, Anthony is angry and he has a plan: he is going to kick his nephew out of the house and move in himself."

On June 20, 2005, Sowell strode through Grafton's corridors for the final time. As he left his housing unit, inmates and staff wished him luck. Several corrections officers—in breach of prison policy—hugged him good-bye.

At age forty-five, Sowell was a free man.

CHAPTER 16

Imperial Avenue

Summer 2005

On an unseasonably warm morning in June 2005, a half-dozen Garrisons, including Anthony Sowell's mother Claudia, his sister Tressa, and his nephew Ja'Ovvoni, pile into a car to bring him home from prison.

For fifteen-year-old Ja'Ovvoni, it would be his first meeting with his Uncle Tony, although he'd read the letters he'd sent from prison to Tressa and Claudia. The third-oldest of Tressa's nine children, Ja'Ovvoni was born in August 1989, one month after Sowell's attack of Melvette Sockwell—the crime that put him behind bars.

Ja'Ovvoni and his siblings had a peripatetic childhood. Tressa moved her family often, never spending more than a year in a home. Because she had an outstanding arrest warrant for grand theft, she was unable to apply for public housing.

"It was tough on my mom having so many kids," Ja'Ovvoni says. "She had a lot of disputes with landlords, so it seemed like we were always on the move. Sometimes we'd live with my grandmother, Claudia, but then my mom and her would get into it and we'd have to leave the house. We'd all get on a bus and go to a homeless shelter until we found a new place or until we moved back in with my grandmother."

Tressa and her family lived with Ja'Ovvoni's father, Sandy Lightbourn, for a while, but the couple fought often. After a particularly bloody brawl in which a stray punch left one of Tressa's sons temporarily in a coma, Tressa left Lightbourn and took her family to Florida.

In Ft. Lauderdale, Tressa resorted to passing several bad checks "to keep us going," says Ja'Ovvoni. The family soon moved back to Cleveland and Ja'Ovvoni enrolled in a charter school. There, he discovered his interests in art and skateboarding.

A soft-spoken, self-contained young man, Ja'Ovvoni says he has never been interested in being "out in the neighborhood environment." He got his first job when he was sixteen, giving a portion of each paycheck to his mother to help with expenses.

He says he embraced skateboarding as both a competitive challenge and an escape. As his skills grew, he participated in regional exhibitions and also learned that he enjoyed teaching the sport to children. He is now enrolled in college and works part-time as a skateboard instructor at a Cleveland nonprofit neighborhood development organization, where, at age twenty-two, he also is a board member.

"I'm someone who wants to make a difference in the world," says Ja'Ovvoni, a self-described community activist. "Growing up in a single-parent family with nine kids, I always felt a responsibility to help out. So working with kids on their skateboarding is something I love doing. I just want to watch people do well and succeed in life."

Ja'Ovvoni says he was optimistic that his uncle would do well in his post-prison life. A month after returning home, Sowell seemed to be on a good track. He was living with Tressa's family and landed a food services job at the Cleveland Indians baseball stadium.

"He was excited," says Ja'Ovvoni. "He was working at the stadium, then coming home and hanging out with us. We'd play video games together and talk sports. He loved the Indians and the Cleveland Browns. And he was proud of what I was doing with my life. 'Keep doing what you're doing,' he'd tell me. He just seemed like an average person; someone who was down-to-earth."

. . .

In late July of 2005, Sowell moved out of Tressa's house, which was crammed with thirteen of her children and grandchildren, and took up residence on the top floor of stepmother Segerna's house at 12205 Imperial Avenue.

Shortly after his arrival, his stepmother was hospitalized with kidney disease, leaving her first-floor suite empty. A month later, a young family who had been renting the second floor also moved away.

Only Sowell remained in the three-story house. But he wasn't alone for long.

That summer, Sowell met Lori Frazier while both were buying beer at a mini-mart. Telling her that he'd like to "buy her something better than beer," Sowell invited Frazier to have a cocktail and dinner at a nearby

Chinese restaurant. They spent several hours chatting. Frazier says she found him charming and easy to talk to.

Sowell was clearly smitten. Frazier was a lively conversationalist and strikingly pretty, with high cheekbones, ebony eyes, and a light caramel complexion. She spoke lovingly of her four children and two grandchildren and her interest in obtaining a college degree someday. When Sowell told her that he was currently unemployed, she hinted that she had a powerful connection in Cleveland's City Hall. Getting Sowell a job with the city wouldn't be a problem, she said.

On the night of their meeting, Frazier accompanied Sowell back to his house. To Sowell, who ostensibly hadn't been with a woman since he'd entered prison in 1990, the attractive, well-connected Frazier must have seemed like a divine gift.

What he didn't know, however, was that Frazier had a raging crack cocaine addiction. Since the late 1980s, she'd compiled a lengthy record of arrests for drug abuse, drug trafficking, theft, and soliciting.

Frazier had been incarcerated several times and had been treated for mental issues, including depression, psychotic disorders, and substance dependence. At one point, she told counselors that she heard voices telling her "to run."

Describing herself as a "strong lady who is spiritual and sensitive," Frazier says her problems began when she fell in with the wrong crowd. "I was always a good girl who never got in trouble. In my teenage years, though, I had a lot of friends who would give me drugs. At first, I just dibbled and dabbled with drugs. I just considered it partying. But then the drugs began controlling me. I ended up with a bad, bad habit."

Frazier says her addiction took over her life. Unable to hold a job or care for her children, she spent her days trolling the streets for crack while her mother took custody of her young children.

Whether or not Sowell knew of Frazier's past, she was soon ensconced in his heart and house, an arrangement that enabled her to, in her words, "stay home all day and watch TV while Tony went to work at a factory on East 55th Street."

Sowell's factory job—he worked as a machine operator at Custom Rubber Corp.—paid for Frazier's crack habit and anything else she desired.

"He took very good care of me," she recalls. "He shopped for me; told me how beautiful I was; he was protective of me. We went to parks and concerts together. He fed me breakfast, lunch, and dinner in bed, if I wanted him to. We were very happy."

Over the next two years, the couple maintained a conventional, monogamous relationship, with neighbors and others remarking that Sowell seemed to adore Frazier.

"Tony treated her so well," says Kendra Robinson, an Imperial Avenue resident. "He bought her anything she wanted—cigarettes, beer, drugs. He was a decent guy."

Segerna Sowell's mother, Virginia Oliver, credits Frazier with "settling Tony down." Noting that Sowell could always be counted on to handle household chores for Segerna, the eighty-nine-year-old Oliver says, "When he was with Lori, he seemed very happy and he liked to work around the house."

Sowell, who had been known to boast about his womanizing in the past, had evidently committed himself to Frazier. Tanja Doss met Sowell shortly after he left prison and just before he met Frazier. "We used to drink beer together and play cards or chess," she says. "He cooked for me a couple of times. He was a good host and a nice guy."

Doss moved to New York in mid-2005 and returned a year later. "I knocked on his door to say hello and he came out and told me, 'I got a woman now, so you can't come around and visit me anymore,'" she recalls. "The woman was Lori Frazier. I'd see them walking around his neighborhood together. It seemed like he was really in love."

While Sowell repeatedly told Frazier that he intended to marry her, their relationship would begin to deteriorate after she discovered that he was smoking crack cocaine.

Since July 2005, Sowell had supported Frazier's crack addiction, without yielding to the drug's lure himself. On some nights, Frazier would be gone until morning, unashamedly telling Sowell that she had spent the night at a crack house. Several weeks later, to see for himself what she was experiencing, Sowell accompanied her to a dilapidated, vacant apartment building populated by addicts—zombie-like men and women sitting on ripped sofa cushions, ardently sucking smoke through their glass stems. What he saw depressed him and left him confused. "I didn't understand her attraction to that lifestyle," he said later. "I was offering this woman everything, but she was choosing that scene."

But at some point, Sowell went from enabler to consumer. In early 2006, while Frazier was in jail for a drug offense, she heard that Sowell was on the streets buying crack. When she returned home, she found him with a small amount of the drug and assumed that he had bought it for her.

"When he didn't give it to me, I felt bad because I knew that he had started smoking crack," she says. "Maybe he just wanted to try it, but I knew then that our relationship was fractured. It wasn't going to work if both of us were smoking. From then on, everything just started to go downhill."

Frazier says that Sowell's personality and appearance changed for the worse. "He'd been nice before he started smoking crack, but now he developed a mean edge and got nasty with me. It didn't take much for him to fly into a rage. Whenever guys were around, he would turn on me and treat me bad."

In April 2006, Sowell received an income tax refund of about $3,600, which he spent, in part, on household appliances and electronic gear including DVD players and video game equipment. The remainder of the money, says Frazier, was spent on crack-fueled parties.

"When he got his refund check, he put me out on the street," she says. "When I tried to come back to the house, I saw that he had girls as young as fifteen and sixteen there. They were all partying, getting high. Anthony told one of the girls to tell me to go away. I still had all my clothes there, but I just left."

Frazier eventually was allowed to return to Sowell's house, which had become noticeably messier and disorganized. Sowell—always neat and well-groomed—had become unkempt as well, taking on a gaunt appearance.

"He looked crazy," Frazier says.

Sam Tayeh knew Sowell and Frazier well. Frazier often bought Chore Boy, a copper cleaning pad used as a filter in crack pipes, at Tayeh's store.

"Lori presented herself well," Tayeh says. "She never cursed. She was well-spoken."

But Tayeh says that Frazier eventually "got on his nerves" because she hung around the front of his store. According to Tayeh, Frazier was a "strawberry," a woman who trades sex for drugs. "Blow jobs, whatever you want, as long as you had crack for her," he says.

He recalls a day after he hadn't seen Frazier for a while. She entered his store and he noticed bruises around her neck. "I asked her about the marks and she said, 'I'm not with that crazy motherfucker anymore. He tried to kill me.'"

Assuming she was referring to Sowell, Tayeh told her to report him to the police. "I can't," Frazier said. "I have warrants on me."

. . .

Despite Sowell's ongoing crack addiction, he was a punctual, productive worker at Custom Rubber, with the company president once describing him as a "very good employee." But in early 2007, Sowell noticed that he was becoming tired at work.

And then, on a Saturday morning in February 2007, he was walking to Tressa's house when he saw an elderly woman struggling to clear snow from her driveway. When he scolded her, she told him that her mailman said she needed to clear the snow from the bottom half of the driveway or he wouldn't deliver her mail.

Sowell shoveled her driveway and then continued on to his sister's. As he walked, he felt tired and achy, but passed it off as flu symptoms. When he arrived at Tressa's house, he collapsed. He was transported to a hospital and soon after underwent heart surgery. Doctors cleared his clogged arteries and implanted a pacemaker.

After a three-month recovery, Sowell was told he'd need daily rehab. Instead, he went back to work at Custom Rubber. Within his first week back, he passed out on the job. Unable to perform the physical requirements of the job, he was terminated in mid-2007.

As a registered sex offender with a drug habit and a serious health condition, Sowell knew he had slim chances of landing another job. So he joined the growing ranks of inner-city scrappers—men and women who scavenge aluminum siding, copper wiring, and plumbing from foreclosed and abandoned homes.

"Scrapping was the only work he could find," says Tressa. "I think he did it for Lori. He was doing everything he could to support himself and Lori. I know he wasn't happy that he didn't have the money he needed. Lori didn't even have enough money to buy a pack of cigarettes. Even her own family wouldn't help her out, but Anthony was willing to go into houses and steal copper pipes to buy her crack. It was illegal, but I guess it's better than holding up banks."

Tressa is candid about her dislike of Frazier, calling her a bad influence and a user. "When Tony met her, he was adapting to life outside prison. He drank, but he didn't seem to have a crack problem until he got involved with her. He was so protective of her that he would ride buses with her to make sure that she didn't go to crack houses."

Tressa says she noticed immediately when her brother began using crack, saying the drug tics were unmistakable. "His face got droopy. He would stay up all night. I asked him if he was doing drugs with her, but he denied it. I blame Lori for introducing Tony to crack. But I blame myself for not doing more to nip it in the bud."

Sowell was now without a steady income and faced with supporting his own crack habit along with Frazier's. He complained to family members that he was overwhelmed with stress and anxiety.

In the spring and summer of 2007, just about the time when women living near Sowell began disappearing, Frazier says she noticed fresh wounds on his body. When she asked him about the gashes on his forehead and leg—and the deep scratch marks on his neck, he'd tell her that someone on the street had tried to mug him. "But I kicked ass. You don't have to worry about me, baby," he told her.

Frazier was now only intermittently living at Sowell's house. On one of her occasional visits, which would end in mid-2008, she noticed blood spots on a floor and holes in a bedroom wall. Sowell's explanation: Someone had tried to rob him, but he fought him off.

Frazier says she noticed other strange occurrences: A window was broken out of a second-floor door. The door to the third-floor sitting room, which had never been locked, was now locked. Once, she found Sowell digging a hole in the backyard. When Frazier asked what he was doing, he initially said he was planting a garden for her. Later, he said he was burying waste from a toilet.

Then there was the terrible smell in the house.

Frazier said she had noticed it as early as 2005. At that time, Sowell blamed it on his stepmother's cooking. In 2008, however, he claimed the stench was coming from next door at Ray's Sausage Co.

By mid-2008, it's likely that there was at least one body in Sowell's third-floor sitting room and another buried in his backyard. Despite neighbors' complaints that the area around Sowell's house—and Sowell himself—reeked of "dead bodies," Frazier says she wasn't aware of a bad odor and denies seeing human remains or suspicious activities in the house.

Twyla Austin, the mother of Sowell's child, says Frazier's story doesn't sell. "Two of my daughters told me that Anthony stunk horribly," she says. "So how can Lori live in a house with him and not get that smell on her clothes? A female is going to try and figure out where that horrible smell is coming from. Why would she believe that the smell was Segerna's cooking at first, and then it was the sausage factory?"

Austin also says that she saw disturbing changes in Sowell. "He seemed depressed," she recalls. "I had heard stories that Lori Frazier was beating him."

Frazier denies any mistreatment of Sowell, saying that his mother is to blame for Sowell's issues and problems.

"Claudia Garrison was a cruel woman," Frazier says. "Anthony used to cry to me all the time about his mother. She called him dumb and useless. She once hit Anthony in the head with a hammer and left a scar. She gave him dolls to play with when he was a kid. She wouldn't let him play with other children. He was very resentful."

Recalling a time when she and Sowell visited Tressa's house, where Claudia was living, Frazier says, "Claudia was hungry, but Anthony wouldn't feed her. He said, 'Fuck you, bitch. Feed yourself.' I was shocked and I asked him why he was talking to his mother like that. He said, 'I hate her.'"

Noting that Sowell's behavior had become increasingly erratic, Frazier said she resolved to leave him. "I wanted to get sober and change my life," she says. "I couldn't do it around him. He was still getting high, flying into rages, and screaming at me. He once threatened to throw me out of a window. I knew I needed to get away from him if I was going to get my life together."

Sowell's sexual requests had also become bizarre, says Frazier. "We had normal intimacy, but then he started asking me if we could bring another girl into our relationship. He would bring a young girl to the house and ask me to have sex with her while he watched. He would also ask if he could use objects on me. One time, he wanted to put a curling iron up me."

Frazier says that Sowell also pressured her to anally penetrate him with dildos. She says she complied once, but didn't find it appealing. "After I did that to him, I became pretty certain that he'd had homosexual experiences in the Marines and while he was in prison. I think that he was actually okay with being in prison. His interests were cooking and sex—and I think that's pretty much what prison was about for him."

When Frazier finally cut her ties with Sowell and moved away, she recalls that he took it well. "We still talked on the phone and he would visit me at my job," she says. Sowell's friends and family, however, say he wasn't so nonchalant about the relationship ending. He told Tressa that Frazier had used him and abandoned him. And Tanja Doss recalls that Sowell was angry and depressed by the breakup—although she also said that he seemed blindly optimistic that he would someday reconcile with Frazier.

September 2009, shortly after his birthday, would be the last time Sowell spoke with Frazier. He visited her at her workplace—a mall food court in downtown Cleveland—to ask why she had neglected to call him to wish him happy birthday.

"He just bitched at me and then left," Frazier says. "I didn't see him again after that."

Sowell would later say that he cried for three days after Frazier left him. "I still love her," he admitted to Tressa. "She was a crackhead, but I loved her and I helped her."

Sowell felt strongly that he was betrayed by Frazier, says Roosevelt Lloyd. "She meant a lot to him," he says. "He once told me that she was the love of his life and the only woman he could trust."

Lloyd recalls a story that Sowell was fond of repeating: "Lori invited him to visit her uncle's house. But she didn't tell him beforehand that her uncle was Frank Jackson, the mayor of Cleveland. Jackson's security guards stopped Anthony at the front door, but they eventually let him in. Anthony was shocked when he walked in the backyard and saw Jackson sitting by his swimming pool. They talked and the mayor supposedly told Anthony that he was going to hook him up with a job. After that, Anthony used to brag all the time that he was dating the mayor's niece."

Lloyd disagrees with Tressa's contention that Frazier corrupted Sowell and sparked his drug addiction. "He was selling crack in East Cleveland before he went to prison," he says. "He was probably smoking it back then also."

Lloyd also says that Frazier wasn't equipped to help Sowell with his complex issues. "It's a very good thing that he went to prison in the first place because it stopped the pattern of violence he was developing. A lot of women's lives were saved when he got locked away for fifteen years."

However, he says that when Sowell was "fresh out of the joint—clean, sober, and healthy—Frazier should have tried to help him stay on the high road. Because once he got involved with crack, it was a done deal for him. On top of his mental illness, now he's got the paranoia and the unrealistic world that drugs create."

Lloyd says that Frazier's decision to move out of Sowell's house could have been triggered by something she saw. "At some point, she may have seen a body or witnessed something bad happen," he speculates. "She knew it was time to move on. Eventually, she would have become a victim, too."

CHAPTER 17

First Blood: Crystal Dozier

Spring 2007

The year was only half over, but 2007 was already a disaster for Anthony Sowell. He'd plunged into crack addiction, suffered a heart attack, and lost his job. And to compound his personal chaos, his relationship with his girlfriend, Lori Frazier, was ending.

Just about every semblance of stability and connection in his life was gone. Following the breakup with Frazier, Sowell told his friend Tanja Doss that he felt betrayed and that he would "get revenge." Although she asked him what he meant, he didn't explain the ominous remark.

In mid-2007, Sowell could often be seen hanging around the parking area of Amira Imperial Beverage. Women who stopped at the store to buy bread, milk, cigarettes, and lottery tickets were likely to be invited to Sowell's house to party. The ladies quickly spread the word that Tony was a friendly guy who was generous with his alcohol and crack.

Several women who partied with Sowell say he initially presented himself as a "helper" who wanted to protect them from the dangers they faced on the streets.

The women were indeed safe with Sowell, if his 2005 psychological evaluation was to be believed. The report, which was standard procedure for sex offenders just out of prison, was used to determine whether Sowell should be classified as a sexual predator and subject to intensive law enforcement supervision.

The evaluator noted that Sowell was generally polite and cooperative during the interview while exhibiting organized and logical thoughts. Sowell stated that he "got along well" with both of his parents and that he was not exposed to violence in his home, school, or community.

According to the report, Sowell had never participated in treatment for sexual offenders and he claimed to have no "deviant sexual preferences and there is no documentation of such." This, despite Sowell having served fifteen years for binding, gagging, choking, and repeatedly raping Melvette Sockwell. And just months after the Sockwell assault, Sowell attacked another woman in an eerily similar fashion.

Sowell told his evaluator that prior to his incarceration, he went to strip clubs only infrequently (despite reports that he was a regular visitor to Okinawa's red-light district while stationed there).

Sowell also said that his current level of sexual desire was "low" and that he had never used a telephone or computer for sex. However, one month before his evaluation, Sowell had set up a profile on a sex fetish Web site.

In his profile, Sowell stated: "If your [sic] submissive and like to please, then this master wants to talk to you. So get you're [sic] ass on over here NOW!"

The evaluator concluded that—based on statistical data—Sowell only had a six percent chance of committing another sex crime. Sowell was pronounced "unlikely to reoffend."

As such, he was classified as a sexually oriented offender, the least restrictive of the three categories in effect in Ohio at the time. He would be required to report his address to the Cuyahoga County Sheriff's Office only once a year for ten years.

However, because he was deemed "unlikely to reoffend," his neighbors weren't notified when he moved to 12205 Imperial Avenue in July 2005.

Sowell was the ultimate wolf in sheep's clothing, says Roosevelt Lloyd. "The last place he should have been was in that neighborhood with those vulnerable women."

In the years that he spent as Sowell's prison bunkmate, Lloyd learned that Sowell possessed a finely tuned observation mode. "When he was in his neighborhood, he was like a leopard in the way he would stealthily watch women," Lloyd says. "He would scope out the area and then lure women into his spiderweb. I think he really enjoyed the feeling of stalking prey. When a woman stepped into his house, he was already in attack mode. It was a dominant, deviant behavior."

During his fifteen years in prison, Sowell hadn't received any sex offender treatment. "He didn't get the tools to cope with his lifelong anger and resentment towards women," says Lloyd. "This was a sick individual who was just tossed back out in the world with all of his demons intact."

Lloyd, who underwent several years of therapy while in prison, says that whatever shred of decency and reason that Sowell possessed had been lost in the haze of his crack addiction.

"He was in personal denial about his problems. His arrogant attitude was 'Why should I explain myself to anyone?' He never learned how to understand or accept himself. Sowell felt shame and guilt for dishonoring the Marines by going to prison. He was now angry at himself for being a crackhead. So he was going to deal with that anger by hurting another crackhead, especially if she dared to reject him—which is his main anger trigger. That goes back to his bad childhood relationship with his mother."

When Lori Frazier rejected Sowell, "she lit a fire that boiled within him," theorizes Lloyd. "When he mixed that anger with the projected animosity that he felt towards crackheads, he was going to take it to the extreme—to the death scene."

Sowell, the great pretender, possessed an ever-changing array of personas. Depending on the situation and his objective, he could be helpful, charming, aloof, or assertive. Not that Sowell needed a winning personality to lure women to his house.

"He had the rock, so that made him a big man on his street," says Robert Harris, a former drug user who now counsels addicts in Cleveland. "He was all-powerful to women with a crack addiction. They didn't need any more encouragement than that. Their own crack addiction was pimping them. Within minutes of walking into Sowell's house, I'm sure they had their clothes off. That kind of power was probably very intoxicating to Sowell. An even more powerful high for Sowell was the knowledge that he could do whatever he wanted to the women—no matter what he wanted."

For Sowell, a "master seeking submissive women," the under-policed and drug-infested Imperial Avenue and its surrounding Mount Pleasant neighborhood must have seemed an urban paradise.

Its residents were beset by poverty and drug abuse. Crime was out of control. Gangs had overtaken Mount Pleasant's streets and uninhabited houses. It wasn't unusual for thugs to move into one of the many vacant bank-owned houses, remove plywood covering the windows and doors, mow the lawn, and move in a little furniture.

They then would order pizza with the intent of stealing the delivery vehicle and robbing the driver. In other iterations of their scheme, drug dealers would run electricity from a neighboring house and set up a crack house or after-hours club.

Crack cocaine was cheap, potent, and instantly addictive. Crack—the "poor man's drug"—was seemingly the only growth industry in the economic wastelands of postindustrial cities such as Cleveland. The social cost of crack addiction was high: junkies spent their nights and days in the streets trolling for drugs, dumping their children on overburdened grandparents or leaving them to raise themselves.

On Imperial Avenue and nearby streets, there seemed to be an abundance of women so desperately addicted that they were willing to trade their bodies for a few rocks of crack, with little regard for personal shame or risk. It's often said that crack is the only substance that can nullify the mothering instinct.

"Where I grew up, I remember seeing my best friend's mom out on the street turning tricks for drug money," says Treasa Mays, a thirtysomething Mount Pleasant resident who works as a nurse's aide. "Your own uncle would crawl through your bedroom window to steal your television set. Mothers would even sell their kids for a fix."

Karen Clemons, a recovering substance abuser who lives on Cleveland's East Side, says that only a crack addict can truly understand the power of the drug's stranglehold.

"It's unbelievably scary what women are willing to do for a fix," she says. "I saw two otherwise normal ladies have sex with a dog just to get a small rock. It saddens me that those two women were so desperate that they did their thing with a Doberman pinscher. The drug dealers made them do it just for the hell of it. The dope boys just sat there and laughed."

Clemons, 47, says the purported stench in Sowell's house would not be a deterrent to a woman seeking crack.

"The smell doesn't matter if he is offering a free high," Clemons says. "Those women who went to his house knew they weren't going into that deep dark hole with a total stranger for nothing. They knew there was only one scenario: they were going to smoke and have sex. But they were manipulating him like he was manipulating them. They knew the smoking was over when the sex was over, so they teased it out. Even when his sex deviant thing was kicking in, the women still wanted to continue smoking. They were greedy for the dope."

Physically, Sowell was strong, says Lloyd, adding, "With his Marine training, most women wouldn't have a chance against him, especially if they were intoxicated. He was a stalker; he was patient. He would wait until the drugs and alcohol had relaxed them. Then a sharp blow to the head would make them woozy and off balance. The strangling then became easy."

For Crystal Dozier, Sowell represented companionship, shelter, and the opportunity to satisfy her drug cravings. But for Crystal and many other women who were locked in the iron grip of addiction, the parties at Sowell's house would go horribly wrong.

In May 2007, Crystal, a thirty-eight-year-old mother of seven, became the first of Sowell's eleven victims. Described by family members as sweet and loving, Crystal grew up in Cleveland's notorious King Kennedy Estates, a sprawling public housing complex infested with drug gangs.

Crystal's mother, Florence Bray, moved her family to King Kennedy after losing her house to foreclosure when her husband died of kidney failure at age thirty-four. Bray, who had her first baby when she was sixteen, worked hard to provide a stable and safe home for her four children.

Bray coached her children to make good choices and avoid negative influences. But the street life was a strong lure for Crystal. At thirteen, she became pregnant by a seventeen-year-old. A year later, she became pregnant again, this time by twenty-one-year-old Anthony Troupe, who had a lengthy arrest record, including charges of grand theft, drug abuse, and breaking and entering. The couple would have five more children by the time Crystal was twenty-one.

Relying on family members to babysit her children, Crystal intermittently attended school. She enjoyed singing and joined her high school's choir. However, when Crystal was seventeen, Bray says she learned that Troupe had been removing her from school and taking her to various public housing projects, where he prostituted her to get drugs.

Crystal and her family lived with Bray until the night she discovered Troupe beating her daughter. "He had punched Crystal so hard that the sound of the impact woke me up," Bray said. "I found them in the kitchen. He had her backed into a corner and was choking her. She was terrified. When he saw me, he said, 'Get back in your room, bitch.'"

Gripping a carving knife, Bray told him, "Let her go or I'll show you how much of a bitch I can be."

The next day, Troupe moved his family into their own apartment. Away from Bray's watchfulness, Troupe resumed beating Crystal while routinely spending their government assistance checks on drugs.

"There were some months when he took all the welfare money and left the kids with nothing more to eat than a bag of potatoes," Bray says.

When Crystal was twenty-one, her older brother visited Cleveland while on leave from the Marine Corps. Told about Troupe's abuse of Crystal, he confronted him, beating him severely. The intervention stopped Troupe from mistreating Crystal. However, he then directed his violence toward his children.

In 1987, a county social worker reported that Crystal's oldest child, Anthony, then five years old, had "marks on his body from beatings." In her report, the social worker described Crystal and Troupe as "unfit parents."

Crystal's family eventually convinced her to leave Troupe. She moved with her children to a federally subsidized apartment. At age twenty-two and on her own for the first time in her life, Crystal was overwhelmed by the responsibilities of raising seven children. Her drug use escalated and she began disappearing for days at a time on crack binges. Concerned family members contacted county social workers, who decided to remove Crystal's children and place them with relatives and foster parents.

"I realized my mother had a very difficult childhood, so I never had hard feelings towards her," says Antonia Dozier, Crystal's oldest daughter. "I always knew that she had a problem with drugs. But there were also times when she really tried to play her role as a parent. There was a Christmas when she took me to get my nails done. I always had the sense that she was trying to get her life in order. She would get clean for a while, but then relapse."

Determined to avoid the pitfalls that ensnared Crystal, Antonia began counseling sessions at an early age.

"I knew that I wanted my life to be different from my mother's," she says. "I saw what she went through and I didn't want that for me. I didn't see any point in struggling like she did."

Enslaved by her addiction, Crystal's life became a relentless hunt for crack. She supported her habit by scavenging scrap metal, panhandling, and various criminal endeavors. She was convicted of a half-dozen drug-related offenses, including trafficking, forging prescriptions, and identity theft.

She'd first met Sowell in 2006, when she was living with a friend on Imperial Avenue. Sowell had invited her to his house on several occasions—with the understanding that he was offering crack in exchange for sex.

Crystal didn't think of herself as a prostitute. As a point of pride, she considered herself "partying" when she bartered her body for drugs. Her appetite for crack was all-consuming. In that state, trading sex was the most expedient way to feed her addiction.

One spring morning in 2007, Crystal told a friend that she needed a "serious" fix. She slipped on a pair of jeans and a blue tank top and then called Sowell.

Only Crystal and her killer know what transpired in Sowell's house that day. But presumably they drank and smoked crack for several hours. Something triggered a mood swing in Sowell. He might have screamed at Crystal and probably struck her. He tied her ankles together with coaxial cable. Her hands were bound above her head, also with cable.

Wrapping a length of knotted cloth around her neck, he held the ends tight until she died. Sowell then pulled a large trash bag over Crystal's upper body—leaving the knotted cloth in place—and pulled another bag over her nude lower body. He wrapped silver duct tape around the bags.

At some point, probably late at night, he dug a pit in his backyard next to the rusted chain-link fence that separated his property from Ray's Sausage Co. He then dragged Crystal's body into the shallow pit. After scraping loose dirt over her, he covered the grave with scrap plywood to keep scavenging animals from digging up her decomposing remains.

Anthony Dozier, who had just returned from Marine Corps service, filed a missing persons report on his mother on June 11, 2007. Over the next two years, he and his siblings searched Cleveland neighborhoods for Crystal.

After receiving a tip that she visited a house on Imperial Avenue, family members posted flyers seeking information about her whereabouts. But the flyers on Imperial Avenue mysteriously disappeared, says Anthony.

That summer, Cleveland's health department began to receive complaints about a foul smell near Sowell's house. After a quick check, inspectors told neighbors the source of the odor was probably a dead animal. Later, they would decide that the smell was coming from Ray's Sausage Co.

It would be a year before Sowell struck again. Tishana Culver, who lived on Imperial Avenue, a half block away from Sowell, was last seen by her family in June 2008. The mother of four worked as a beautician. Her remains would be found on the third floor of Sowell's house, stuffed in a crawl space.

The next woman to go missing, Leshanda Long, had a history of disappearing for days and weeks at a time. So when she vanished in August 2008, her father, Jim Allen, just assumed she was on one of her adventures.

Leshanda was born in 1984 to a drug-addicted mother and Allen, who self-admittedly was not a consistent presence in her life. Allen attempted to raise their six children alone, but struggled to balance his job as a county corrections officer with his domestic duties. Because Leshanda's mother, Jewell, was only an occasional visitor to the family, Allen enlisted his elderly grandmother to help with parenting duties.

The family unit was broken apart, however, after Allen's grandmother complained to the county that the children—ages one to thirteen—were often left home alone. In her complaint, the grandmother said the children's parents didn't contribute to their care. She begged the county to take custody of the children.

Social workers made plans to put the children into foster care, but one of Jewell's sisters stepped in and took custody. Initially, Leshanda thrived. Her aunt remembered her as "strong-willed and sassy." She earned good grades in school and had perfect attendance.

But at age fourteen, Leshanda became defiant, often running away from home to search for her mother Jewell in the streets and crack houses she was known to inhabit. That year, Leshanda became pregnant. She would have two more children over the next three years.

Leshanda's juvenile troubles landed her in detention facilities several times. During one of her stays, she wrote to a juvenile court judge, asking for "another chance at life." In the letter, she stated: "Sir, I am sixteen and I have two daughters. I can honestly say that at the rate I am going, I'll be dead before I am eighteen. Lord knows I've made a concious [sic] decision to begin a new and productive life for my kids and myself . . . I am ready to step up to the plate and admit my problems, get help, and take care of my responsibilities."

However, by the time she reached her late teens, county social workers had deemed her an unfit parent. After her children were taken from her and placed with relatives, Leshanda got in trouble with police for kidnapping her children away from their new homes. She was also arrested for a number of drug-related offenses.

Despite the dissonance of his daughter's life, Allen says she never forgot to call him on his birthday. But in August 2008, he didn't get his call.

Police discovered her skull in a bucket in Anthony Sowell's basement. The rest of her remains weren't found.

Two months later, in October 2008, forty-five-year-old Michelle Mason was reported missing by her mother, Adlean Atterberry. Police and family members searched continually for her, focusing on the Mount Pleasant area where she was last seen.

"Michelle was living near Imperial Avenue, so we posted flyers at the beverage store on East 123rd and Imperial, right by Sowell's house," Atterberry says. "But the flyers kept disappearing. We now think that Sowell was removing them."

Michelle's body would be found a year later in Sowell's backyard, buried under eight inches of dirt, with a brown sock tied around her neck. Her partially mummified body was wrapped in a black comforter, orange carpet padding, and black plastic bags. She was wearing a sweater and a brown shirt.

"She was a sweet person, with a big, beautiful smile," says Atterberry, 67. "She did what she did. She was no angel, but she never hurt anyone. She didn't deserve to be killed and left out there in the backyard like that."

Discussing the challenges her daughter faced in her life, Atterberry says, "When she was sixteen, she decided to leave home for New York. I didn't hear from her again until five years later when she came home. We found out that she had contracted HIV from drug use. She was also bipolar, but as long as she was on her medication, she was fine."

While in New York, Michelle had given birth to two sons. Now in Cleveland, she was gripped by a crack addiction and unable to care for her boys. Atterberry raised one; the other was placed with Michelle's sister, Mary.

Between 1993 and 2001, Michelle was arrested nearly a dozen times, mostly for drug abuse and prostitution. Although Atterberry says her daughter quit drugs ten years ago, Michelle still found it difficult to stay away from the streets. In the mid-2000s, she was involved in a dispute that ended with her getting shot in the face. She was left for dead, but managed to make it to a neighborhood store to request help. During surgery, one of her eyes was removed and replaced with a glass eye.

A friend of Michelle's says she was shot by a man who was angry that she'd had unprotected sex with him without disclosing her HIV infection. Mary Stewart, who met Michelle while both were in the Ohio Reformatory for Women, says, "Michelle was a really nice lady who had a difficult time kicking drugs and the drug lifestyle." Michelle was a "little thing with a big heart," says Stewart. "Unfortunately, in prison and county jail, other inmates avoided her because they were afraid of catching AIDS."

A "big-hearted woman" is also Atterberry's remembrance of her daughter. "That's probably how she got caught up with Sowell," she says. "She was just like me—she'd give you the coat off her back. He probably said hello to her on the street and charmed her. In her mind, she was just making friends with him."

On November 10, 2008, Tonia Carmichael told an acquaintance that she was going out to "have some fun." After her family hadn't seen her for three weeks, they attempted to file a missing persons report, telling police that Carmichael had a drug problem. Carmichael's mother says police dismissed her concerns, saying Tonia would "come home when the drugs ran out."

An FBI cadaver dog led investigators to her body a year later. Wrapped in clear plastic, she was buried in Sowell's backyard. She had been strangled with the charger cord from an electrical device. Her hands were tied behind her back.

A month later, Gladys Wade told police that she was attacked by Sowell after encountering him on Imperial Avenue. In her complaint, Wade says Sowell punched her in the face and dragged her into his house, where he attempted to kill her. She escaped, flagging down a police car. When police went to Sowell's house to investigate, they reported that they saw blood droplets on the walls and steps—exactly where Wade told them to look.

Although Sowell was now classified as a Tier Three sex offender, the most dangerous classification, Cleveland prosecutors decided not to pursue charges against him, saying there was "insufficient evidence."

Sowell's killing spree was escalating. After Wade's complaint was dropped in late 2008, six more women would lose their lives in his house of horrors.

Kim Yvette Smith would be his first victim in 2009. Known to her friends as Candy, she was last seen January 17.

Born in 1965 to Donald Smith, who worked at a bottling factory, and Virginia Herndon, a bookkeeper, she was a talented singer who developed a substance-abuse problem in her last year of high school.

Kim had blossomed into a very attractive lady at an early age, says her father. "Her body grew before her mind. Older gentlemen gravitated towards her and turned her onto marijuana, cocaine, and crack."

Kim's parents split up when she was young, but her father maintained contact with her. She graduated from high school and later attended community college, where she studied art and dance.

But her substance abuse led her into criminal trouble, including convictions for theft and several drug offenses. Her father says that in jail, she didn't get any drug treatment.

"The judges and prosecutors didn't send her away to rehabilitate—just incarcerate," he says. "In fact, she ended up getting her hands on drugs in most of the institutions she was sent to."

Saying his daughter was "his heart," Smith took her to various rehab programs. "They'd help her get off one drug, but she'd end up with a different addiction. That was her demise—trading one addiction for another."

Kim's last prison stretch was in 2007. When she was released, she learned that her father had a surgery that had left him wheelchair-bound.

Her aunt, Christine Shobey, says Kim wanted to get her life together and take care of her father. "She wanted to be there for her father the way he had been there for her."

On the afternoon of January 17, Shobey took Kim shopping to buy her new clothes. "She wanted a new outfit because she was singing in the church choir," she says. "We bought her a coat, designer jeans, and a designer sweater."

Shobey recalls that "Kim seemed stressed out and worried about her father's condition because he had undergone so many surgeries. After we got home, Kim took her father Chinese food. Then she said she was going to her boyfriend's house. But she must have gone someplace else because we found out later that he hadn't been at home."

That "someplace else" was Anthony Sowell's house. Kim Yvette Smith was found buried in his backyard. She was wrapped in plastic; her ankles and wrists were bound with cloth.

While she was missing, her father and aunt posted flyers and a $500 reward. "On the street, that amount of money is like a million dollars," says Smith. "We got lots of phone calls, but no credible leads. It was tough. Every hour seemed like it lasted a day. The days turned into weeks." When Kim went missing, her family had been planning her upcoming birthday. "No matter how hard you try to help someone, it's tough on the streets," says Shobey. "Once in a while, Kim asked me to pray for her. And I always did."

Amelda "Amy" Hunter's family didn't file a missing persons report when she vanished in the summer of 2009. Her son, Bobby Dancy Jr., had become accustomed to her disappearing for days at a time on drug binges.

He enjoyed the times he spent with his mother, cooking and singing, but he also knew that it wasn't unusual for her to choose the streets over her family.

Amy, 47, and her seven siblings grew up on Chicago's South Side. At age fourteen, she became pregnant by a teacher who gave her alcohol at a party. Amy's daughter, Kelly, was born deaf and with cerebral palsy.

After moving to Cleveland with her family, Amy met Bobby Dancy Sr., who was seventeen years her senior. They became a couple and had two sons together, Bobby Jr. and Andrew. They also had a daughter, Victoria, who died of a birth defect. Dancy and Amy never married but lived together for many years.

Dancy says his relationship with Amy was complicated by her drug use. "I didn't like her disappearing from the house and leaving the kids alone," he says. "We'd have fights over it. Afterwards, she'd promise not to get high anymore. But then I'd wake up in the morning and she'd be gone again. It was frustrating for me and tough on the kids."

Amy's family says she may have sought comfort in drugs, desperate for respite from the grief she felt about her daughter Kelly, who has multiple disabilities and lives in a group home.

Others say she was introduced to crack by her own siblings, several of whom struggled with addiction. She attempted rehab several times, but was unable to extricate herself from her drug problem. Amy was arrested several times on drug and theft charges. She served a sentence at the Ohio Reformatory for Women.

Dancy, who once owned a record store on the East Side of Cleveland, says Amy worked as a hairstylist and a home health care aide. Her family says she enjoyed watching TV quiz shows and reading classic novels, including the works of Charles Dickens.

According to her sister, Lynnette Hunter Taylor, when Amy Hunter left her house to get high, she often ended up at Anthony Sowell's. "She used to live up the street from him," says Taylor, adding that her sister considered Sowell her "buddy," and a "nice man" who would do whatever he could to help her.

Amy's decomposed body was found in a shallow grave in Sowell's backyard. Nude from the waist down, her remains were infested with insects. The shoulder strap of a suitcase or briefcase was wrapped around her neck. Her killer had wrapped her in heavy-duty garbage bags.

"My sister had a good heart," says her brother, John Hunter. "I remember that she took care of me when I was younger and I had a football injury. I had been tackled and my teeth were knocked out. She cared for me like a nurse."

Hunter says that his sister's kindness sometimes got her in trouble. "There were times when people took advantage of her good nature," he says. "She'll never have to worry about that anymore. My sister is in a better place now."

CHAPTER 18

Great White Shark

2009

In the four years since he'd been released from prison, seven women had lost their lives to Sowell's murder-lust.

His compulsion to kill was intensifying. By the time of his arrest in October 2009, four more women will be dead. Three other women will manage to survive his demonic rage.

Despite a 2005 evaluation that rated Sowell as a "low risk" to reoffend, each of his post-prison attacks seemed to mirror his 1989 sex assault of Melvette Sockwell.

Sowell's criminal repetition is not surprising, says Dr. James Knoll IV, a forensic psychiatrist with extensive experience studying serial sexual offenders.

Knoll, the director of forensic psychiatry at SUNY Upstate Medical University in Syracuse, New York, has worked extensively with Roy Hazelwood, a former FBI agent who pioneered the profiling of sex predators.

"Serial offenders such as Sowell are typically driven by deviant sex fantasies they need to repeat during their crimes," Knoll says. "It's clear that Sowell was repeating his pattern. He was aroused by the fear and suffering experienced by his victims."

The term "psychopath" has generally fallen out of favor with the psychiatric profession, replaced by the catchall Antisocial Personality Disorder.

However, if psychopathy can be considered as a highly distilled, predatory form of Antisocial Personality Disorder, then Sowell possessed many of the hallmarks of a psychopath: the ability to instantly turn on superficial charm and glibness, lack of remorse for others' suffering, enjoyment in conning and manipulating people, and the inability to accept responsibility for criminal behavior.

135

"Psychopaths are the great white sharks of society. They are the predators among us," says Knoll, explaining that psychopaths approach emotions very differently than the majority of the population. "They have a cold, cruel approach to people's suffering. They are more callous and unempathetic."

Sowell's behavior, says Knoll, is indicative of a sexual sadist. "They find it highly erotic, stimulating, and satisfying to have women completely under their control—to torture them, strangle them to unconsciousness, then let them wake up and do it all over. We've even seen cases where a [sadist] performed CPR on his unconscious victims to revive them so that he could strangle them again. It wouldn't be surprising if Sowell had even indulged his sexually sadistic behavior on dead victims. Necrophilia is not unusual for deviants like him."

According to Knoll, the heart of sadism isn't the pain and torture that's inflicted—it's the feeling of being a victim's personal god. Sadists find that feeling to be "endlessly gratifying and exciting," he says. "They love the control. With Sowell, we see that he binds and restrains his victims, which gives him total and complete control. The element of choking and strangulation is another one of his behaviors that is designed to inflict considerable fear, terror, and domination over his victims."

The origins of Sowell's sexual sadism?

Knoll says he strongly suspects that the brutality exhibited by Sowell's mother, Claudia Garrison, left psychological wounds and contributed to his apparent hatred of womankind.

"Sowell witnessed child abuse and neglect; he didn't have a loving, caring mother," he says, explaining that his tremendous anger at women was reported by his surviving victims.

Knoll says that two women who lived through Sowell's attacks said he screamed at them for being "no-good crackheads" who were doing drugs instead of staying home to take care of their kids. The survivors also say he told them, "It's crazy women like you who make me want to hurt women."

Sowell was projecting all of his hatred onto his victims, says Knoll. "He had intense anger towards women. We are lucky that we have the reports of survivors. They give us evidence of what he did and what he said during the crimes. The survivors' stories of what happened are very similar to what happened to the deceased victims. With serial offenders, there is very often a repetitive component to their behavior. They have a fantasy in their heads and they are trying to enact it. But the reality is never as good as the fantasy, so they have to repeat it and repeat it until they get it right."

Knoll says he's intrigued by the stories of women who managed to talk their way out of an attack by Sowell.

"When I hear about those situations, I wonder what they did to turn him off or cause him to step out of his normal program of getting more and more aroused and ultimately killing them. What did they do to take him out of his fantasy?"

On April 21, 2009, Tanja Doss became one of the few who somehow survived Sowell's murderous rage. Tanja, 43, had known Sowell since the summer of 2005 when he first left prison. She lived near him on Imperial Avenue and they'd partied and hung out at his house many times.

Their friendship stalled in 2006 when Tanja, who had just returned from an extended stay in New York, stopped by his house to say hello. Sowell told her not to come around anymore because he was involved with Lori Frazier. When his relationship with Frazier floundered a year later, Tanja and Sowell resumed their friendship.

On an April night in 2009, Tanja had planned to hook up with her childhood friend Nancy Cobbs.

"Nancy's birthday was in five days, so I was going to take her to Anthony's to party," Tanja recalls. "I wanted her to meet him. But I never heard back from her, so I went to his house myself."

Sowell had invited his neighbors to join them for a front-yard barbeque, but he found no takers. While the locals were appreciative of his hospitality, they did not want to be around that horrible smell that enveloped his premises.

Tanja and Sowell spent the evening playing cards and drinking beer on his front porch. "We always had a good time," she says. "He was a very good host, always offering me a beer when I came over."

She says Sowell's hospitality extended to not only his friends and neighbors but also to the local street people. "He was kind to hookers," she says. "He'd let them stop by and use his shower, and then leave. It wasn't about sex."

Tanja recalls that Sowell was a good cook, preparing shrimp, chicken, and steak for her. He'd told her that he'd trained as a "chef," although she'd later learn that he acquired his cooking skills in a prison kitchen.

When she asked him why he'd been incarcerated, Sowell fabricated a story about "taking a fall" for his brother on a drug case. Tanja herself had multiple convictions for drug possession and theft. She once served a stint in the Ohio Reformatory for Women for drug trafficking.

In the spring of 2009, Tanja spent a lot of time with Sowell. "Mostly inside his house, because I was dating a couple guys and it would have gotten complicated if we were going out in public," she says.

Occasionally, Tanja would take Sowell to her family's house for dinner. Her mother, Edna, who worked as a Cleveland Police dispatcher, told Tanja that the reserved and polite Sowell seemed like a gentleman.

Tanja, a mother of three children and grandmother of two, says that Sowell was a romantic, adding that he was sometimes aggressive during sex but never rough. "When we were dating, he was a one-woman man," she says. "He was a pleaser. He liked performing oral sex. In that department, I'd say he was a professional."

On the night of the attack, Sowell and Tanja sat on the porch until darkness fell. They went into the house, where they drank a few more beers, smoked crack, and watched a Cleveland Cavaliers game on TV. At some point, Sowell showed Tanja a purple jogging suit that he planned on giving to Frazier for her birthday, which was two months away. Tanja was confused because she knew that Sowell then had an acrimonious relationship with Frazier, but she offered assurances that Frazier would like the jogging suit.

Suddenly, Sowell's mood turned dark. Whether he was experiencing a hard crash from his crack high or he was angered by sour memories of his breakup with Frazier, he became aggressive.

"I was sitting on the edge of his bed watching the Cavs game," Tanja says. "We were talking about walking up to the corner store for beer. Then he just flipped out."

Without any warning or provocation, he lunges at the 98-pound Tanja, knocks her to the floor, and begins to choke her. As she struggles to breathe, Sowell tells her to knock three times on the floor if she wants to live. She knocks. Sowell releases the pressure on her neck, but his anger hasn't dissipated.

"You don't know the real me," he screams. "I could kill you like any crackhead bitch on the street and no one would give a fuck about you, bitch."

Tanja tries to placate him, saying, "Tony, why are you doing this?" He then slaps her across the face several times and tells her to remove her clothes.

"I could feel my face swelling," she says. "I was shocked. He had never spoken to me like that. I realized that he was not playing, so I told myself just to be cool and go along with whatever he told me."

Sowell allows Tanja to walk to the bathroom. She checks her face in the mirror, then starts putting her clothes back on. "He then yelled at me to get back to the bedroom," she says.

When she returns, he is laying on his bed naked. "Bitch, I should have killed you before," he tells her.

He orders her onto the bed. Tanja says she laid down on the edge of the mattress, curled up in a fetal position. Sowell lay on the bed beside her. "He didn't rape me; he didn't even touch me," she says. "Every so often, I glanced at him. He was just staring into space. I laid there thinking about my children and praying."

Tanja cries herself to sleep, unsure if she'd survive the night.

The next morning, Sowell acted as if nothing strange had happened the previous night. Experts in criminal behavior say Sowell's instantaneous rage of the previous night and his preternatural calm the next day are typical of the "heating-up, cooling-down" cycle often seen in sexually sadistic killers.

"It was so strange. He casually asked if I wanted a beer," Tanja recalls. "He was right back to being a good host. I didn't want a beer, but I figured I should accept his offer. Then I picked up my phone and acted as if I was talking to my daughter. I told him that I had to help her with something. He said, 'okay,' and then I just left."

Tanja says Sowell called her the next day "just to see if everything was okay."

During this point in time, there would have been at least seven dead bodies scattered throughout Sowell's house and in his backyard, but Tanja says she didn't see any evidence of crime or notice any unusual odors. She offers the explanation that her "sense of smell is impaired."

Days later, Tanja would realize that Sowell had once before said to her, cryptically, "You don't know the real me." She'd thought he was hinting that he was selling drugs. "I never thought he was talking about his violent side," she says. Tanja considers herself "lucky" to have escaped Sowell. However, Melvette Sockwell offers her opinion that Tanja's ability to stay calm and not scream was probably the key to her survival. "In my case, when Sowell was threatening to kill me, I sensed that if I screamed, he would have killed me—either because he was afraid of being caught or because my fear was arousing him," she says. "I didn't panic, so I threw him off his whole game. By not showing panic, I didn't fuel his fire and give him what he craved. I defused him."

Tanja did not report Sowell's attack to the police, mainly because she had been a rape victim the previous year and was unhappy that her attacker had received a light sentence. "The guy who raped me only got six months at the county workhouse. And he had in-and-out privileges," she says. "It wasn't even worth the hassle of filing the police report."

But her decision not to report the April 21 incident would haunt her. Unbeknownst to Tanja, her best friend since grade school, Nancy Cobbs, was also acquainted with Sowell and had made plans to party with him.

"I told Nancy that Sowell had choked the fuck out of me," Tanja says. "But she never admitted that she knew him, even after I told her that he was crazy."

Three days after Tanja was attacked, Nancy Cobbs would become one of Sowell's victims.

A forty-three-year-old mother of three, Nancy doted on her five grandchildren, taking them on bike rides and walks in the park. Her relatives say Nancy lived her life in extremes. She was a tireless worker, whether as a housekeeper or restaurant employee. She was also a loyal and devoted friend. But she also fed a demanding crack addiction. Her daughter, Audrey Williams, says Nancy turned to drugs shortly after a messy breakup with her boyfriend. "She was depressed and started hanging out in the streets," Williams says.

Nancy served two stretches in the Ohio Reformatory for Women after convictions for drug offenses. Her children were placed with relatives while she was in prison. Williams, admitting that she felt neglected, would have her first child at the age of thirteen.

Family members last saw Nancy on April 24, 2009. She had spent the day with Williams and her children. When Nancy left that evening, she said she was going to a neighborhood store and would return later. When Williams hadn't heard from her mother by the next day, she became concerned and filed a missing persons report with the security force that oversaw her mother's apartment complex. Over the next two weeks, family and friends posted flyers on utility poles and storefronts in their neighborhood.

Williams says she also contacted the Cleveland Police Department's Fourth District, but she says they "didn't offer much help."

Nancy's remains were found in a third-floor crawl space in Sowell's house. She had been strangled with a ligature that seemed to be hastily constructed of rope and cloth. Her body was wrapped in black plastic bags and a cloth comforter; her wrists were bound with rope. Autopsy photos show she was wearing a bracelet, a watch, and a cross necklace.

Saying she is wracked by survivor's guilt, Tanja Doss regrets not reporting her attack. "If I had gone to the police and they would have listened, maybe my friend would still be here," she says.

Sowell would kill three more women after Nancy Cobbs. Telacia Fortson would be his next victim.

A mother of three, Telacia disappeared in June 2009. She had promised her daughters that she would braid their hair. When she didn't show up, family members became concerned.

She was found seminude on Sowell's third floor. She had been strangled; a cloth ligature was still wrapped around her neck when she was discovered. Police found a knife next to her body.

Janice Webb, 48, was last seen in early June of 2009. She was reported missing to Cleveland Police a month later.

Following her disappearance, police canvassed local hospitals and homeless shelters, but they were unable to find any information on her whereabouts. Janice, a mother of one son, typically notified family members if she was going to be away for an extended period. Audrey Webb says she spoke to her sister nearly every day. "The last time I talked to her, she said she was coming over," says Audrey. "It wasn't like her to not show up."

Concerned about Janice, family members printed up missing persons flyers and posted them in various Cleveland neighborhoods. They were mystified that the flyers posted near Imperial Avenue kept disappearing.

A drug user since her late teens, Janice tried to maintain her family connections. Despite the shame she felt about her addiction, she could be counted on to attend holiday gatherings and family birthday parties.

"She knew that we loved her, no matter what," says Janice's oldest sister, Joanne Moore. "She was a loving person."

Janice's drug use spanned two decades, resulting in a dozen felony convictions for offenses ranging from drug abuse and trafficking to carrying a concealed weapon and receiving stolen property. She served several prison sentences.

Janice made several attempts to get clean, but drugs and the drug culture were endemic in her Buckeye Road neighborhood. "Buckeye just wasn't good for her," says a family member.

Janice's remains, which weighed ninety-six pounds, were found under a mound of dirt in Sowell's basement. Her autopsy was performed by Dr. Elizabeth Balraj, who determined that she had been strangled with a green belt. Her hands were bound with shoelaces and situated in front of her body. She had been gagged with a shirt that encircled her head and face. The shirt was knotted in the back of her head.

Balraj, who served as the Cuyahoga County coroner before Frank Miller, was called out of retirement to assist with the autopsies of Sowell's victims. She performed the postmortem examinations of five of the eleven victims.

Based on her thirty-eight years as a forensic pathologist, Balraj says it's not unusual in forensic work to see strangulation and sexual assault "go together hand in hand."

Strangulation is a rather common form of homicide against women, says Balraj. "My own thinking about this case is that the killer acted out of anger. The strangulation probably gave a completion to the sexual gratification he was seeking. He strangled them so that he could enjoy seeing them lose consciousness."

Balraj adds that it's "somewhat unimaginable that all of these women were being killed and nobody even knew about it. A dead body is the worst smell and a very distinctive smell. That's the thing that distinguishes this crime from others. How could someone have bodies laying around his house and live with the horrible smell? It's way beyond bad housekeeping. It just shows so much callousness towards life."

Balraj says she has always tried to separate her emotions from her work. "But this case made me sad," she says. "When I think of what happened to the eleven victims, I wonder why a person would have done this."

When the Cleveland Police SWAT team entered Sowell's house on October 29, 2009, to arrest him, they discovered Diane Turner's remains laying on the floor of the third-floor sitting room. A black plastic bag was wrapped around her ankles and calves. According to her autopsy report, Diane's cause of death was homicidal violence, but the type was undetermined.

Diane's body, which was next to Telacia Fortson's, was extremely decomposed, and it would take five weeks to determine her identity.

Diane, 38, had disappeared September 2009. Her last known address was about a mile from Sowell's house. She occasionally worked as a dishwasher at a Jamaican restaurant in Cleveland. When her coworkers didn't hear from her for a week or so, they alerted her family.

She would be the last of the eleven victims identified. The county coroner had difficulty identifying Diane because her family members were slow to come forward to provide DNA. Eventually, James Martin, the father of one of Diane's daughters, brought the girl to the coroner's office to submit a sample.

Diane's life, which Martin describes as "rough," was checkered with numerous arrests for drug use and prostitution. She reportedly suffered from epileptic seizures and became alienated from most of her family members because of her substance abuse.

County social workers removed all five of Diane's children from her custody. Relatives say that each time one of Diane's children was taken, she would sink lower and lower into a funk of shame and guilt. In a report recommending removal of Diane's month-old baby, a county employee stated: "Mother frequently passes out and often requires excessive amounts of sleep due to her epilepsy, which prevents mother from providing proper care for the child."

"It was hard on her to lose her kids," says her brother, John Turner Jr. Her typical reaction, he added, was to seek escape through drugs.

In an ironic footnote, James Martin had been hired in October 2009 to help renovate a house next to Sowell's. Martin recalls smelling a "terrible odor that was hard to describe." Like so many others, he assumed the smell was coming from Ray's Sausage Co.

When the identities of Sowell's eleven victims were released, Martin realized that he knew nine of the women "from around the neighborhood walking the streets."

Sowell's penultimate act of brutality—and the incident that would lead to his arrest—would be his September 22, 2009, assault of Latundra Billups.

On the second floor of Sowell's house, Latundra endured a horrific attack in which she was raped and strangled with an extension cord until she lost consciousness. Sowell, thinking she had died, was surprised when she awoke.

Although he had tried to kill her only hours earlier, he graciously took her to his basement, where he offered her a sweater to replace the one he had torn. He allowed her to leave his house, making her promise that she wouldn't tell police about the incident. Latundra went to a hospital emergency room and reported the attack.

While police were completing their investigation of Latundra's complaint, Sowell met Shawn Morris at a bus stop on October 19.

In the early morning, he invited her to his house to smoke crack. She left his house several hours later, but she returned to retrieve her ID card.

Sowell, without any provocation, wrapped his arms around Shawn's neck in a choke hold and dragged her upstairs to his second-floor bedroom. He then forced her to strip naked and raped her. When he began to close windows throughout the second floor, Shawn realized that he intended to kill her.

While he was out of the bedroom, she jumped from a window, landing hard on a section of pavement between Sowell's house and Ray's Sausage Co.

Sowell ran downstairs and attempted to drag the naked, bloodied Shawn back into his house. Passersby saw the bizarre scene and called an ambulance. Shawn would spend eight days in the hospital with several broken bones and a fractured skull.

Fearing that her husband would be angry with her for partying with Sowell, Shawn lied to police, telling them that her injuries were caused by an accidental fall from Sowell's second-floor balcony.

On October 29, 2009, Cleveland Police secured warrants to search Sowell's house for evidence related to his attack on Latundra. A SWAT team entered Sowell's house and discovered the decomposed bodies of Diane Turner and Telacia Fortson in the third-floor sitting room.

While coroner's deputies were removing human remains from Sowell's house, he was several blocks away, playing video games with his nephew.

Anthony Sowell, one of the most prolific serial killers in Ohio history. Sowell was convicted of the aggravated murder of 11 women and the attempted murder of three others. Courtesy Cuyahoga County Prosecutor

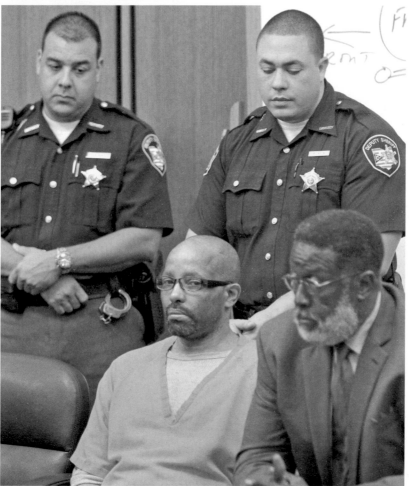

Sowell's trial, the most expensive publicly funded criminal defense in Cuyahoga County's history, cost taxpayers nearly $700,000. Sowell is on Ohio's death row awaiting execution by lethal injection. At right is defense attorney Rufus Sims. Courtesy *Cleveland Plain Dealer*

Crystal Dozier, 38, was the first of Sowell's eleven murder victims to go missing. Last seen in May 2007, investigators dug up her body in Sowell's backyard. Courtesy Cuyahoga County Prosecutor

Tishana Culver, 31, was a nursing assistant and beautician. Missing since June 2008, her body was found in a trash bag on Sowell's third floor. Courtesy Cuyahoga County Prosecutor

Leshanda Long, 25, was the youngest of the eleven murder victims. Her skull was found in a bucket in Sowell's basement. Her body has not been recovered. Courtesy Cuyahoga County Prosecutor

Michelle Mason, 45, was last seen in October 2008. The mother of two was HIV positive and suffered from bipolar disorder. Courtesy Cuyahoga County Prosecutor

Tonia Carmichael was 52 when she vanished in November 2008. Her family said police turned them away when they tried to file a missing persons report. Courtesy Cuyahoga County Prosecutor

Kim Yvette Smith, 44, was last seen in January 2009. Nicknamed "Candy," she was an artist and an accomplished singer. Courtesy Cuyahoga County Prosecutor

Nancy Cobbs, a grandmother of five who lived near Sowell, disappeared in April 2009. Cobbs, 43, was a construction worker. Courtesy Cuyahoga County Prosecutor

Amelda "Amy" Hunter, 47, a beautician and mother of three, went missing in April 2009. Courtesy Cuyahoga County Prosecutor

Left: Janice Webb, 48, vanished in June 2009. She left behind one son. Her body was found under a mound of dirt in Sowell's basement. Courtesy Cuyahoga County Prosecutor. Center: Telacia Fortson, 31, missing since June 2009, was found in the third-floor sitting room. Courtesy Cuyahoga County Prosecutor. Right: Diane Turner, a 38-year-old mother of five, went missing in September 2009. Her body was found next to Fortson's on the third floor. Courtesy Cuyahoga County Prosecutor

Impromptu memorial erected across the street from Sowell's house in November 2009. Author photo

Guided by cadaver dogs, police and cornoer's investigators discovered five bodies buried in Sowell's backyard. Most of Sowell's victims were bound with wire or rope and wrapped in plastic bags. Courtesy Cuyahoga County Coroner

Former Cuyahoga County Coroner Dr. Frank Miller (center) oversees the removal of a body from Sowell's backyard. Using small shovels and rakes, workers unearthed the bodies, then slid tarps under them to lift them from their shallow graves. Courtesy Cuyahoga County Coroner

Police SWAT officers discovered the first two bodies in a third-floor sitting room of Sowell's house. Towels had been shoved against the bottom of the door to keep the smell of decomposing flesh from escaping the room. Cadaver dogs led police to two other bodies that had been hidden inside the visible crawl space. Both had ligatures around their necks. Courtesy Cuyahoga County Coroner

Under the basement stairs, buried beneath a layer of dirt, police found a partially decomposed body that had been wrapped in duct tape. Courtesy Cuyahoga County Coroner

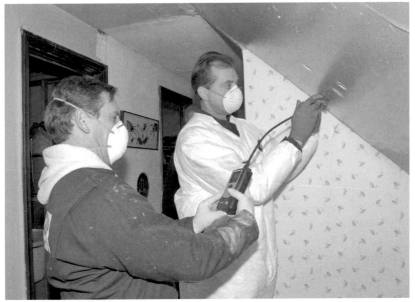

Searching for additional bodies, FBI agents and police use thermal-imaging equipment and X-ray scanners to examine walls in Sowell's house. Courtesy Cuyahoga County Coroner

A skull, wrapped in black plastic, was found in this bucket in Sowell's basement. The bite marks on the bucket are from rodents. Courtesy Cuyahoga County Coroner

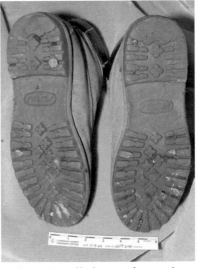

Anthony Sowell's boots. The treads were caked with maggots and blowflies, presumably from the third-floor sitting room, which was covered with flesh-eating insects. Courtesy Cuyahoga County Coroner

Sam Tayeh, former owner of the Amira Imperial Beverage store. Across the street is Ray's Sausage Co., which is next door to Sowell's house. Ray's was blamed for the stench that plagued the neighborhood for three years. Author photo

Sgt. Dan Galmarini, Cleveland Police SWAT supervisor. His team discovered the first two bodies in Sowell's house. Author photo

Anthony Sowell's third-floor bedroom, which was only a couple of feet from the sitting room that contained four corpses. Courtesy Cuyahoga County Coroner

The first floor of Sowell's house, which was occupied by Sowell's stepmother until she moved into a nursing home. Courtesy Cuyahoga County Coroner

Coroner's technicians, FBI agents, and homicide detectives removing bodies from Sowell's yard. The extreme decomposition of the bodies made identification difficult. Courtesy Cuyahoga County Coroner

An array of jewelry found at Sowell's house. The jewelry was helpful in enabling family members to identify their loved ones. Courtesy Cuyahoga County Coroner

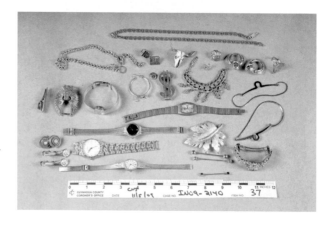

The house on Page Avenue in East Cleveland where Sowell spent much of his childhood. He returned here after his Marine Corps service. In 1989, he kidnapped and assaulted Melvette Sockwell in the house. She escaped by crawling out the third-floor window and screaming for help. Author photo

Melvette Sockwell was brutally assaulted by Sowell at 21, but she survived. Sowell pleaded guilty to the assault and served 15 years in prison. Author photo

Roosevelt Lloyd, Sowell's best friend in prison. Lloyd told trial jurors that the Sowell he knew in prison was a "nice, loving, caring person." Author photo

Left: Lori Frazier, Sowell's girlfriend from 2005 to 2007. Sowell has implied that his breakup with Frazier, who is a former drug user and the niece of Cleveland Mayor Frank Jackson, might have triggered his killing spree. Courtesy Cuyahoga County Sheriff. Right: Shawn Morris, 51, who was attacked by Sowell in October 2009. Afraid of retribution from Sowell, she didn't file police charges. Author photo

The paved area between Sowell's house (left) and Ray's Sausage Co. Shawn Morris escaped from Sowell by jumping from a second-story window. She suffered a fractured skull and other injuries. Author photo

Gladys Wade (Thomas) and her husband, Leander Thomas. She was attacked by Sowell in December 2008. Sowell was arrested, but he was not charged by Cleveland prosecutors. Six women died in Sowell's house after Wade's attack. Author photo

Latundra "Lala" Billups and her mother, Harriet Billups. Billups survived a near-fatal assault by Sowell in September 2009. Her complaint to police led to Sowell's arrest and the discovery of his House of Horrors. Author photo

Vanessa Gay (left) with her attorney Melanie GiaMaria. Gay was attacked by Sowell in his house in September 2008. He allowed her to leave the next day, on the condition that she not report the attack to police. Author photo

Tanja Doss, a friend of Sowell, was inexplicably punched and choked while partying with him. She credits her ability to remain calm for her survival. Author photo

Sowell's half sister, Tressa Garrison. In support of her brother, she says his health issues and turbulent childhood are to blame for his crimes. Author photo

One of several heated exchanges during Sowell's trial. From left, prosecutor Lauren Bell, Judge Dick Ambrose, prosecutor Pinkey Carr, defense attorneys Rufus Sims and John Parker, and lead prosecutor Rick Bombik. Courtesy *Cleveland Plain Dealer*

Forensic psychiatrist Dr. James Knoll IV. Testifying for the prosecution, Knoll said Sowell's behavior was indicative of a sexual sadist. According to Knoll, Sowell enjoyed gaining complete control over his victims. Courtesy James Knoll

The discovery of bodies on October 29, 2009, triggered media attention on Imperial Avenue that persisted for several years. Author photo

Calling Sowell's house a "menace to public health," the City of Cleveland demolished it December 6, 2011. The debris was shredded to prevent anyone from pilfering memorabilia. Author photo

CHAPTER 19

Discovery

October 29, 2009

On a quiet Thursday evening at Tressa Garrison's house, her son Ja'Ovvoni, 22, is sitting on the living room couch next to her brother Anthony. Uncle and nephew are playing Halo, a combat-oriented video game that rewards players for performing "assassinations."

The popular game, a favorite of fifty-year-old Anthony, enables combatants to maim and kill in a multitude of creative ways, including snapping opponents' necks or stabbing them in the skull, spine, or eyeballs.

Ja'Ovvoni hears a knock at the door and recognizes Anthony's neighbor, Debbie Madison, on the porch. "She seemed very upset," he recalls. "At first, she led us to believe that my uncle was dead. Then she spotted him in the living room and she was surprised. She got real nervous and started going on about dead bodies in his house. Anthony had to keep telling her to calm down."

Madison told Sowell that he should ride back to his house with her so that he could "clear up any confusion" with the police. After he agreed, Madison suggested that Ja'Ovvoni ride along.

"I was all set to go, but Anthony told me to stay home," says Ja'Ovvoni. "They pulled away and then they came right back. Anthony came into the house and picked up some of his things. He was quiet, but he looked worried. He told us, 'I'll just go back to Imperial by myself.' My brothers and sisters were here. We said good-bye to him and he walked off. Debbie Madison was crying when she drove away."

The Garrisons hadn't been watching television that evening, so they weren't aware of the police activity at Anthony's house. Shortly after Madison left Tressa's, however, she was back with two detectives.

"The officers didn't give us much information, except to say they had found bodies in Anthony's house," Ja'Ovvoni says. "They asked if we had seen the bodies. Then a couple more policemen came and they all searched our house. Social workers came to the house later to make sure all of the kids were safe. It was a long night."

In the morning, Ja'Ovvoni and his family were up early to watch the news coverage. "We kept seeing bodies being taken out of Anthony's house," he says. "Then the TV trucks started coming to our house. Reporters kept knocking on our door. My mom couldn't take it. Some of the younger kids were getting upset."

While Ja'Ovvoni says he was surprised by news of the discovery at Anthony's house, he says he wasn't shocked. "I couldn't imagine him doing the things he was accused of, but for me to say he's not capable of those things would be foolish. Some people get pushed to do unbelievable things. For all the stuff he had been through with Lori Frazier, maybe it was in his cards."

Ja'Ovvoni says his uncle had been spending a lot of time at Tressa's house in recent months. He played video games with the kids and made breakfast for his mother Claudia, who lived with the Garrisons.

"I could tell something was wrong," Ja'Ovvoni says. "He was real good about hiding his emotions because of all he'd been through in the military and prison. He didn't talk about his personal life that much—I think he just didn't want to burden us. But I knew that he was very upset about how Lori played him."

On October 29, Sowell's twisted world imploded. Cleveland police had gone to his house expecting to arrest him for the September 22 attack of Latundra Billups. He wasn't there. Instead, they encountered a ghoulish scene in his third-floor sitting room—two mummified bodies lying in open view.

Sowell, riding with Debbie Madison toward his house, saw the commotion of emergency vehicles and TV vans and told her to return to Tressa's house.

"That girl made me do it," he told Madison.

Over the next two days, as Sowell eluded a police manhunt, investigators found more bodies dumped in his house and buried in shallow graves in his backyard.

The discovery of Sowell's heinous graveyard sparked horror and anger among community residents—and morbid fascination throughout the world.

Sowell was arrested while walking near his neighborhood on October 31 and hurried to Cleveland Police headquarters. He spent the next eight hours being questioned by detectives from the Sex Crimes and Homicide units.

His bail set at six million dollars, Sowell is held in solitary confinement, charged with the murders of eleven women. Initial reports determined that Sowell had strangled his victims. The coroner found a variety of ligatures, mainly household items such as belts, rope, extension cords, and purse straps, still wrapped around the victims' necks.

The victims all shared a common profile: they were poor, black, and living on society's fringes. All had a history of drug abuse. Most had fractured family relationships and weren't likely to be missed. Investigators theorized that Sowell lured the women to his house with promises of alcohol and crack cocaine.

News accounts of "the Cleveland Strangler" triggered comparisons between Sowell's alleged crimes and the city's "Torso Murders" that occurred from 1935 to 1938.

In the unsolved Torso Murders, thirteen men and women were decapitated, dismembered, and scattered around an area called Kingsbury Run, a jagged ravine that cuts through the East Side of Cleveland near the Mount Pleasant neighborhood. Heading the police investigation was legendary crime fighter Eliot Ness, who, at age thirty-four, was Cleveland's safety director at the time.

During the 1930s, Kingsbury Run was a forbidding shantytown populated by hobos, prostitutes, nameless drifters, and other unfortunates who had been forced there by the blight of the Great Depression.

In Sowell's crimes and the Torso Murders, the big similarity is that the victims were people who were down on their luck, vulnerable, and desperate to some degree, says Rebecca McFarland, a Cleveland-area librarian and Eliot Ness/Torso Murders historian.

"While Sowell used drugs to lure his victims, the Torso Killer's bait was more likely food," she says. "It depends what you're hungry for: If you're a hobo living in a box during the Depression, then food would be very attractive to you. For the women who ended up at Sowell's place, their need for crack made them susceptible to him."

In the era of the Torso Murders, forensic scientists struggled to identify the mutilated victims, but nearly all remain anonymous.

Sowell's eleven victims—so decomposed that their race and gender were barely discernible—would also present challenges to the pathologists tasked with identifying them. However, Cuyahoga County Coroner Frank Miller and his staff had the advantage of DNA technology.

Calling the Imperial Avenue murders a "forensic pathology case to the extreme," Miller said that police and researchers from the coroner's office constructed a missing persons database and then publicly requested DNA samples from relatives of women who had disappeared in Cleveland over the past two years or so.

On November 12, the first victim's funeral is held. Family and friends remembered Telacia Fortson as a kind, thoughtful mother who had a warm smile and a wonderful sense of humor. The final funeral—for Diane Turner—would be held on December 11.

As Sowell's victims were memorialized at tearful funeral services, a Cuyahoga County grand jury was considering evidence against him. On December 1, Sowell was indicted on eighty-five counts, including eleven counts of aggravated murder with a "mass murder specification," meaning multiple people were killed in a similar fashion.

Along with multiple charges of kidnapping, abuse of a corpse, and tampering with evidence, Sowell was charged with rape, attempted rape, felonious assault, and attempted murder in connection with his attacks on three survivors—Gladys Wade, Latundra Billups, and Shawn Morris.

Sowell's attorneys entered a plea of not guilty by reason of insanity, but soon they would change it to simply "not guilty."

Cuyahoga County Prosecutor Bill Mason, at a press conference to announce Sowell's indictment, says it's possible there are other victims. Noting that Sowell threatened his victims and warned them not to contact police, Mason asked anyone who has been attacked by Sowell to come forward if they have not already done so.

But there are many in Cleveland's black community who view Mason's request as disingenuous and little more than political posturing.

"Where were the police when I needed help finding my daughter?" asks Barbara Carmichael. According to Carmichael, police officers in Cleveland and neighboring Warrensville Heights refused to let her file a missing persons report when her daughter, Tonia Carmichael, who had a history of drug abuse, disappeared in November 2008.

"I pleaded with them to investigate, but they told me to go home," Carmichael recalls. "They said 'once he stops feeding her crack, she'll come home.'"

Calling police "negligent," Carmichael says, "Not to sound racist, but if it was a white woman who was missing, I'm sure they would have taken more interest in looking for her."

Black community activists point out that the Sowell indictment incorporates charges related to his attack on Gladys Wade. However, on December 8, 2008, when Wade first reported that Sowell tried to kill her, the city prosecutor declined to pursue her case, saying that a detective in the Sex Crimes Unit did not believe that Wade was credible. Six more women would die in Sowell's house after Wade's attack.

Police tended to dismiss the concerns of the families of missing women, says Art McKoy, founder of Black on Black Crime Inc., a grassroots group that combats inner-city crime and racial inequality in Cleveland.

"The cops shrugged off a serial killer," McKoy says. "They told the family members to look into their missing persons cases for themselves. But when numerous families, in frustration, started coming to our organization, it quickly became clear that there was a pattern to the disappearances."

McKoy says that the socioeconomic status and race of Sowell's victims was the determining factor in whether police diligently investigated their disappearances. "Let's keep it real. The police and the city didn't care," he says.

According to McKoy, the ongoing stench near Sowell's house and a naked woman falling out of his second-floor window should have been a red flag that something was seriously amiss on Imperial Avenue. "Anthony Sowell was not a perfect criminal. He did stuff that Stevie Wonder could detect. But nobody cared enough to investigate this man."

Sowell's house and yard, which is overgrown by weeds, is now encircled by a tall chain-link fence. The fencing was requested by prosecutors to protect the crime scene. But it doesn't deter gawkers from slowly driving past the house at all hours.

"These people driving in from the suburbs in their Range Rovers don't care about the dead women," says Cleveland council member Zack Reed. "If they want to see dead people, they should go to a cemetery."

The people of Imperial Avenue need a sense of closure, says Reed. "The victims were women who did not deserve their fate. Their families knew them as daughters, mothers, nieces, sisters, and aunts. What was done to them is terrible. The healing is going to take a long time."

Reed says it's unimaginable that police and sheriff's deputies couldn't pinpoint the smell on Imperial Avenue. "Back in spring 2007, I got a call about a foul smell," he says. "We called the city health department, but nothing happened. A month later, another call was made to the city about the smell. In October 2007, yet another call was made. The people on the street had to live under that stench, falsely believing that it was coming from Ray's Sausage. The health department, state inspector, public utility people, sheriff's department, and police were all informed. At least some of those people must have recognized the smell of dead bodies. But they all missed it."

Reed points out that sheriff's deputies might have missed an opportunity to end Sowell's carnage when they conducted a routine sex offender compliance visit.

"But they couldn't enter the house because they needed probable cause," he says. "In 2005, a change in the law reclassified Sowell as a Tier Three offender, the most dangerous classification. Yet he wasn't required to notify anyone in the neighborhood because he didn't move to a new residence. The laws and the system that are currently in place protected Sowell."

Despite his frustration and anger that Sowell's murder spree continued unabated for more than two years, Reed doesn't blame any one person or entity.

"We need to evaluate the entire system," he says. "There are 100,000 sex offenders in the U.S. whose whereabouts are unknown. The system is overworked. Clearly we need to do some things differently or this will happen again somewhere. There are more Anthony Sowells out there. It's not just Sowell who is on trial—it's the system."

Reed, who is black, also takes exception to the unspoken selection process that occurs when women go missing. Society turns its back on poor black women, he says, "But if these were blonde-haired, blue-eyed women, this wouldn't have happened. The common denominator of Sowell's victims is that they had crack use in their background. We need a national conversation about addiction because it happens everywhere—not just on Imperial Avenue. If you go to Wyoming, you'll find addicted people. It's not necessarily a criminal mind that does drugs."

If we are to prevent another Imperial Avenue tragedy, says Reed, it's going to take the combined effort of police, the community, and family members.

"From the family's standpoint, their loved ones were addicts who often left for several days at a time. So maybe it's understandable that a lot of the families didn't file missing person reports right away. Because when the addicts are gone, the families can bring out their fine silverware and not have to hide the jewelry box. They can relax until they come back home. But how can a mother of seven disappear and no one ever report her missing?"

The "no snitch crap" in neighborhoods has to stop, says Reed. "Anthony Sowell wasn't crazy. He knew the streets went dark at night. On one street corner, he buys crack; on another corner, he buys alcohol. So now he's the man—all for five to ten dollars. It shouldn't have been an eye-opener that women weren't coming back from his house. Someone out there must have seen red flags and decided not to tell anyone. It seems that people in the inner city just aren't comfortable talking to the police."

. . .

With the public thirsty for a glimpse into the maniacal mind of Sowell, the nation's leading forensic psychiatrists and criminal profilers weigh in with their suppositions.

Their consensus? Sowell is a serial sexual killer in the vein of Ted Bundy, whose brutal crimes were rooted in a need to exert control and power over his victims. Like Bundy, who confessed to thirty murders in the 1970s, Sowell is a coldhearted predator driven by an intense hatred of women.

Dr. Phillip Resnick, director of forensic psychiatry at the Case Western Reserve University School of Medicine, says individuals like Sowell use sex as a weapon to dominate and cause humiliation.

"He gets sexual excitement from taking sex rather than having a willing partner," says Resnick, who has consulted on many high-profile criminal cases, including Jeffrey Dahmer, Scott Peterson, Andrea Yates, and Ted Kaczynski, better known as The Unabomber.

While Resnick says it's somewhat unusual for sexual sadists to keep bodies stashed around their house, he theorizes that Sowell may have kept his victims' decaying bodies out of laziness or convenience, rather than "trophy-collecting" or for cannibalism, as did Dahmer.

"After a while, if you live in a house with a bad smell, you get used to it," he explains.

Sowell's house and yard, in fact, served as ideal burial sites. Many of the houses on his street were vacant while Ray's Sausage Co., which was directly to his east, was a serendipitous scapegoat for the smell of decomposing flesh.

When asked if psychiatric treatment could have helped to stanch Sowell's murderous urges, Resnick says it's doubtful. "Overall, psychotherapy is not all that helpful with sexual sadism crimes. It's not likely that somebody like Sowell would be open with his therapist. If he told the truth about what he was doing, he would be caught."

Resnick and other serial crime experts say it wouldn't be surprising if there are more than eleven victims. Dr. Cathleen Cerny, a Cleveland forensic psychiatrist who has worked with Resnick, says the odds are good that Sowell has been involved in other cases.

Cerny says many experts believe that serial killers just keep going until something external, such as their death or arrest, stops them. "It didn't seem like he was that concerned about being caught," she says. "He didn't make much of an effort to hide what he was doing."

Retired FBI agent John E. Douglas, who is credited with creating the FBI's criminal-profiling program, told the *Plain Dealer* that law enforcement officials should investigate cold-case files from North Carolina, California, and anywhere else Sowell was stationed while he was in the Marines.

"I can guarantee you, every place [the killer] lived, you're going to find cases of women just like these being raped and killed just like this," said Douglas: "There is no way he only started killing a few years ago."

Although coroner Frank Miller holds a less certain view than Douglas, he says, "It's reasonable to expect that Sowell committed other rapes and murders while he was in California. Those military bases are huge, with thousands of acres to bury a body."

Miller says there may still be "secrets" in the Page Avenue house, where Sowell lived as a child and also after he returned from the Marines.

He adds that it's troubling from an investigative standpoint that the only body part of Leshanda Long's that was recovered was her skull.

"It begs the question of whether there are other burial grounds and other victims," Miller says. "Sowell had access to the industrial dumpster at Ray's Sausage and also at the corner beverage store. Ray's was getting a lot of attention from the city health department, so that may have prompted him to alter his plans of using their dumpster. We thoroughly searched Sowell's house, but we didn't find Leshanda's body. Where is it?"

Noting that Sowell seemed to have a pattern of escalating crime, evolving from rapes to murders, Miller echoes the sentiments of community activists and victims' families when he says, "Maybe if Sowell had been caught for rapes he committed years ago, there wouldn't be eleven Imperial Avenue victims."

"The key is that if we have a rape kit, it needs to be turned in [to a lab] and processed. The Cleveland police have a backlog of more than 3,000 rape kits that are unprocessed. How many of them might have Sowell's DNA?" Miller explains that rape kits are unprocessed for a variety of reasons. For example, he says, "They don't process the kits for rape victims who don't cooperate. They kind of just drop it. But if we went ahead and processed all of the kits, we could include the DNA in a database. The DNA could be a match for someone who is involved in an unrelated murder or robbery."

But at a cost of $500 to process each kit, he admits that his idea may not be practical. "We don't have an endless amount of money for an endless amount of forensic testing. The big question is 'how much do we want to spend per bad guy to catch more?'"

In a December 2009 press conference, County Prosecutor Mason announces that he's reopening dozens of older unsolved cases of murdered women who fit the profile of Sowell's victims: drug-addicted, transient, and not likely to be missed.

Mason says his team of cold-case investigators is analyzing at least seventy-five homicides from within a three-mile radius of Sowell's Imperial Avenue residence and also his former home at Page Avenue. He then once again asks any other victims of Sowell to contact police or his office.

In response to Mason's plea, a thirty-nine-year-old woman from suburban Cleveland Heights comes forward to report that on April 15, 2009, she was raped by a man whom she believes is Sowell. After the attack, the woman was treated at an emergency room, where DNA evidence was collected in a rape kit.

But Cleveland Heights police failed to submit the rape kit to a testing lab. If they had done so, it's possible that DNA matching could have led investigators to Sowell, whose DNA sample had been logged into a statewide database in 1997 while he was in prison. Tragically, a review of Sowell's murder timeline show that five of his eleven victims had gone missing after the April 2009 attack.

In the woman's police report, she describes an assailant whose appearance, behavior, and house are remarkably similar to Sowell's.

The woman told police she was waiting at a bus stop on the evening of April 15 when she was offered a ride by a friend in a car driven by a man named "Tony." Her friend got out of the car, leaving the woman alone with Tony, whom she described as a light-skinned black man about fifty years old, with a slight build, shadowy beard, and a short receding hairline.

The woman said that after she got in Tony's car, he began driving in the opposite direction of her house. When she complained, he slapped her and then drove in a circuitous manner, eventually ending up at a house fitting the description of 12205 Imperial Avenue.

Tony then put her in a "choke hold" and pulled her into the house, she reported. Later, she would tell police that the house smelled "stagnant, possibly of garbage or mold." She was taken "forcefully" to a third-floor bedroom, where, on the top of a dresser, she says she saw a crack pipe, lubricant, lottery tickets, and a fillet knife.

According to the police report, Tony told her that he was going to "train her like an animal" and that she needed to call him "master." He told her to remove her clothing and raped her orally, vaginally, and anally for forty-five minutes. At times, he yelled at her in a very "manic" manner, sometimes not completing ideas or sentences. He also repeatedly bragged about having been in the Marine Corps.

The woman said she was raped a series of four times between the night of April 15 and the morning of April 17. Each time, Tony performed cunnilingus to "wake her up."

At some point, he tied her to a bedroom chair with several neckties and went to a nearby store to buy Cobra beer, cheap wine, and cigarettes. Upon his return, he forced her to take a pill—which she believed was Ecstasy—and wash it down with a mixture of beer and wine. Tony then performed anal sex on her until she passed out from the pain.

She woke up to find him asleep with his arm draped over her. She said she pulled a framed glass picture off a wall and smashed it over his head, then tried to escape. In the ensuing struggle, he pulled her hair and she "bit him on his forearm and poked him with broken glass."

She then escaped, but in her haste, she became disoriented and failed to note the house's location. She called a friend who took her to the hospital. She was treated for numerous scratch marks on her neck and hands. She also had scalp wounds where hair had been ripped from her head. In addition, the attending nurse noted that the woman's voice was "raspy, due to strangulation."

The Cleveland Heights police officer who took the woman's report said he attempted to find her attacker's house but was unsuccessful. The DNA evidence from the rape kit, which should have been passed on to detectives from the Sex Crimes Unit, sat instead in a desk drawer unprocessed for two years. A Sex Crimes detective reported that he tried to contact the victim, but she didn't respond to repeated messages.

When Sowell was arrested on October 31, the victim recognized his face on TV and contacted the Cleveland Heights police, who relayed her information to Cleveland Police Sex Crimes detectives. They retrieved the rape kit from Cleveland Heights and had it tested. The DNA evidence was a match for Sowell.

In the days after the DNA snafu was discovered, the Cleveland Heights police chief at the time defended his department's evidence procedures, saying, bluntly, "We send all rape kits for testing."

But the Lake County Crime Lab, which handles testing for the police department, confirmed that Cleveland Heights police had never sent the rape kit for analysis. If it had been submitted, said the Lake County prosecutor, the test would have been completed in seven to ten days. He added that a match for Sowell's DNA would have likely been discovered in the state's database shortly afterwards.

The Cleveland Heights police chief also told the local media that his department had no records of any sexual assaults reported in April 2009. However, when reporters looked at the April 15 victim's case file, it was clearly labeled "rape/kidnapping."

Later, the chief conceded that his department—like nearly half of the police departments in the United States—does not have a computerized system to track the flow of evidence.

The evidence from the April 15 rape case is damning against Sowell. But county prosecutors decide not to seek an additional indictment after a judge ruled that Sowell's defense team would not have enough time to independently analyze the DNA results in time for the upcoming trial.

As Sowell awaits the start of his trial, which is scheduled for June 6, 2010, he sits in a six-by-eight jail cell, isolated from other prisoners and headline-seeking reporters.

Newspaper and TV stations gear up for Cleveland's most sensational murder trial since Dr. Sam Sheppard was tried in 1954 for killing his pregnant wife, Marilyn.

The Sheppard case, which was the inspiration for the TV series and movie *The Fugitive*, generated media coverage so extensive and lurid that the U.S. Supreme Court said a "carnival atmosphere" had permeated the trial.

The *Plain Dealer*'s heavy coverage of the Sowell case includes news articles and opinion pieces from more than a dozen staff writers. Breaking updates and videos are posted on the newspaper's affiliated Web site, Cleveland.com.

Despite the newspaper's large allocation of resources, *Plain Dealer* reporter Stan Donaldson has concerns that relatively few black reporters have been assigned to the Sowell case.

"There were a few of us reporters of color who believed that this story involved the black community—which was our community—and we should be working on it," says Donaldson. "Initially, when I tried to get involved in the story, I was told to just focus on my shift [the evening police beat]. But I could see that CNN, TruTV, and other news networks were getting better details about the case than we were. A large part of that is because many of our reporters were too comfortable staying in the newsroom."

Donaldson, anxious to get into the field to cover the human interest aspects of the Sowell story, pressed his case with the *Plain Dealer* editors.

"After a group of us black reporters talked to middle and upper management, we were able to work on the stories that we needed to do," Donaldson says. "Everyone else wanted to cover the crime part of the story; everyone wanted to find out about Sowell; but we wanted to find out about the eleven women who lost their lives."

In collaboration with black reporter Margaret Bernstein, Donaldson wrote in-depth pieces about each of the eleven victims. The stories detailed the women's struggles against drug addiction and the guilt and shame they felt for neglecting their children.

Donaldson also profiled some of the sons of the victims, reporting that the young men had vowed to stop the cycle of neglect by being good fathers to their own children.

Born in the rust belt city of Youngstown, Ohio, Donaldson saw first-hand the devastating impact of drug addiction. "Even as a five-year-old, I saw the poverty, depression, and abuse caused by crack," he says.

While covering the Sowell case, Donaldson says, "My heart went out to all the young children who were left behind when their mothers were taken. It took me back to when I was young, and how I wanted my dad to be there for me."

Donaldson's father, a casualty of the crack epidemic, was absent for much of his childhood. "I was blessed to have a good support system. My mother made sure we had a lot of love," he says. "But I yearned to have a relationship with my father."

Being in the field and writing about the families of Imperial Avenue victims helped inform Donaldson of what he calls the "new normal" of the black community. "I learned that the new normal is to have kids out of wedlock and not be educated. The new normal is to live a street life and be 'in the game' and never be 'out of the game.' There seems to be a lack of respect for the traditional family structure. It seems like now it's okay to be raised by grandma."

Ultimately, young women, in particular, need their fathers in a "great way," says Donaldson. "It's not enough for a man to make a bunch of babies and not be a manly presence. It's not about how many women you can conquer. The men need to be a part of their daughters' lives. Because women who have weak fathers who aren't there for them are going to make poor decisions in the men they choose."

Not only would the *Plain Dealer* provide extensive coverage of the Sowell story, but the newspaper would also find itself as a player in the story. The newspaper's unusual and inadvertent involvement would lead to the removal of two judges from Sowell's trial.

Cuyahoga County Common Pleas Judge Timothy McGinty was the first judge scheduled to preside over the Sowell case, receiving his assignment on December 8, 2009. But McGinty recused himself a week later, citing a potential conflict. Later reports said McGinty stepped down because he'd sent emails to the *Plain Dealer* expressing his views on the Sowell case.

McGinty also erred when he showed Sowell's court-ordered psychological evaluation to a *Plain Dealer* reporter. The evaluation, which was completed when Sowell left prison in 2005, was ordered to determine whether Sowell should be classified as a sexual predator. The report revealed personal details about Sowell and concluded that he was a "low risk" to reoffend.

Sowell's lawyers lambasted McGinty's actions, arguing that his release of the report—and its subsequent inclusion in a *Plain Dealer* article— would make it difficult to find an impartial jury for their client's trial.

The next judge assigned to the case, Shirley Strickland Saffold, was promptly removed by the Ohio Supreme Court after she was suspected of posting inflammatory online comments about Sowell and one of his attorneys, Rufus Sims.

The comments, which were posted under the name of "lawmiss" on the *Plain Dealer*'s Web site, Cleveland.com, disparaged the courtroom competency of Sims.

The *Plain Dealer* traced the postings to Saffold's court-issued computer. After filing a public records request, the *Plain Dealer* found that someone used the computer to access Cleveland.com at the exact times and dates of several comments posted under the lawmiss username, which was created through the judge's personal e-mail account.

Many of the numerous lawmiss comments revealed a familiarity with Saffold's court cases. One of the postings criticized Sims's defense work in a previous trial presided over by Saffold. "Rufus Sims did a disservice to his client," the post read. "If only he could shut his Amos and Andy style mouth. What makes him think that is [*sic*] he insults and acts like buffon [*sic*] that it will cause the judge to think and see it his way. There are so many lawyers that could've done a much better job. This was not a tough case, folks. She should've hired a lawyer with the experience to truly handle her needs. Amos and Andy, shuffling around did not do it."

Both Sims and Saffold are black.

When Sims learned of the link between Saffold and the lawmiss comments, he demanded that she remove herself from the Sowell case. "I am through with her, finished forever," he told the *Plain Dealer*. "She can never be involved in another case of mine."

When questioned about the online comments, Saffold said she had nothing to do with any postings by lawmiss. Later, the judge's twenty-three-year-old daughter would claim that she actually posted the comments under the lawmiss screen name.

The lawmiss imbroglio was not Saffold's first run-in with the newspaper. In the mid-1990s, Saffold was angry that *Plain Dealer* reporter Jim Ewinger reported that she told a woman charged with credit card fraud to find a better man.

"Men are easy," Saffold told the woman. "You can go sit at the bus stop, put on a short skirt, cross your legs and pick up twenty-five. Ten of them will give you their money. It's the truth. If you don't pick up the first ten, then all you got to do is open your legs a little bit and cross them at the bottom and then they'll stop."

After her removal from the Sowell case, Saffold sued the *Plain Dealer* for fifty million dollars, saying the newspaper violated her privacy.

With McGinty and Saffold gone, Cuyahoga County Common Pleas

Judge Dick Ambrose was selected to oversee the Sowell trial. A judge since 2004, Ambrose's thoughtful and even-tempered disposition belies the crushing tackles he delivered as a linebacker for the Cleveland Browns from 1975 to 1985.

Nicknamed "Bam Bam" during his playing days, Ambrose began law school when the NFL players went on strike in 1982. Square-jawed and fit, Ambrose tells reporters that he's ready for the biggest trial of his career.

Lead prosecutor Rick Bombik is also ready and prepared for the trial that he calls his "Super Bowl."

Before being assigned to the Sowell Case, Bombik was set to retire after a thirty-three-year career with the Cuyahoga County Prosecutor's Office.

"After doing this for so long, I realized that a case like this doesn't come around too often," he says. "I thought it was a fitting way to end my career—to be handed the reins of prosecuting someone who is one of Ohio's most notorious killers. This guy was so over the top in what he did and how he was able to accomplish it over a couple of years."

Bombik, a self-described "old school guy" with a traditional work ethic, grew up in what he calls a "lunch-pail, blue-collar" neighborhood. The son of a steel mill worker, he was the first in his family to go to college and graduate.

After working as an accountant for two years, Bombik served a couple of weeks on jury duty and found himself interested in pursuing a career in law.

Criminal law was a natural fit for him, he says, explaining, "If you're going to work in the criminal arena, you need to be competitive. I've always liked competition—I'm a legal warrior in the courtroom, but I also take my oath very seriously. I never had a desire to convict an innocent person. For me, it's not 'win at any cost.' It's play fair, play hard—but play by the rules."

Bombik, the blue-collar lawyer with a shock of white hair, became frustrated by the defense team's many motions to delay the trial. "The Empire State Building took one year and forty-five days to build. They've had eighteen months and they are still digging, digging, digging," he said.

Sowell's defense lawyers, Rufus Sims and John Parker, have repeatedly appealed to Ambrose for more time to "properly prepare" their client's defense. The trial, which was originally expected to begin in June 2010, has been postponed four times and is now scheduled for June 2011.

Parker claims the defense needs at least four more months to review 2,000 hours of video footage obtained from six cameras mounted on the exterior of Ray's Sausage Co., which is next to Sowell's house. He adds that their mitigation expert is still reviewing thousands of pages of documents. And defense expert Dr. George Woods Jr. says he needs six months to "adequately review the material provided and conduct the appropriate interviews." Ambrose has said there will be no more delays—whether defense experts are ready or not.

Noting that Sowell's trial is expected to cost taxpayers $600,000, the most expensive in the county's history, Bombik says, "His attorneys were able to get the faucet opened for financial resources. Sowell has shattered spending records for indigent representation. His attorneys went as far as the West Coast for expert witnesses."

In Bombik's view, the women who survived Sowell's attacks will probably supply the most important prosecution evidence against Sowell. "He had a specific scheme of doing things," he says. "He had a pattern. The guy has a thing for choking people. And the women who lived to escape are able to tell us about it."

Assisting Bombik will be Pinkey Carr, a tall, charismatic black woman who professes mixed emotions about the death penalty. "I don't know if I'm a proponent," she says. "It's case by case. I'm comfortable with whatever decision the jury makes. It's my job to prove my case beyond a reasonable doubt."

Carr has been an assistant criminal prosecuting attorney since 2002. Before that, she spent nine years as law director for the City of Cleveland.

A spirited competitor in the courtroom, she boasts one of the highest conviction rates among her colleagues. The Sowell trial may be her last as a prosecutor. Carr hopes to win a seat as a Cleveland Municipal Judge in the upcoming November election.

On the defense side, Rufus Sims is one of Cleveland's top criminal defense lawyers. Sims, 59, is an Air Force veteran who worked as a city meter reader to finance his law school education.

"I just kind of drifted into law," he says. "I'm a civil rights–era baby and there were issues of discrimination. I wanted to make the world a better place."

Sims said preparing for the Sowell case required a "tremendous" amount of work. "To understand the case, we went through thousands of pages of documents and thousands of photographs," he says, adding that the Imperial Avenue murders are a "tragedy for everyone."

In his spare time, Sims is an amateur comedian. "But just for fun," he says. "I've always been the clown of the family."

John Parker, the defense co-counsel, said the trial preparation was a "massive, massive" undertaking. "We had a team of paralegals, mitigation experts, and crime scene experts all working on it," he says. "At one time, I had five people working on this case in my office. On any death penalty case, it's just not possible for one or two people to do it all."

Still, Parker says he wishes he would have had more time to prepare. "There are various aspects of his life that we didn't get to explore. Sowell was fifty when he was arrested. He lived a long and full life. We could have gotten into that more if we had time."

A native of Southeast Ohio, Parker began his law career in the Cuyahoga County Public Defender's Office. He's been in private practice since 1993.

"Once a public defender, always a public defender," Parker says. "I see myself as working for the little guy, the underdog. I've seen how unfair the political system can be. Innocent people go to prison. People in a position of power and authority shaft the little guy often. When I went to law school, I had no intention of practicing criminal defense. But it just spoke to me that the little guy needs someone to fight for them." Parker says he has enjoyed his conversations with Sowell. "He's been very cooperative. As a client, I liked him."

When asked if he is concerned that the public may have a negative perception of him because he is defending an accused serial killer, Parker says, "It doesn't bother me at all if people don't like me. My job is to defend Sowell to the best of my abilities. The point isn't to blame the victims. You can certainly defend someone like Sowell and respect the victims."

In the weeks leading up to the start of Sowell's trial, new business ventures emerge that are geared to leverage—or shamelessly exploit—his notoriety and publicity.

An Akron-area heavy metal band, Fistula, releases a Sowell-themed album. The disk features Sowell's face superimposed on the forehead of a goat and contains songs titled "Ohio Death Toll Rising," "One Chair and an Electrical Cord," "The Ones That Got Away," "So Far Sowell So What," and "Mission Accomplished."

Fistula guitarist and songwriter Corey Bing says the inspiration for the album came when he first saw a mug shot of Sowell. "His eyes just looked black, like a demon," Bing says.

And SerialKillersInk, a Web site that sells so-called "murderabilia" from infamous criminals, offers one-gram bags of soil purportedly from the front yard of Sowell's house. The sealed baggies, which cost twenty-five dollars apiece, include a copy of a CBS News story titled: "Anthony Sowell's House of Horrors, Who's Buried There?"

When questioned about the authenticity of the Sowell soil, Eric Gein, the operator of SerialKillersInk, says, "An associate of mine went to the Sowell house, parked his car, put his blade against the chain-link fence, took his hand and started scooping up dirt into plastic sandwich baggies."

Gein tells Cleveland's WKYC-TV, "We don't put fakes on our site. We take pride that we are the premier [murderabilia] site."

CHAPTER 20

Trial

June 5, 2011

In 2009, *Time Magazine* pronounced the Anthony Sowell case as the number two crime story of the year in its top ten list, overshadowed only by the rescue of Jaycee Dugard, the California woman who had been held hostage for eighteen years by a registered sex offender.

On June 5, 2011, however, when Sowell's long-anticipated capital murder trial began, media and public attention were riveted elsewhere. The courtroom drama of Casey Anthony, the young, pretty Florida woman accused of murdering her two-year-old daughter, had become a watershed media event that uniquely encompassed elements of entertainment, news, and criminal justice.

Although coverage of Sowell's proceedings was not insubstantial, relatives of his victims were heard to say the disparity in coverage of the two trials reflected our nation's disinterest in the plight of black inner-city women.

But the disparity shouldn't have been all that surprising, says Ed Gallek, a reporter with WOIO-TV in Cleveland. "There were a couple of factors involved," he says. "Casey Anthony was an attractive mother, whereas Sowell's victims were all poor women who were labeled as 'crackheads.' And there was no mystery to the Sowell case: We knew how it was going to end up. But we didn't know what would happen in Casey Anthony's trial."

On October 29, 2009, when SWAT officers discovered bodies at Sowell's house, Gallek—after receiving a tip from police—was the first reporter on the scene.

"It quickly went from a routine crime scene to an unusual crime scene," he recalls. "There have been a lot of interesting challenges and layers to this case. You had the 'whodunit.' You had the element of police accused of not looking for missing persons. Also, why didn't Sowell's neighbors notice what was going on? And did the city drop the ball by not investigating the smell?"

As the case has evolved, Gallek says he has taken a broader view of the Imperial Avenue crimes. "There's a whole lot more to look at than who did it and why. We need to look at what the city and the police are going to do differently to investigate missing persons and sex crimes. And then there's the cost of the trial. It's setting records for spending and that's a big issue with taxpayers."

The less-than-expected media coverage was not the only surprise for courtroom participants and observers. In a dramatic move just days before the trial started, the victims' families pleaded with county prosecutor Bill Mason to strike a plea deal that would spare them from having to relive their tragedies in the public spotlight.

A petition, signed by members of eight of the eleven women's families, stated they wanted to avoid a trial that would become a "media spectacle where our loved ones' lives and the details of the horrendous criminal acts inflicted upon them are spotlighted."

The one-page statement called for offering Sowell life in prison without parole in return for a guilty plea.

The plea deal would spare Sowell from a possible death sentence.

"The death penalty for Anthony Sowell isn't necessary or even desirable, in comparison to the grief we families will continue to suffer under the realities and uncertainties of the criminal justice system," the petition said.

An attorney for the families said prosecutors should consider the feelings of the family members when deciding whether to seek a last-minute deal.

Jim Allen, the father of Leshanda Long, whose skull was found in a bucket, said a trial would be especially distressing for him, especially if a conviction led to a lengthy series of appeals.

"I need closure," he says. "I've never been able to put my daughter's body to rest."

But prosecutor Rick Bombik is committed to seeking the ultimate punishment. "No plea deal—absolutely not," he tells reporters. "If ever there was a reason for the death penalty, this is the case. I don't relish putting a man to death, but very few people can match his deeds in the history of Ohio."

In Bombik's view, allowing Sowell to plead out would be tantamount to sweeping his atrocities under the carpet. To give him a life sentence would, in essence, allow him to commit eleven murders for the price of one.

"Where's the punishment in that?" Bombik asks. "He has to be sent back with something heavy over his head. They won't make him suffer in prison. He has to face the same sentence that he carried out on others. At some point in time, we [as prosecutors] exist to do this. Fortunately, we live in a county that can afford it."

Gallek and other courthouse veterans didn't expect the prosecutor's office to miss an opportunity to try a capital case as notorious as Sowell's.

"Everyone wants a piece of Sowell for their own reasons," says Gallek. "Everyone is getting something from this case that they can use to push their agenda."

To Bombik, on the crest of retirement, the trial is a fitting swan song. For Pinkey Carr, the trial's publicity could help vault her into a judgeship.

Defense lawyers build their brands through high-profile criminal cases like Sowell's. And activists have leveraged the Imperial Avenue tragedy to vent their anger and frustration about the police department's supposed bias against the black community.

. . .

"You are about to begin a rather disturbing journey . . . where you will hear about the unspeakable," Bombik tells jurors in his opening statement. "It will be burned in your memories as long as you live. What happened over a period of two years was a total of eleven atrocities and up to five near-atrocities. Make no mistake about it, when the case is over, you will be convinced beyond a shadow of doubt that the person who committed these atrocities sits in this courtroom. Make no mistake about it. I look forward to bringing Anthony Sowell to justice."

Bombik then walks jurors through a timeline of Sowell's murder spree—victim by victim, beginning with Crystal Dozier, who disappeared in June 2007. As Bombik outlines the details of each murder, the jurors watch images of the victims on a TV monitor.

Bombik also speaks about Sowell's relationship with his ex-girlfriend Lori Frazier, saying she played a large role in his life. After the relationship ended, he says, "Things started to happen."

Defense Attorney Parker, in his brief opening statement, concedes that there are eleven homicide victims but tells jurors, "There are no eye-witnesses. There are no fingerprints. There is no DNA linking Mr. Sowell to any of the victims." Parker also says that the crime scene was mishandled by police.

In his statement, Parker notes Sowell's health, explaining he had a heart attack while shoveling snow in 2007 and received a pacemaker. "He checked himself out of the hospital early to be with Lori Frazier," Parker says. "He tried to make a living as a scrapper. There was no planning here, with respect to the homicides."

Regarding the women who say they were attacked by Sowell, Parker says they all have "sad stories of drug abuse and serious credibility issues."

"You will find Mr. Sowell not guilty of aggravated murder," says Parker, adding, "Do not draw any hasty conclusions."

The first prosecution witness is Cleveland Police SWAT team member Richard Butler, who describes the night of October 29, 2009, when he entered Sowell's third-floor sitting room and discovered two bodies. "It took a second or two for us to realize the people in front of us were deceased," Butler says. As he speaks, the prosecution team shows jurors photos of the bodies. In one of the photos, a body is clothed in a dress—and a plastic bag is wrapped around the feet.

"The odor was considerably strong [in the sitting room]," Butler recalls.

As Butler testifies, Bombik questions him methodically and patiently. Although the state's case against Sowell seems—on the surface—open and shut, the prosecutors are working largely with circumstantial evidence, albeit a houseful of it. Bombik is not leaving anything to chance. With thirty-three years of trial experience, he knows all too well the vagaries of a jury.

His counterpart, Parker, who will handle the bulk of the witness cross-examination, is also methodical and thorough. He grills law enforcement and forensic witnesses about their testimony, attempting to cast doubt on their competency and their performance while at the crime scene.

When Cleveland Police detective Melvin Smith testifies about finding women's underwear and jewelry in Sowell's bedroom, Parker insinuates that Smith and other police officers didn't properly process the crime scene and bungled their handling of evidence.

Noting that several beer cans were found on Sowell's porch, Parker asks Smith why investigators didn't take fingerprints from all of the cans. In reply, Smith says, "Because we knew how many people were connected to the crime at that time."

"How many were involved?" Parker asks.

"One," says Smith.

During the testimony of Dr. Elizabeth Balraj, who performed autopsies on five of the victims, jurors view graphic photographs of the crime scene and autopsies.

Sowell, dressed in a striped polo shirt and wearing tortoise-shell eyeglasses, listens impassively as Balraj describes the autopsy of Leshanda Long, whose skull was discovered in a plastic bucket in Sowell's basement.

"The cause of death was undetermined, but it was violent," says Balraj. "The skull is skeletonized; there is no soft tissue attached to the bones. The maxilar is intact, the maxilar teeth are present. Some of the anterior and posterior teeth are absent postmortem. The mandible is not present."

Defense attorneys, in their cross-examinations, pepper Balraj with questions about whether there were traces of drugs in any of the bodies she autopsied. Several of the victims autopsied by Balraj showed evidence of cocaine and antidepressant usage.

Parker also questions Balraj about her autopsy report on Amelda Hunter in which she stated that Hunter was strangled by "a male."

"How could you know that information based on her autopsy?" Parker demands.

Balraj, an experienced expert witness, calmly replies that she bases her findings, in part, on information from police reports.

Parker also took issue with the accuracy of reports compiled by forensic scientist Kristopher Kern.

In his testimony, Kern described the clothing worn by the women and the items that were used to strangle them and bind their wrists and ankles. Speaking of the shoelaces that were wrapped around Janice Webb's wrists, Kern said, "They were bound so tightly, I had to cut them to remove them."

In a grueling and lengthy cross-examination, Parker pointed out a clerical error in one of Kern's reports. Parker also focused the jury's attention on bed sheets and women's underwear and other clothing that were tested for semen and found to contain none. Under questioning, Kern admitted that ropes and shoelaces used to restrain the victims were not tested for DNA.

The first week of the trial included testimony from Assad "Sam" Tayeh, owner of Amira Imperial Beverage, the neighborhood store that Sowell visited daily to purchase beer and cigarettes.

When asked if he ever smelled a bad odor in the neighborhood, Tayeh, a native of Palestine, waved his hand in front of his nose and said, "Oh my, that smell. It was unbelievable. Forget about it."

"When did it start?" Bombik asks.

"Oh, a long time ago, it started . . . I don't remember the exact date but it was a very, very bad smell."

At about the same time he noticed the odor in the neighborhood, says Tayeh, Sowell began to buy boxes of garbage bags from his store. Tayeh recounts a conversation with Sowell in which he specifically asked him for extra-strength bags.

"He came up to me said, 'Can you get me the heavy-duty garbage bags?' I told him next time I order my groceries I get a box for the store. So one time, I will never forget, he bought five boxes of Glad trash bags. I told him, 'Why you buying so much garbage bags, my God?' He said, 'Oh, I am going to be cleaning around the house.'"

Tayeh also tells jurors that he suspected Sowell was using his trash dumpster and the dumpster at Ray's Sausage Co. for his own disposal purposes.

"One day, a very bad smell was coming out of my dumpster, so I took my store clerk and we walked over to it, and I opened it, and the smell is so bad," Tayeh says. "And I saw like a big garbage bag stuffed and wrapped with duct tape and I can't stand the smell of it, so I shut it fast. We thought that maybe a dead animal was in the bag. I told him [the store clerk] to get a bottle of bleach and pour it in."

Tayeh, while being cross-examined by Parker, says that Sowell's appearance changed dramatically in 2006 or so. "Everything changed, big time. First time I met him he wore nice clothes, was a nice-looking guy. Then dirty clothes."

Over the three-week course of the trial, the prosecution called more than sixty witnesses, including forensic experts, Sowell's relatives and neighbors, and law enforcement. Some of the most powerful testimonies were provided by Sowell's ex-girlfriend Lori Frazier and the women who had lived through Sowell's brutal attacks.

Lori Frazier testified that during the time she lived with Sowell—from 2005 until 2007—she saw evidence of suspicious injuries.

According to prosecutors, those injuries could have been caused by women who were fighting off an attack.

Under questioning by Pinkey Carr, Frazier says she saw several disturbing wounds on Sowell, including a deep laceration on his forehead. At the same time, she noticed blood spots on a wall and the carpet. He told her he incurred the gash when he fought off a home intruder.

"Another time his neck was stripped down to the white meat," Frazier says, adding that the wound required numerous stitches. She says he claimed he got the injury when someone had mugged him while he was walking through a park.

She tells Carr that she observed other strange behavior. She once saw Sowell digging a hole in his backyard and emptying a pail into it. She also noticed that the door to a third-floor room, which had always been unlocked, was mysteriously locked in 2007.

Frazier, a self-described recovering addict, says Sowell was attentive and nice to her when they first met. But he began smoking crack and acting mean and aggressive toward her. "He would just get off base and scream and holler in my face," she says. "Once, he smacked me and I fell on the table. I tried to kick him."

Sowell seems uncomfortable while Frazier testifies. She tells Carr that she decided to move out because she wanted to get off drugs and spend more time with her family.

Parker's cross-examination of Frazier is brief. He highlights her past drug addiction as evidence of her lack of credibility.

In October 2009, Shawn Morris, 51, escaped near-certain death at Sowell's hands by jumping out of a second-floor window. Landing on pavement between his house and Ray's Sausage Co., she suffered a fractured skull and other injuries that required eight days of hospitalization.

During her testimony, she tells jurors that she was sitting at a bus stop when Sowell approached her and invited her to his house to party. Suddenly, after a day of drinking beer and smoking crack, he inexplicably attacked her.

Morris explains that she didn't want her husband to know that she had been partying, so she lied to hospital personnel about the cause of her injuries, saying they came from being hit by a car.

Prosecutors then introduced a picture of a naked Sowell standing over Morris, who was also naked and laying semiconscious and bloodied between Sowell's house and Ray's Sausage. The image was recovered from security cameras that were mounted on the exterior of Ray's building.

The defense objects to the introduction of the picture, saying they had not previously seen it. Ambrose allows the picture to be admitted.

Under cross-examination that quickly turns argumentative, Parker ruth-lessly attacks the apparent discrepancies between Morris's testimony and the statements she made to police immediately after her attack.

Although she had earlier testified that she was knocked out when she landed on the pavement and didn't wake up until several days later, she admits to Parker that she remembered getting into the ambulance and that Sowell, to her consternation, rode with her to the hospital.

Noting that there were city workers outside of Sowell's house, Parker asks Morris why she didn't yell for help. In reply, Morris says she didn't try to summon help because Sowell had threatened to kill her if she talked.

Losing her composure, Morris calls Parker an "idiot," and yells, "Don't play with me, okay? This is my life, not yours. I did what I had to do to save it."

After Ambrose reprimands Morris for her outburst, she tells the court that she was traumatized by the attack and Sowell's threats.

"So this man threatened your life, but you had those city workers right out in front and you couldn't scream for help?" Parker presses.

"I was trying to save my own life," she says. "I was trying to get away alive. Not in one piece, but alive."

Parker then drills Morris about her long history of drug abuse and the numerous aliases she has been known to use. Parker also notes that Morris had willingly gone to Sowell's to party, implying that she had consensual sex with him.

In turn, Morris becomes so upset that Ambrose has to scold her again.

When Parker asks her if she paid for the crack she had smoked at Sowell's, she says, "No, and nobody else did either. But those women paid with their lives. By the grace of God, here I sit. The devil didn't win."

After stepping down from the stand, Morris walks past the defense table, flipping her middle finger in Parker's direction.

On a late evening in early September 2008, Vanessa Gay was ap-proached by Anthony Sowell as she prowled the Mount Pleasant neigh-borhood in search of drugs. She accepted Sowell's invitation to return to his house. What followed were several hours of heart-stopping terror.

Testifying at the end of the first week of the trial, Gay transfixes jurors with her dramatic account of a brutal rape and a nightmarish sight that she says she'll never forget.

A thirty-seven-year-old black woman with a confident manner and a warm smile, Gay says Sowell initiated a conversation with her on a street corner on that September night. "He said, 'You know, it's my birthday and I don't have anyone to celebrate it with,'" recalls Gay. "I told him, 'I don't celebrate birthdays, but happy birthday anyhow.'"

Sowell then told Gay that he didn't like to get high by himself. "We started talking about cooking and recipes," she says. "When I told him that I liked to cook, he said he could 'cook me under the table.' He told me he'd cook me pinto beans with brown gravy that would blow my mind."

As they walked to Sowell's house, he talked about his service in the Marine Corps and his interest in chess. Gay noticed that several people greeted Sowell and said hello to him. "So I thought he was okay," she says.

It was dark when they reached his house. When they stepped inside, Sowell began locking doors and closing windows. "My gut told me to leave," she says. "But I followed him up the stairs. As we climbed, I noticed boxes of old food. There was a whole chicken that looked spoiled and there was a musty, moldy smell in the house. He told me the smell was from the sausage factory next door."

In his third-floor bedroom, Gay says she was enjoying their conversation, but she noticed that he was repeatedly walking in and out of the room. She began to doubt whether he really had any drugs.

"I told him that maybe I should leave. I didn't really want to leave. It was nice to get off the streets and chill in a house for a while. But I was looking to get high."

In hindsight, says Gay, she realizes that Sowell wanted her "to make a move." She explained that Sowell expected her, as a crack addict, to rummage around his bedroom to see if there were any drugs that could be stolen.

"That would have given him an excuse to do whatever he wanted to me," Gay says. "But I just sat on the bed and waited patiently. I didn't complain, although I was getting creeped out by the overabundance of flies in the house. They were obviously there for the spoiled food and the dead bodies."

Explaining to Sowell that she has a phobia about flies, Gay says she finally asked Sowell, "What's up?"

At that, Sowell punched Gay, dazing her.

Then he said, "Take your clothes off, bitch."

"He told me if I refused, he was going to put me in a closet and nobody would ever find me." Gay said he then began ranting about his exgirlfriend and women who smoked crack who had hurt him in the past.

"My thoughts at that moment were, 'Nobody knows I'm here. Is this how it's going to end for me?'"

Terrified, but sensing that if she showed fear, it would only incite him, Gay disrobed. "We got into bed and he told me, 'You don't deserve what I'm about to do to you.' It was all bad after that," said Gay.

At this point in her testimony, Gay, a mother of four, began to cry. Dabbing her eyes with tissue, she continued. While she spoke, Sowell watched blankly, his chin propped in his hand.

Bombik then asked her if there was sexual activity. "He raped me orally," she answered. "What does that mean?" asked Bombik.

"He put his penis in my mouth."

Sowell then climbed on top of her and raped her vaginally. He continued to rage about the women who had done him wrong. Seeking to placate him, Gay says she nodded her head in agreement. But he punched her several more times.

While she was being raped, Gay says she felt tears roll down her face, but she didn't want Sowell to know she was crying. "I can't let this man see me cry, I told myself. I kept saying to myself that if he knew that I was scared, it would excite him more or give him more power."

At some point in the night, Sowell gave Gay permission to use his bathroom. As she walked down a hallway, she passed a room that had a black tarp hanging from the ceiling to the floor.

Gay then stops her testimony. She begins crying, her head down. After a pause to gather herself, she resumes, telling Bombik that a corner of the plastic tarp was pulled up. "Behind the plastic, I saw something on the floor. I realized it was a body and it didn't have a head on it," she says, now wracked with sobs.

Through her sobs, Gay says the headless body was propped up in a seated position on the floor. Its hands were by its side and it was wrapped in clear plastic.

Gay pauses again, using a tissue to cover her eyes. Judge Ambrose whispers to her and she nods. In the silent courtroom, jurors and spectators are spellbound.

Continuing her testimony, her voice becoming stronger, Gay says that she somehow managed to continue on to the bathroom without collapsing from terror. As she used the bathroom, Sowell stood outside the door. "There wasn't even any toilet paper," she recalls. "I had to use a rag and throw it in a corner of the bathroom afterwards."

Sowell then escorted her back to the bedroom. Gay recalls thinking at the time, "This isn't real. I couldn't have seen what I thought I saw. It's not possible. I guess I deserve this for smoking crack."

In the bedroom, Sowell told Gay that he had an "insatiable sexual appetite" and resumed raping her. On several occasions during the assault, Sowell would "pop out" of his manic behavior and speak normally, says Gay.

"All I could do was pray that I would make it through the night. I just tried to keep calm."

Both Gay and Sowell fell asleep at some point. She recalls waking up in the dawn light and realizing that his arm was around her "as if they were a couple."

Because she had seen a corpse in his house, Gay didn't think Sowell would let her leave alive. But she was relieved when he permitted her to put her clothes on and then call her sister. During the phone call, she made plans with her sister to get together and make macaroni and cheese.

When Gay told Sowell that she was leaving, he said, "You're going to tell, aren't you?"

Gay tried to convince him that he'd done nothing wrong. "I said, 'tell what? You were a little rougher than what I'm used to, but what am I going to tell?'"

To Gay's surprise, Sowell gave her his phone number and walked her to the door. He told her to come back on the following Monday when he "gets paid."

Once Gay was outside and a block away, she relaxed. "I thanked God that I was alive. I kept walking, but my body was torn up. It was a Sunday morning and I saw people walking to church. I wondered what I must have looked like to them."

Gay said she called the Cleveland police and tried to report the rape, but she was told that she needed to come down to the station and speak with an officer in person.

Melanie GiaMaria, Gay's attorney and advocate, says that Gay's previous negative experiences with police officers had made her less than confident about filing a report.

"She had been raped in the past and the police did absolutely nothing for her," says GiaMaria. "And the attacker got acquitted. So that was her experience. Vanessa feels that the police have failed her. They've made her feel less than human."

GiaMaria suspects that Sowell allowed Gay to live because she had made him feel like they had a connection. "He probably let her go because he really believed that they were going to be boyfriend and girlfriend," she says, noting, "Sowell told her that she wasn't like the 'other ones.'"

In GiaMaria's view, Gay actually is different than the "other ones." She explains that Gay didn't start using drugs until she was thirty-three. "She doesn't fit the profile of a typical crackhead. She was a wife and mom. Her husband turned her onto drugs by lacing some marijuana with crack and getting her to smoke it. It was a control thing on his part."

Once she was addicted, Gay quickly spiraled downward. "My TV started walking; my stereo started walking," she says. "We were selling everything to pay for crack. Even my kids' toys."

Spending fifty to one hundred dollars per day on crack, Gay prostituted herself and occasionally turned to petty theft. She began spending days at a time on the street, chasing her high. "I didn't take showers; I didn't brush my teeth," Gay says. "I had gotten so bad, that I had completely left home. My children were with my father."

On one occasion, Gay says her mother was searching for her to bring her home. She found Gay on a street corner. "I had just made eye contact with a guy who was driving some kind of company vehicle," she says. "My mom started screaming at me, 'Are you out here prostituting?' I told her that I was with a friend, and I got in the guy's car. My mom was disgusted."

After she was attacked at Sowell's house, Gay was emotionally and physically traumatized. Reeling from the grisly sight of the decapitated body, she wanted nothing more than rest. She ended up in the attic of a crack house, where she numbed herself in a drug haze. After sleeping for several days on a cot, Gay went to a friend's apartment.

A year later, on October 29, 2009, Cleveland police would discover the bodies in Sowell's house. After recognizing Sowell's face on TV, Gay contacted police to report her attack.

Toward the end of her trial testimony, Bombik showed Gay a photo of Leshanda Long, a victim of Sowell's whose skull was found in his basement. Gay began to cry. She was friends with Long, who was nicknamed "Thick."

The two ladies knew each other from the streets. Gay now is certain that the headless body she saw in Sowell's house was her friend Thick.

On July 18, the prosecution rests its case after calling sixty-two witnesses and offering more than 400 pieces of evidence, including a video-tape of police interrogating Sowell over a two-day period.

The next day, when Judge Ambrose offers defense attorneys their opportunity to present witness testimony, Parker says, simply, "We will rest."

Trial spectators and media representatives are surprised by the defense team's decision to call no witnesses. The move indicates that Sowell's attorneys are essentially conceding the guilty verdict and focusing on the sentencing part of the trial in which they'll present evidence to persuade the jury to sentence him to life in prison without parole instead of death.

Although Parker didn't present a single witness, he attempts to introduce as evidence the criminal and psychiatric reports of several of the women who survived Sowell's attacks and testified against him.

To win a death penalty against Sowell, prosecutors must demonstrate proof that the murders were committed with prior calculation and design. To ensure that jurors understand that Sowell is a calculated killer, Bombik tells them it takes at least three minutes of constant pressure on a person's neck to cause death.

"That is a long, long time," he explains. "That is a blueprint of prior calculation and design . . . because he can stop at any time. He was on a hell-bent mission to cause their deaths." Bombik then calls Sowell a "vile and disgusting serial killer."

Parker, in his closing statement, posited a new theory that the bodies found in Sowell's house and backyard could have been dragged there from elsewhere.

"We know where the bodies were found, but we don't know where they were killed," Parker says.

He uses the majority of his closing statement to bash the credibility of the five women who testified that Sowell attacked them. He calls Shawn Morris a "liar who just can't tell the truth" and claims that another survivor's testimony was motivated by "financial interests."

Parker reminds the jurors that the women all have histories of drug addiction and psychiatric problems. "A lot of these women were selling their bodies for drugs," he says. "And just remember that the way they appeared here in court is not the way they appeared on the streets."

In his summation, Parker repeats his contention that police and the coroner's office mishandled the murder investigation. Calling their actions "equally horrifying," he notes that they didn't perform DNA tests on important pieces of evidence, including the ligatures that were wrapped around the victims' necks.

"To prove who strangled these women, wouldn't you want to test the ligatures? Just one of them?" he asks, his voice rising.

"This man is an honorably discharged United States Marine Corps veteran," Parker shouts. "He deserves better. But the state didn't even try."

Carr then begins her rebuttal closing argument. "Let me give you eleven reasons why he should be found guilty," she says, displaying photographs of each of the victims, one at a time.

"When you strangle somebody, it's personal," Carr says. Then, in a theatrical gesture, she walks behind one of the prosecution's assistants and wraps her arm around his neck as if to strangle him. "And Tony likes to choke a girl. Tony was so close to these girls, he could smell their fear."

"And what about the girls he strangled from the front?" she asks. "He looked them in the face and sucked the life out of them . . . That's a killer."

Carr also disputes Parker's theory that the victims were brought to Sowell's after being killed elsewhere. "I guess he ran an all-night cemetery," she says, facetiously.

On July 22, after deliberating for fifteen hours, the jury reaches a verdict: Sowell is guilty on eighty-two of eighty-three counts, with the lone "not guilty" verdict coming on the charge that he stole eleven dollars from Gladys Wade. He had originally faced eighty-five counts, but Ambrose had dismissed two of the counts at the beginning of the trial.

Sowell stands, blinking rapidly, as the verdicts are read aloud. At the end of the reading, when Ambrose tells him he has the right to appeal, Sowell yawns.

Then, as sheriff's deputies approach to lead him away, Sowell raises his shackled hands above his head and looks directly into a TV camera, his face showing no expression.

Verdict and Victory

August 2011

Ohio has the dubious distinction of being the birthplace of a lengthy list of serial killers, including Jeffrey Dahmer; Charles Manson; serial sniper Thomas Dillon, who targeted hunters and fishers; Gary Heidnik, who imprisoned and tortured women in his basement; and Russell Ellwood, a suspect in as many as seventeen murders in New Orleans.

Michael Swango, a physician, was living in Ohio when he poisoned an estimated sixty patients and colleagues. The uncaptured Torso Murderer killed at least thirteen transients in Cleveland.

And now there is Anthony Sowell, convicted of one of the most heinous serial killings in Ohio history.

As the sentencing—or mitigation—phase of his trial begins, his attorneys bring forward witnesses who try to convince jurors that Sowell's military service, his troubled childhood in an abusive home, his work history, and his good behavior in prison while serving fifteen years for attempted rape are reason enough to spare him the death penalty and let him live out his life behind bars.

Even Sowell—the heartless strangler of eleven women and attacker of at least five more—has backers. His best friend from prison, Roosevelt Lloyd, tells jurors that the Sowell he knew at Grafton Correctional Institution was a good basketball player and "perfect" at his job as a food handler, which he called a "very responsible position in prison . . . had to make sure there was enough food for 1,300 . . . 1,600 inmates."

Sowell uses his sleeve to wipe away tears as Lloyd testifies that he loves him like a brother.

"Y'all only see what Anthony Sowell did for one period of time," says Lloyd, who was serving a twenty-year sentence for rape when he met

Sowell. "He's a disturbed young man. I didn't know how disturbed until this happened. But if you knew him fifteen years ago, you would have known that he was a nice, loving, caring person."

In a heartfelt plea to jurors, Lloyd then says, "Regardless of what he done, he deserves not to die. I'm here to ask the court . . . ask the jury . . . ask the judge . . . to have mercy on him. Let him live . . . let him live."

The fifty-five-year-old machine operator says he doesn't "appreciate" what Sowell did. "What he did was wrong, very wrong. I'm sad for the families. But we all make mistakes. Killing him ain't going to bring nobody back."

Assistant County Prosecutor Lauren Bell, in her rebuttal questioning of Lloyd, pounces on his characterization of Sowell as someone who simply "made a mistake."

She reminds Lloyd that Sowell killed eleven women and attacked five others. "Made a mistake?" she asks incredulously. "And another mistake . . . and another mistake . . . and another mistake."

"So this is the loving, caring man who is your best friend, correct?" Bell asks.

"Yes, ma'am," Lloyd replies.

When Bell notes that Lloyd's rape involved a juvenile victim and that he is a registered sex offender, he says, "Regardless of what ridicule I might go through. My neighbors might find out about me. I might have stones thrown at me. But I'm willing to risk my life and freedom for that man because he's my friend. Ain't but a handful of people going to stand by his grave. But I want him to know that I'll stand by it."

But Bell scores points for the prosecution when she gets Lloyd to admit that Sowell, his bunkmate for seven years, had never mentioned that he was abused as a child or that he had heard voices—which were two of the defense team's fundamental arguments for a life sentence, rather than execution.

Lloyd also testifies that Sowell would go into "military mode" whenever someone "messed with his stuff" in prison. "His eyes would get all red," Lloyd says.

When Bell turns the cross-examination over to Rick Bombik, he restates Lloyd's depiction of Sowell as a "nice, loving, caring" person.

"Roosevelt Lloyd, what planet is he from?" Bombik asks the courtroom. He then suggests that prison would be too easy for Sowell, saying, "It's a place where he can become the best of friends with child rapists."

Tressa Garrison, Sowell's half sister, also provided testimony that—while intended to help her brother—was of questionable value to his defense.

Tressa and Sowell both blinked back tears as she pleaded with jurors to spare his life. "My brother is my right-hand man," she said. "He's truly been my best friend since I had my children. He tried to be that man in my life because I didn't have a man in my life . . . my dad died when I was two. And now I need Anthony more than ever."

Citing her brother's kindness, she said, "He's loved by a lot of people. He loves children. He had cookouts for the kids in his neighborhood because a lot of them weren't being fed."

Under John Parker's questioning, Tressa said that many factors are to blame for the eleven murders. Along with his ex-girlfriend Lori Frazier leaving him, Tressa said her brother was a victim of a bad childhood as well as a genetic tendency toward depression.

Tressa also faulted the Marine Corps for not discovering his heart condition and for teaching him how to kill, and the Cleveland police for repeatedly blaming Ray's Sausage Co. for the stench on Imperial Avenue. "How could the police not recognize the smell of decomposing bodies?" she asked.

"I'm not going to say that this was all my brother's fault," she told the jury. "I think it was my fault; I think it was my mother's fault; I think it was the police's fault. Everybody played a certain fault."

Tressa, becoming agitated, said that if her brother had gotten the help he needed over the years, "this thing" would have never happened.

"Life has its ups and downs," she said. "Sometimes we make the wrong turns, not always by choice. Life just turned him the wrong way and he didn't know how to come back."

However, during cross-examination, Tressa unwittingly buttressed the prosecution's argument that Sowell was prone to violence toward women.

While denying Pinkey Carr's suggestion that her brother had anger issues, Tressa inexplicably conceded that he "sometimes got angry," especially if he drank alcohol and smoked marijuana at the same time.

And then, ostensibly to demonstrate her brother's loyalty to her, Tressa told Carr that he had once punched a girl who "was being aggressive" toward her during an argument.

"She just kept talking and Anthony got mad," Tressa testified, smiling at her brother. "He hit her . . . just once. The girl started bleeding all over the place."

Later in her testimony, Tressa—again unprodded by Carr—complained that the East Cleveland police didn't properly investigate Sowell's 1989 attack of Melvette Sockwell. This was the first time the jury heard about the sexual assault that had led to his incarceration for fifteen years. Before the trial began, Judge Ambrose had barred any mention of the incident to avoid prejudicing the jurors.

But now Tressa had opened the door for Carr to question her about the attack.

With Tressa unaware of her gaffe, Carr—masterfully, in a soothing voice—cajoled damaging details from her, most importantly that Sockwell was partially clothed and her wrists had been tied. Many of Sowell's eleven victims had also been bound and partially disrobed.

Tressa, now a runaway train, also volunteered her theory that Sockwell had not been kidnapped and raped by her brother. In Tressa's version, Sockwell had been caught breaking into the house. "At the time, my brother was selling drugs," she said.

"So she broke in to steal his marijuana?" Carr asked.

Parker, anticipating Tressa's answer, screamed, "Objection!" Ambrose overruled and Tressa said, "It wasn't marijuana; it was crack."

Until that moment, the jury hadn't known that Sowell had been involved with crack cocaine as far back as 1989.

Tressa then went on to say that the East Cleveland police were somehow involved in a conspiracy against Sowell and other members of her family. "They paid that girl [Sockwell] to say he raped her," she said. "East Cleveland [police] played some sort of part in this."

After the trial, Pinkey Carr would joke that Tressa Garrison was the best witness the prosecution had. "It was Tressa who brought up the 1989 rape and Sowell being in prison," Carr said. "She let the cat out of the bag. Sowell's attorneys just kind of threw their pens in the air."

The defense team then called to the stand two former teachers of Sowell's, both of whom remember him as an enthusiastic student who seldom missed school.

His junior high school science teacher, Cary Seidman, said Sowell was an "average" student who became excited during science experiments. Cathy Whelan said that Sowell was "just a nice little kid."

Jamison Abernathy, a fellow worker at Custom Rubber Corp., where Sowell worked as a molder until his 2007 heart attack, told jurors that Sowell did his job well, kept to himself, and took the bus to work.

A human resources manager at Custom Rubber, Christine Angiocchi, testified that Sowell "came in and did his job." Angiocchi added, "I never had any issues with him."

The defense's next witness, Dr. George Woods Jr., a California-based forensic psychiatrist, testified that Sowell suffered from numerous neuropsychotic disorders, including obsessive-compulsive disorder, posttraumatic stress disorder, sexual obsessions, and a "cognitive disorder not otherwise specified."

Woods, who was paid $350 per hour for his work on the case, as were most of the expert witnesses, said that children who experience or witness chaotic and abusive home environments, such as Sowell's, can be traumatized. "That trauma lays the foundation for obsessive-compulsive disorder and post-traumatic stress disorders," he explained.

As an example, he referenced his interview of Roosevelt Lloyd, who told Woods that Sowell was obsessed with counting. He counted inmates, food, utensils, and clothing.

When Sowell discovered that an item of his was amiss, he would "go off," said Woods, adding that it would be "almost impossible" to calm him down.

Sowell thrived in the structure and regimentation of the Marines, prison, and the workplace because he was able to channel his obsessive-compulsive tendencies, Woods said. But when Sowell lost his job after suffering a heart attack, he found himself without structure, leaving him susceptible to his sexual obsessions.

Without explicitly drawing the link, Woods implied that Sowell's sexual obsessions led to the killings of the eleven women found in his house and yard.

Woods also said that Sowell told him he mimicked sex with a Chatty Cathy doll when he was three or four. He remembered "spreading feces on the doll," said Woods, explaining that Sowell's actions with the doll are indicative of post-traumatic stress from abuse that he suffered as a child.

He noted that Sowell remembered biting the hand of someone who had abused him when he was very young, although Sowell was unable to provide "specifics" about the event.

While not directly saying that Sowell suffered from "dissociative amnesia," Woods suggested that he was afflicted with the condition. Woods explained that someone with severe dissociative amnesia may not remember what they've done.

Dr. Dale Watson, a neuropsychologist also based in California, was the next defense witness. Watson told jurors that it's likely that Sowell's 2007 heart attack caused a moderate brain injury.

After evaluating Sowell's performance on a series of puzzles, Watson says he found that it took Sowell "considerably longer" to solve certain puzzles than most people. Estimating Sowell's IQ in the mid-eighties, he said Sowell's below-average mental processing speed could have been caused by his heart attack, which reduced the oxygen reaching his brain.

When Watson depicted Sowell's early life as dysfunctional and told jurors that he didn't have a single friend throughout his childhood, Sowell's eyes welled with tears.

Watson also said that Sowell's possible brain injury could have also been caused by a hard impact, such as a car accident or football injury. Sowell has said that he suffered a concussion playing football as a youngster.

In reply to questioning by Parker, Watson said he believes that Sowell has auditory hallucinations. "The voice had a name and the name was Arnie?" Parker asked. "Yes," answered Watson.

During cross-examination, Bombik questioned Watson's finding that Sowell was severely depressed. Watson had evaluated Sowell while he was in jail awaiting trial.

"There could be a lot of reasons that make a person depressed," Bombik said. "At least one of them could be being incarcerated for a year and being charged with eleven counts of aggravated murder."

The prosecution's first rebuttal witnesses, Dr. Diana Goldstein, told jurors that despite the testimony of Drs. Woods and Watson, she could find no evidence that Sowell has a cognitive disorder.

Goldstein, a neuropsychologist who operates a private practice in Chicago, said that she "could not rule out" malingering as a reason for Sowell's below-average performance on Watson's tests.

After reviewing Sowell's pre–heart attack and post–heart attack medical records and assessments, Goldstein said she detected no indications of cognitive impairment. She added that a CT scan performed in 2008 also showed no sign of brain damage.

Goldstein said that Sowell is not a person who grew up with a cognitive disorder or suffers from a severe psychotic disorder. She explained that "An individual who cooks for himself, who plays chess, who manages his finances [as Sowell does] . . . This is not dysfunction. This is not a person who qualifies for a disability check."

"So was Mr. Sowell's brain function normal, even after his heart attack?" Carr asked her. "Other than raping and murdering people, yes," Goldstein replied.

Goldstein became testy at one point when Parker, in his cross-examination, challenged her opinion that Sowell might be faking his mental issues.

"Living with four decomposing bodies does not show some cognitive dysfunction?" he asked. "No, absolutely not," Goldstein responded.

"So it's no cognitive dysfunction in the brain to be living with four decomposing bodies in the same house for a long period of time?" Parker asked again.

"I think there's a more parsimonious explanation for that," she answered. "Mr. Sowell is an individual with antisocial traits and a serial rape-murderer."

In her view, Sowell is not cognitively impaired; he's simply a monster.

Dr. James Knoll IV, the next rebuttal witness, agreed that Sowell didn't seem to exhibit any form of cognitive impairment. Instead, said Knoll, Sowell's actions toward his eleven victims were typical of methodical sexual sadism.

After reviewing Sowell's videotaped police interrogation, in which he claimed he heard voices, Knoll said it's likely that Sowell was lying about the auditory hallucinations.

"It's important to keep in mind that this was a lengthy interview," said Knoll. "Mr. Sowell was articulate and logical. Some people who are hearing auditory hallucinations will look around, but I didn't see any of that behavior."

Knoll noted that Sowell first told detectives that his crimes seemed like they were a dream, but then he blamed the crimes on his ex-girlfriend. "This is a sign of malingering," Knoll said. "He's saying, 'Here's one explanation. And if you don't buy that, here's another explanation.'"

Knoll told jurors that Sowell's murders and disposal of his victims showed a "pattern of very deliberate, purposeful, planned action, as opposed to loss of control or irresistible impulse, as Dr. Woods suggested in his testimony."

Knoll also faulted Woods for not testing more thoroughly for malingering. He explained that in a forensic setting, malingering should always be suspected.

The behavioral evidence at the crime scene itself indicates that Sowell had the ability to interact with his victims, set them at ease, and find a way to get them to come into his house, explained Knoll. "That in itself requires some amount of interpersonal skills, cognitive functions, and mental wherewithal."

Continuing, Knoll said that Sowell would need normal cognitive functioning to be able to bind and restrain the women, rape them, and strangle them. After that, he would have had to wrap them in plastic and place them in a hole that he dug in the backyard or in a crawl space in the house. All of this had to be done without detection.

"All of this requires intact attention, concentration, memory, and the ability to organize," he said. "These are complex actions."

Put simply, Anthony Sowell is a sexual sadist, Knoll said. "The individual gets aroused, gets sexual pleasure from suffering. It's not uncommon to see things such as binding or restraint in these situations. This gives the offender complete and utter control. This helps the offender instill dominance and fear in the victim."

On August 8, Sowell took the stand and offered an apology of sorts to his victims' families.

In an unsworn statement, Parker carefully guided him through thirty minutes of question-and-answer testimony.

In a low monotone voice, Sowell spoke about being beaten with canes, whips, and a switch as a child. "It was like a war," he said.

Sowell cried softly when Parker asked him if his mother had ever hugged or shown any affection toward him. "No, that didn't go down," he replied.

Sowell recounted his time in the Marines, saying that he misses his ex-wife Kim Yvette Lawson, who divorced him in 1985 and is now deceased. "The relationship was good," he said. "It was good. It was the best time of my life. She handled me better than anyone else ever did. She was one of those touchy-feely kind of females."

Sowell told jurors that he had been a good chess player until he suffered a heart attack in 2007.

"I'm a good chess player; I play on the Internet all the time. I mean I used to play," he said. "After the heart attack, I was depressed and had mood swings. I could not win a game of chess anymore."

Parker then said, "You know why you're here, obviously."

"Correct," said Sowell, leaning forward, adjusting his eyeglasses. "Well, the only thing I want to say is, I'm sorry. I know that might not sound like much, but I truly am sorry from the bottom of my heart."

Glancing at the jurors, Sowell added, "I don't know what happened.

It's not typical of me. I can't explain it. I know it's not a lot, but that's all I can give you."

Sowell then returned to his seat, walking stiffly.

Some family members of his victims dabbed their eyes with tissues; others shook their heads in apparent skepticism of Sowell's words.

Because the prosecution wasn't allowed to cross-examine Sowell, his statement seemed to generate more questions than answers.

The victims' relatives, many of whom were sitting in the front rows of the courtroom, asked later: What was he apologizing for? Why did he kill the eleven women? And are there other victims?

On August 9, Parker began his closing remarks by appealing for mercy. Sowell's crimes, he said, were products of his abusive childhood. Although Sowell didn't experience the same whippings as his nieces and nephews, he witnessed them. That was enough to traumatize any child and set the stage for a lifetime of dysfunction.

But Sowell worked hard to overcome his childhood, said Parker. He served in the Marine Corps, was honorably discharged, and went to work. "He worked. He paid taxes. That is mitigation. That is to be considered."

Parker blamed Sowell's heart attack in 2007 for the unraveling of his life and dreams. Not able to work, Sowell became depressed and fell victim to his demons. No matter what atrocities happened at 12205 Imperial Avenue, Sowell is a human being, said Parker.

"What the state is asking you to do is eliminate this man from the face of the earth. But what you need to keep in mind is that when you execute a person, you are killing their entire life. You are executing the abused child. You are executing the honorable Marine. You are executing the well-behaved prisoner. You are executing the man who held down a job."

Continuing, Parker said, "The prosecution mocked Roosevelt Lloyd . . . fine . . . fair game. But there are human qualities there that Mr. Lloyd tried to express to you. Yes, we knew [Mr. Lloyd] was a convicted rapist, but we hoped you could see beyond that."

Parker then shifted direction, telling jurors that anyone who lives in a house with the decomposing bodies of his murder victims must have a serious mental problem. "This man is sick in the head. Something's wrong with this man, folks. That can't be disputed."

Pinkey Carr then took her turn, rejecting Parker's argument that Sowell has to be mentally ill because no normal person would live in a house full of dead people.

"Defense counsel would say that by the mere fact that he has four dead bodies in his house there's something wrong with him," said Carr. "Yeah, there is something wrong with him. He's crazy like a fox. He's evil."

Bombik began his closing argument by saying that a sentence of life in prison would hardly be a penalty for Sowell. "A life sentence, ladies and gentlemen?" he asked. "Where's the punishment? You're sending him home to a place where he does well."

After a pause, Bombik told the jury, "The house at 12205 Imperial Avenue had a long, respectable history until Sowell moved in. He soiled it, he ruined it, and he condemned it."

The jurors then filed out of the courtroom to consider Sowell's fate. Because Sowell had been ruled a "violent sexual predator" at a bench trial the week before, the jury has only two options: Life in prison without parole—or death.

Less than a day later, the jury returns. While relatives of victims hold each other, Judge Ambrose announces the juror's recommendation: Sowell should be put to death.

When Ambrose finishes reading the verdict documents, the family members applaud. Sowell, wearing an orange jumpsuit, nods slightly in their direction as he is escorted from the courtroom.

Per Ohio law for capital murder cases, Ambrose has the discretion of accepting or modifying the jury's recommendation.

Two days later, Judge Ambrose tells a packed courtroom that he has reached his decision. But before he announces whether Sowell will live or die, the family members of the murder victims are given the opportunity to speak about the heartbreak, grief, and anger they feel.

Speaking directly to Sowell, Donnita Carmichael says, "I don't want to give you the satisfaction of standing up here and telling you how you destroyed our family. You are an animal and hell awaits your arrival."

Donnita, the daughter of Tonia Carmichael, who went missing in November 2008, adds, "I'll never forgive you . . . The way you sat here during these court proceedings without an ounce of remorse. The only time you showed any type of emotion was when your family . . . tried to defend you or spoke about some sentimental memory that brought a tear to your eye. Well, we've been crying since November 10, 2008. You thought these women were worthless, that no one knew they were gone, that no one cared about them. You were wrong."

Florence Bray, the mother of victim Crystal Dozier, tells Sowell, "No matter how much time you have left on this earth, I hope you never have peace. One thing is for sure—you will have to answer to God for what you have done."

The father of Kim Yvette Smith cries as he tells Ambrose that Sowell "took my heart, my life." Donald Smith, wheelchair-bound, his voice cracking, says, "I might as well die, too, because he killed a part of me." (Donald Smith died several weeks after making his courtroom statement.)

Sowell sits impassively, refusing to look in the direction of the family members, even those who say they have forgiveness for him.

"First of all, I must forgive Anthony Sowell for what he did to all these women," says Jim Allen, father of Leshanda Long, whose body has never been recovered. "I know love conquers hate, and it always will."

Gladys Wade, one of the survivors of an attack by Sowell, also expresses forgiveness for Sowell. "I just want to say that he didn't kill me, but he killed what I was," she tells the courtroom.

When the family members concluded their impact statements, Ambrose asks Sowell if he wants to speak. Sowell, not responding, doesn't look at the judge.

Ambrose then tells the courtroom that he agrees with the jury's recommendation. Sowell will die by lethal injection.

Addressing the family members, Ambrose says that he is not certain that Sowell will ever feel remorse for what he has done. "Even though he said he was sorry from the bottom of his heart," says Ambrose, "He failed to take responsibility for his crimes when he added, 'I don't know what happened. I can't explain it.'"

Then, speaking to Sowell, who remains seated, his head tilted back and his eyes closed, Ambrose says, "If you did feel bad, then I would have some hope for you. Not for your physical well-being here on earth, because that's been decided in court, but for your eternal well-being."

In the lobby outside of Ambrose's courtroom, the prosecution team is joined by their boss, county prosecutor Bill Mason. With their arms around each other's shoulders, Rick Bombik, Pinkey Carr, and Lauren Bell grin at the semicircle of TV cameras and microphones gathered in front of them.

Referencing the petition from the victims' families that begged Mason to seek a plea deal with Sowell, Mason says the story of the eleven women who died on Imperial Avenue was one that needed to be told.

"The death penalty was designed for killers like Anthony Sowell," he says.

Bombik, with a wry smile, adds, "Sowell is a hopeless soul. There's nothing redeeming about him, and there never will be."

Standing alone, twenty feet away from the prosecutors' celebration, Vanessa Gay leans against a wall as a media surge moves past her.

Several jurors would say in TV interviews that Gay's gut-wrenching story of rape and survival was a key factor in their decision to sentence Sowell to death.

Gay watches the prosecutors as they strike victory poses. After the ten-week trial, she is weary and curiously solemn.

Later, she would say: "I wondered what they were celebrating. Were they celebrating for themselves? They will move on to the next case . . . the next victory . . . the next career. But this is my life. I've lived with my pain for three years and I will continue to live with it every day for the rest of my life. Eleven women are dead. Now a twelfth life is going to be taken . . . It feels like a hollow victory. There just aren't any winners here today."

Epilogue

The House of Horrors is gone.

The City of Cleveland condemned the three-story structure in September 2011, saying there were problems with the roof, plumbing, heating, and water supply, and it was infested with roaches and rodents

At sunrise on December 6, 2011, a city backhoe began demolition, tearing into the double-decker porch on the front of the house. Less than ninety minutes later, only a pile of rubble remained. The debris was carted away to a dump, where it was shredded to prevent anyone from pilfering macabre memorabilia.

According to the city's condemnation notice, the house "was a menace to public health, safety and welfare."

But the crowd of neighbors and victims' families who gathered in the cold rain to watch the demolition said razing the house was necessary to stop sightseers.

Over the past three years, a steady stream of gawkers have cruised Imperial Avenue, curious to see the house that hid the remains of Sowell's victims.

With the house gone, so are any secrets that remained within.

Anthony Sowell, now on death row in the Chillicothe Correctional Institution, has taken his secrets with him.

During the three years I spent writing this book, I spoke to more than a hundred people who have been impacted by Sowell's crimes, including the families of victims, survivors, his relatives and neighbors, community activists, police officers, and others. I heard the same question dozens of times: "Why did he do it?" Despite the theories of the forensic psychiatrists, neuropsychologists, and FBI profilers, I knew that only Sowell had the answer.

Through a half-dozen phone interviews with him, I was able to ask him the questions that seemed to be on the collective mind of the community.

I first wrote to him in September 2011 to request a phone conversation. He promptly and politely replied to my letter, stating that he wasn't interested in speaking to any journalists because he didn't want to jeopardize his chances of appealing his conviction.

I was surprised when he called me a week later to say he needed to "get a few things off his chest."

We small-talked for a few minutes, mainly about the food and living conditions on death row—both are "okay," he said.

Sowell is amiable, an easy conversationalist—looser than he appeared in court. His glibness isn't so surprising, since that was the tool—along with crack cocaine—that he used to lure victims into his house.

He then told me that he had been unhappy with his attorneys' performance during his trial. He complained that they seemed more interested in generating fees than presenting a staunch defense for him.

"I think money played a big issue in their minds," he said. "It was crazy money that they got paid—$600,000 to $700,000—just to drag the case out longer than it should have taken."

Sowell contends that his attorneys didn't allocate enough money for diagnostic tests that might have pinpointed a cause for his behavior.

"I didn't even get a chance to get all the medical tests that I was supposed to take," he said. "My doctor had wanted me to get an MRI and a CT scan to see if I had any brain damage."

I considered that Sowell could be disingenuously criticizing his attorneys in order to support a motion for a new trial, but his anger at their defense strategy seemed authentic.

I then asked him if he thought that his actions on Imperial Avenue stemmed from physical/medical issues or the childhood abuse that he said he experienced.

When he didn't answer right away, I thought that perhaps my question had overstepped a boundary. But then I heard a guttural sound. When he spoke, his voice was choked up.

"It bothered me seeing my nieces and nephews getting whipped. It happened to me, too, but I didn't look at it like some people do. My punishment was different. I would get hit and it would just roll off my back. I could handle being hit, but I didn't like being called dumb and stupid."

"Who called you stupid?" I asked.

After several seconds of silence, I heard what sounded like sniffling.

"Did your mother call you stupid?"

More silence.

"I can't . . . I don't want to talk about that now."

I waited.

"It's hard to grow up like that," he said. "My childhood was rough—the love just didn't happen. But she did the best she could. I love my mom."

His voice then became strained and emotional. "I didn't even know that my parents were never married. I found out in court. That was a blow to me."

Switching topics to keep the conversation moving, I asked him why he thrived in the Marine Corps.

"First of all, you guys don't know anything about my military service," he said, his voice regaining its normal timbre.

"Do you even know how many commendations I got?"

"Not sure," I answered.

"I'm looking at my Marine pictures right now," he said. He then rattled off the names of a half-dozen medals and ribbons that he'd received. "I got three letters of appreciation. Did you know that?"

"Why did you do so well in the Marines?"

"Me and the Marines were a natural fit. I fit in because there's a lot of physicality in the Marines. I've always been an athlete. I was gifted in the athletic area. I played every sport. I bowled. I was on the swim team. I was on the diving team. I was in the roller derby when I was young."

He added that he was a good football player, "except I didn't like training," he said, laughing.

Continuing to speak about his time in the Marine Corps, Sowell said, "I joined because my mom said I couldn't cut it in the Army. I showed her—I joined an even tougher outfit. In the Marines, I got to be me finally. I always had it in me."

Sowell said he enjoyed the camaraderie of the Marines, particularly in Okinawa where he was posted for a year. "It was crazy there. I have a picture of my platoon on my cell wall. About forty of us would go out to the bars; each guy would buy a round. It was men competing with each other; drinking and chasing women. That's where I learned how to drink. I felt like I had to drink to be normal in the Marines."

He met Kim Yvette Lawson in Okinawa. Sowell said Kim not only helped him to moderate his drinking but also to be more open about his feelings.

"I loved Kim and she loved me," he said. "Kim could have had her pick of any man, especially in Japan where all the foreign men wanted her. But she picked me. I don't even know why she loved me. I brought a lot of my childhood problems into my marriage. I didn't grow up being hugged. And Kim helped me to be able to do that."

Sowell was transferred to Chillicothe in January 2012 when the Ohio prison system relocated its death row there from the Ohio State Penitentiary in Youngstown.

During a conversation shortly after his transfer, Sowell said he had more liberal phone privileges ("they bring the phone right to my cell"), but he complained that "they don't let me have my arts and crafts here."

When I told him that his house on Imperial Avenue had been torn down, he said, "Yeah, I heard. Why did they tear it down? It was a good house. They could have at least turned it into a homeless shelter."

Sowell said he keeps himself busy in prison by reading—mostly mystery novels—and answering letters. He said he averages about three a day, from all over the world, including many from Denmark, the UK, and other European countries that are opposed to capital punishment.

Denmark, paradoxically, has no death penalty but is home to a pharmaceutical company that produces the drug used for lethal injections in Ohio.

"I get a lot of mail from women who say they want to save me," Sowell said. "And religious people are big letter writers. They say they are praying for me."

"Are you spiritual?" I asked.

"I grew up in the church. I am still a God-fearing man."

"How do you feel about your execution?"

"I am prepared to die," he said. "Whatever, whatever."

Sowell added that he occasionally gets letters from "kooks who want to get inside his head." Then, in utter irony, he said, "You wouldn't believe how crazy some of these people are."

Two weeks later, he called me. After the standard recorded message, he said "Hello" and then laughed.

"What's so funny?"

"Lawyers," he said.

He explained that the attorneys handling the automatic appeal of his conviction had learned that he had been speaking with me, an author.

"They bitched me out," he said. "They told me that they were worried that I would say something that would blow my appeal."

"Probably not a bad idea to listen to your attorneys," I said.

"Yeah, but when they were done bitching me out, they told me that they had their own writer who was going to do a book on me," he said, chuckling.

(Sowell has since been assigned new appeals attorneys.)

With Sowell in a good mood, I stepped up my questions. "Do you care what people think about you?"

"I couldn't give a damn," he said.

"What happened on Imperial Avenue, Anthony?"

After a pause, he said, "It just built up. The pressure just kept building . . . and building."

"The pressure of Lori Frazier leaving you? The pressure of not having a job? Your crack addiction?"

"All of that," he said. "All of it. I just had to release it."

I then told him that Sam Tayeh, the owner of the corner beverage store on Imperial Avenue, had said there might have been a dead body in his dumpster.

"Was that Leshanda Long's body?"

"Sam wouldn't know anything about that," Sowell said. "He's full of shit. He had sold the store to his brother by the time I . . . "

When I realized he wasn't going to finish the statement, I asked, "Where is Leshanda's body?"

"I'm not going to tell you that over the phone."

"In person?"

He then told me that if I wanted to visit him, I'd have to first purchase $300 worth of items for him from the prison commissary.

Jim Allen, the father of Leshanda, had spoken emotionally about his desire to find his daughter's body so that he could have closure. I would have liked to help facilitate Allen's closure, but I wasn't willing to pay ransom to Sowell.

I sensed that Sowell was becoming impatient and irritated with my pointed questions. Knowing this would likely be our last conversation, I said, "What would you say if someone were to ask you, 'Why did you do it?'"

Instantly, he answered, "Four words: Abused children grow up." I received a letter the next week with the following list of items:

4-gigabyte MP3 player

24 prepaid songs

12 Pac-Man games

Various electronic adapters and modulators

Next to each item, he had printed the serial number and item price. At the bottom of the list, he printed: Total price—$295.97.

. . .

Amid the extreme tragedy of Sowell's crimes, several positive developments have begun to emerge. The Cleveland Police Department revamped its sexual assault policies. Police inventoried all of their untested rape kits, finding more than 4,000. Going forward, CPD says it's committed to testing all submitted rape kits.

Ohio Attorney General Mike Dewine launched discussions about the standardization of rape kit testing across the state. His staff surveyed police departments throughout Ohio to learn how each department handles evidence.

In Cleveland, Mayor Frank Jackson formed a commission to study the city's procedures on missing persons cases and sex crime investigations. The commission recommended dozens of changes, including improving partnerships among regional police departments, mandating sensitivity training for police officers who handle missing persons cases, and creating a new missing persons Web site.

Called the Northeast Ohio Missing Person Database, the site includes information for the public and allows family members of missing persons to print flyers.

While the Imperial Avenue murders have spurred institutional and systemic improvements in the way sex crimes and missing persons cases are handled in Cleveland, the case has also helped to open much-needed conversation among law enforcement, the criminal justice system, and people in the community.

The Sowell case has shown that sexual assault perpetrators are often very good at finding the most vulnerable victims. Sowell targeted women who had criminal histories, drug problems, and weak or nonexistent family structures.

It's an unfortunate societal problem that these are the victims who, because of their problems, are the least likely to be believed by police and also not likely to engage with the criminal justice system, notes Rachel Dissell, a *Plain Dealer* reporter who focuses on the impact of violence against women and children and other social justice issues.

"Since we know this problem exists, we can work on ways as a society to address it, if we choose," Dissell says. "Since the Sowell murders and

attacks, I think this topic has been really discussed in-depth pub
the first time in at least a decade. It's a conversation that has to per
law enforcement and people in the community— all potential jurors
are often judgmental and non-believing of victims as well."

Dissell, who has written about Sowell's victims, says, "As we dug into
the Sowell case, we were shocked that he was able to operate for so long
without scrutiny. There were victims who were not believed, there were
rape kits not tested, and there was even DNA taken from Sowell that
somehow didn't make into CODIS-linked databases."

Calling Sowell "one lucky serial killer," Dissell says, "It seems like a
number of factors played into this—some based on failures of specific
systems or institutions—and others that are part of broader misunder-
standings and misconceptions related to violence against women."

Dissell says there is "absolutely no excuse for blowing off" a victim
such as Gladys Wade, who was attacked by Sowell but, despite her visible wounds, was deemed "not credible" by Cleveland city prosecutors.

But Dissell also recognizes that limited manpower and funding has
placed tremendous strain on police detectives and others who respond
to cases.

In Cleveland, she says, "The city has taken some steps and promised to
take more to assure victims they will be treated with respect. They have
made commitments at the top to change things on a number of levels."

It remains to be seen whether those commitments will filter down to
the police and other people on the street who encounter victims daily.
However, Dissell says, "If, because of the publicity generated from the
Sowell case, there are wider community conversations, then that will
make things better for victims in the future."

eline of Events

Aug. 19, 1959: Anthony Sowell is born. He is raised in a large home at 1878 Page Avenue in East Cleveland, where he lives with his extended family. During his childhood, Sowell witnesses his mother and grandmother frequently strip and beat his nieces and nephews.

Jan. 24, 1978: Sowell drops out of East Cleveland's Shaw High School and enlists in the Marine Corps. During his eight-year hitch, he serves in North Carolina, California, and Okinawa. A Marine buddy of Sowell's would later say that Sowell engaged in deviant sex with strippers and prostitutes in Okinawa.

Jan. 18, 1985: Sowell is honorably discharged from the Marines and returns to his family's home at Page Avenue.

July 28, 1989: Melvette Sockwell tells police that Sowell lured her to the Page Avenue home, where he gagged, bound, and raped her. She escaped by crawling out of a third-floor window. Sowell is arrested but skips bond.

June 24, 1990: While a fugitive from the Sockwell case, Sowell is accused of choking and raping a Cleveland woman inside a home. Police arrest him, but no charges are filed because the victim refuses to testify.

Sept. 12, 1990: Sowell pleads guilty to attempted rape in the Sockwell assault. He serves fifteen years in prison.

June 20, 2005: Sowell is released from prison. He moves into his stepmother's house at 12205 Imperial Avenue. Shortly afterwards, she moves to a nursing home. Sowell registers with the Cuyahoga County Sheriff's Office as a sex offender and is required to check in with them once a year.

July 2005: Sowell begins his relationship with Lori Frazier, a drug user and the niece of Cleveland Mayor Frank Jackson. Frazier would live in his house for the next two years. Sowell says he supported Frazier's crack habit through his job as a machine operator at Custom Rubber Corp. in Cleveland.

Feb. 2007: Sowell suffers a heart attack and loses his job at Custom Rubber. He earns money as a "scrapper"—scavenging and selling copper and aluminum siding.

April 2007: Sowell is smoking crack on a regular basis. His relationship with Frazier begins to erode. She moves out of his house, but she continues to see him intermittently. Frazier notices that Sowell occasionally has suspicious scratches and wounds on his body.

May 2007: Crystal Dozier tells a friend that she needs a "serious fix." She arranges to party with Sowell. Dozier is never seen again.

June 29, 2007: A woman who lives across the street from Sowell calls Cleveland City Hall to complain about a foul odor in the neighborhood, which she says smells like a dead person or animal. Cleveland health inspectors investigate, but they can't trace the origin of the smell. They eventually blame the odor on Ray's Sausage Co., which is next door to Sowell's house.

June 2008: Tishana Culver vanishes.

August 2008: Leshanda Long, 25, disappears.

Sept. 2008: Sowell lures Vanessa Gay to his house to party. He rapes her repeatedly but allows her to leave the next day. While in his house, Gay sees a headless body. She does not report the attack to police.

Oct. 2008: Michelle Mason, 45, is last seen by her family.

Nov. 10, 2008: Tonia Carmichael, 52, tells an acquaintance that she is going out to "have some fun." Carmichael's pickup truck is found several days later, but there is no sign of her.

Dec. 8, 2008: Two Cleveland policemen are flagged down by a distraught Gladys Wade, who tells them that Sowell dragged her into his house, where he choked her and tried to rip off her clothes. Police went to Sowell's home and discovered evidence of a struggle. He was arrested, but the Cleveland prosecutor decided not to file charges, saying that Wade's story is "not credible." Sowell was released.

Jan. 2009: Kim Yvette "Candy" Smith disappears.

April 15, 2009: A suburban Cleveland woman reports that she was raped. After the attack, the woman was treated at an emergency room, where DNA evidence was collected in a rape kit. But police failed to submit the rape kit to a testing lab. Months later, the woman would realize that the rapist fit the description of Anthony Sowell and would contact the police. If the rape kit had been processed, it's possible that DNA matching could have led investigators to Sowell, whose DNA sample was on file.

April 21, 2009: Tanja Doss, a friend of Sowell, is visiting him at his house when he suddenly attacks her. Doss is choked but is allowed to leave the next morning. She doesn't report the incident to police.

April 2009: Several days after Doss is attacked by Sowell, her best friend Nancy Cobbs disappears. Amelda "Amy" Hunter also vanishes.

June 2009: Janice Webb and Telacia Fortson are last seen by their families.

Sept. 2009: Diane Turner doesn't show up for work. Her coworkers say her disappearance is mysterious, but a missing persons report is not filed with police.

Sept. 22, 2009: Sheriff's deputies pay a surprise visit to Sowell's Imperial Avenue home to verify that he lives at the address he has given them. Sowell speaks to the deputies at the door. Several hours later, Sowell persuades Latundra "Lala" Billups to come to his house and party with him. She later tells police that he became enraged, choked her with an extension cord, and raped her until she passed out. Billups was able to get away after promising Sowell she would not tell police about the incident. She files a police report.

Oct. 19, 2009: An ambulance is sent to Sowell's house after neighbors report a naked woman falling from a second-floor window. Sowell tells police that he and the woman, Shawn Morris, had been doing drugs all day and that she accidentally fell out the window. Morris, who would spend eight days in the hospital, corroborates Sowell's story.

Oct. 27, 2009: Latundra Billups meets with Sex Crimes detectives. The next day, they secure an arrest warrant for Sowell and a search warrant for his home.

Oct. 29, 2009: A Cleveland Police SWAT team goes to Sowell's house to arrest him. He is not at home, but they discover two decomposing bodies in a third-floor sitting room.

Oct. 30, 2009: Police find the remains of four more bodies—two are discovered in a crawl space on the third floor, another is in a shallow grave under the basement stairs, and the fourth is found buried in the backyard.

Oct. 31, 2009: Police begin a manhunt for Sowell. After receiving a tip, police arrest Sowell on a street a mile from his home.

Nov. 3, 2009: Prosecutors charge Sowell with five counts of aggravated murder. Although six victims have been found so far, the coroner is uncertain that the sixth died of homicidal violence. On the same day, police discover five more victims at his house—four bodies are unearthed from his backyard and a skull is found in a bucket in his basement.

Nov. 4, 2009: Coroner Miller reports that all eleven victims are black women. At least eight of them were strangled. He makes the first identification of a victim: Tonia Carmichael. Miller says the advanced decomposition of the bodies is making it difficult to identify the victims. He appeals to the families of missing women in Cleveland to come forward and provide DNA samples.

Nov. 12, 2009: The first of eleven funeral services is held for Sowell's victims. The community expresses concern and anger that police didn't do enough to detect and stop Sowell's killing spree. The FBI brings in thermal imaging to search for more victims at Sowell's house. The FBI is also analyzing Sowell's military service to determine if there are unsolved crimes that may have occurred in locations that he was stationed at.

Dec. 1, 2009: Sowell is charged with eighty-five counts including murder, kidnapping, rape, and abuse of a corpse.

June 6, 2011: Anthony Sowell's capital murder trial begins.

July 22, 2011: The jury, after deliberating for fifteen hours, finds Sowell guilty of multiple aggravated murder charges.

August 10, 2011: The jury recommends death for Sowell. Two days later, Judge Dick Ambrose upholds the jury's recommendation. Sowell is sent to Ohio's death row.

Dec. 6, 2011: The City of Cleveland demolishes Anthony Sowell's House of Horrors.

Letters to the Author

During his research, the author corresponded with the incarcerated Anthony Sowell. Sowell had specific demands before he would allow interviews.

Bob   2/8/12

I am having a visitation form sent out to you, you must fill this out and return it. Then you will be put on my friend visitation list. If you want to visit me and do an interview. I want 300°° for this interview. This is to be paid by ordering online the items I will list on the next page, so let me know,

order online at
www.ohiopackages.com
(Access SecurePak)

Amp'd 4 GB MP3 Player
Item # 51908010N $112.30

Amp'd outlet Adapter
Item # 51911010N $16.05

Prepaid Songs $5.00 increments
Item# 51848010N (24) $5.00 increments =
$120.00

PAC-MAN 12 Games
Item# 51876010N $30.50

Rf modulator
Item# 51932010N $17.12

295.97

Hi Bob   2/14/12
I received your letter and
I would like to start by saying
that when I make a deal, I keep
my word no matter what.
    That's cool that you will put
$100⁰⁰ on my account when you
are approved for a visit, but
I will not visit with you unless
I have Received ether the
Items on the list or the money
has been put on my account
100 the + 300. once I have confirmed
that one or the other has been
done you can visit the one
time. Also you have 10⁰⁰ Phone
time left.

$104
$4 + 30⁴

Mr Sberna   3/30/12

I am not going to keep on
wasting time on this thing. I'm
not going to change the deal thats
been made. I am only going visit
with one of you guys. so if you
don't want the chance you need
to let me know because your not
the only one who wants to see
me. So if you have not done
what you are to do and have
made your visit by April 30 2012
I will move on to the next person
Also because of the questions that
you were asking me over the
phone, I will not be calling
any more.

①
4-5-12

Bob
There is nothing to think about
you don't have to visit with me then.
I have been more then honest
and fair with you. All you had to
do was to stick to the deal and
everything would have worked out
fine, Frist of all you have been appeared
to visit with me. You said (not me)
that when this happend that you
would put $100⁰⁰ in my account. Did
you do this? now you want to ~~act~~
try and say that anything can
happen to cancel a visit, but this
is not the case, I am the only
one who can cancel my visit. This
is why I will not change my mind.
You are to busy worrying about
things that are none of your business
and I'm kind of pissed about this.
who I talk to or visit with. for what
ever reason is none of your business. But I'm going to tell you —

②

this because I wont you to see
how foolish you are. The guy you
are talking about (miller) to me is
a asshole. In his very frist letter
to me he writes.
Anthony
Here we are. I am your biographers
and I guess there's not a lot either
of us can do about it I am a crime
writer and you're a convicted
criminal and I am writing your
story, and on and on. now this is the
way he thinks that he can talk to
me, so I go along with it, I put him
on my phone list then he ask to be
put on my visiting list, so I do that
also, so now he is on my phone list
and on my visiting list, but guess
what? I don't have to call him
and I don't have to visit with him
and I'm not unless we can
  come to a under standing also.

③

So you see the way you came
was very disrespectful. Good Luck!

Bibliographic Note

The research for this book was compiled primarily through the author's interviews with dozens of individuals who had firsthand experience with Anthony Sowell. Extensive interviews were conducted with Sowell's family and friends, his neighbors, Cleveland Police officers, family members of his victims, and—most significantly—the many women who survived his brutal attacks. Source information was also gathered from trial testimony, prosecution and defense documents, forensic reports, and published news accounts from the *Plain Dealer,* Associated Press, WOIO-TV, WEWS-TV, and others.